Mary Through the Centuries

Jaroslav Pelikan

Mary
Through the Centuries

Her Place in the History of Culture

Yale University Press   New Haven and London

Title page illustration: Giovanni Bellini, *Madonna and Child* (*Lochis Madonna*), detail. Galleria dell'Accademia Carrara, Bergamo. (Alinari / Art Resource, N.Y.)

Designed by Rebecca Gibb
Set in Joanna type by The Composing Room of Michigan, Inc., Grand Rapids, Michigan.
Printed in the United States of America by R. R. Donnelley & Sons Company, Harrisonburg, Virginia.

Library of Congress Cataloging-in-Publication Data

Pelikan, Jaroslav Jan, 1923–
    Mary through the centuries : her place in the history of culture / Jaroslav Pelikan.
        p.   cm.
    Includes bibliographical references and index.
    ISBN 0-300-06951-0 (cloth : alk. paper)
    1. Mary, Blessed Virgin, Saint—History of doctrines.   2. Mary, Blessed Virgin, Saint—
Theology. I. Title.
    BT610.P45   1996
    232.91—dc20   96-24726
                                                           CIP

A catalogue record for this book is available from the British Library.

The paper in this book meets the guidelines for permanence and durability of the Committee on Production Guidelines for Book Longevity of the Council on Library Resources.

10 9 8 7 6 5 4 3 2 1

To Martha and Anne Therese

Each in her own special way Mulier Fortis (Proverbs 31:10 Vg)

Contents

Attributed to Saint Luke the icon painter, *Our Lady of Częstochowa, Queen of Poland*. (Photo courtesy of the Polish Institute of Arts & Sciences of America, Inc., New York City)

Preface

Already while I was planning and writing my *Jesus Through the Centuries*, which Yale University Press published in 1985, I was simultaneously planning a companion volume on Mary. In spite of the obvious chronological precedence of the Mother over the Son, however, both the relative amounts of the material dealing with them throughout history and the absolute difference in their theological importance required that the book about the Mother be published second—and that it be slightly shorter. In both books, the number of images and metaphors, leitmotivs and doctrines—and therefore, even after combining two (or more) of these into one as I have throughout, the number of chapters—could have been proliferated almost at will. But, as I did in *Jesus Through the Centuries*, I wanted to present, in roughly chronological order, a series of distinct but related vignettes of the Virgin both in their continuity and in their development across various cultures and "through the centuries."

This book has been made possible by the invitation of President Richard C. Levin of Yale University to return to the podium of the William Clyde DeVane Lectures in the autumn of 1995 for my final semester of teaching as a professor at Yale, concluding fifty years in the classroom here and elsewhere. I am pleased as well to acknowledge the stimulation and insight, and in some cases the bibliographical suggestions, that came from the students who took the DeVane Lectures as a course. My thanks are due also to my editors at Yale University Press, John G. Ryden, Judy Metro, and Laura Jones Dooley, and to the many readers, known and unknown, who have commented on the manuscript in whole or in part at various stages of its development.

In most cases I have quoted, or sometimes adapted, the Authorized ("King James") Version of the English Bible, except as indicated, where I am translating a translation, for example, "The Woman of Valor" in the title of chapter 6, as a rendering of *mulier fortis* from the Vulgate (abbreviated "Vg") of Proverbs 31:10, the Latin title that I am also pleased, in the Dedication, to award to my beloved daughters-in-law. Translations of other works are sometimes borrowed or adapted from existing versions and sometimes are my own.

Mary Through the Centuries

Russian school, twelfth century, *The Virgin of the Great Panagia* (called *The Virgin Orant of Jaroslavl*). Tretyakov Gallery, Moscow. (Scala / Art Resource, N.Y.)

Introduction
Ave Maria, Gratia Plena

Hail Mary, full of grace: the Lord is with thee.
—Luke 1:28 (*Vg*)

The second sentence of the Introduction to *Jesus Through the Centuries*, the companion volume to this book, posed the question: "If it were possible, with some sort of supermagnet, to pull up out of that history [of almost twenty centuries] every scrap of metal bearing at least a trace of his name, how much would be left?"[1] The same question may be appropriately asked also about Mary. There are, on one hand, many fewer such scraps of metal bearing the name Mary. But on the other hand, she has provided the content of the definition of the feminine in a way that he has not done for the masculine; for in a distinction of linguistic usage about which it may be necessary to remind present-day readers, it was "man" as humanity rather than merely "man" as male that he was chiefly said to have defined—to the point that some speculative thinkers were willing to portray him as androgynous. Even in the absence of reliable statistical data, however, it is probably safe to estimate that for nearly two thousand years "Mary" has been the name most frequently given to girls at baptism, and, through the exclamation "Jesus, Mary, and Joseph" (or just "Ježiš Mária!" as I used to hear it in Slovak from my father's Lutheran parishioners during my childhood), and above all through the *Ave Maria*, which has been repeated literally millions of times every day, the female name that has been pronounced most often in the Western world. Almost certainly she has been portrayed in art and music more than any other woman in history. To mention only one example for now, not only did Giuseppe Verdi compose an *Ave Maria* in 1889 (as well as a *Stabat Mater* in 1897); but Arrigo Boito's adaptation of Shakespeare's *Othello* for Verdi's opera in 1887 followed Gioacchino Rossini's opera *Otello* of 1816 in adding an *Ave Maria* to Shakespeare's text for Desdemona to sing just before her death.[2] It came in anticipation of the question Othello asked Desdemona in Shakespeare's play before he strangled her, "Have you pray'd to-night, Desdemona?"[3]

The Virgin Mary has been more of an inspiration to more people than any other woman who ever lived. And she remains so in the twentieth century, despite its being conventionally regarded as secularistic by contrast with previous so-called ages of faith. The last empress of Russia, Alexandra, who at her marriage to the czar had converted from Hessian Protestantism to Russian Orthodoxy, wrote a few weeks after the October Revolution: "An uncultured, wild people, but the Lord won't abandon them, and the Holy Mother of God will stand up for our poor Rus."[4] It was only a coincidence, but a striking one, that two years later, in 1919, the powerful icon *The Virgin of the Great Panagia*, shown here, was discovered in the Convent of the Transfiguration (*Preobraženie*) at Jaroslavl. Rose Fitzgerald Kennedy, in speaking near the end about all the tragedies she had endured in her long life, said that she had constantly found inspiration and consolation above all in "the Blessed Mother," who had not lost her faith in God even when her Son had been "crucified and reviled."[5] One of our most sensitive commentators on current affairs, the Hispanic-American man of letters Richard Rodriguez, has suggested that "the Virgin of Guadalupe symbolizes the entire coherence of Mexico, body and soul. . . . The image of Our Lady of Guadalupe (privately, affectionately, Mexicans call her La Morenita—Little Darkling) has become the unofficial, the private flag of Mexicans."[6] For the portrayal of the Virgin Mary in this Mexican image, as another twentieth-century writer has suggested, "contains the . . . basic themes of liberation."[7]

Secularistic or not, this century has, for example, witnessed a continuation, and probably an acceleration, of the phenomenon of apparitions of Mary, for which the nineteenth century became almost a golden age.[8] The Mariological scholar René Laurentin estimated some years ago that there had been well over two hundred of them since the 1930s, and they have continued unabated. Television reporters and print journalists, who sometimes seem to become interested in the phenomena of religious experience and expression only when they are politicized or bizarre or both, have managed to keep the public well informed about these sightings. In Bosnia-Herzegovina, which in 1914 was the fuse that ignited the First World War and which throughout the century has continued to be a venue for religious hatred and ethnic violence, the Virgin appeared in 1981, at Medjugorje, a Croatian-speaking village of 250 families.[9] Since then, more than twenty million pilgrims have visited it, despite the land mines and the sniper fire, and it has been given credit by no less an authority on such matters than the president of Croatia, Franjo Tudjman, for "the reawakening of the Croatian nation."[10] Nor is this phenomenon confined to Roman Catholic countries; in Orthodox Greece, for example, apparitions of the Virgin in the twentieth century have become a major force.[11]

Because, as was said just when the twentieth century was beginning, it was traditionally held that "in Mary, we see in the little that is told of her what a true woman ought to be,"[12] the twentieth century's dramatic upsurge of interest in the question of exactly "what a true woman ought to be" has likewise been unable to ignore her.[13] It has become a widely held historical consensus that "the theology of the Virgin Mary has not altered women's inferior status within the Church."[14] Indeed, one of the most articulate spokeswomen for the position that the modern woman cannot be truly free without a radical break from tradition, above all from religious tradition, has characterized the traditional picture of the Virgin Mary as follows: "For the first time in history, the mother kneels before her son; she freely accepts her inferiority. This is the supreme masculine victory, consummated in the cult of the Virgin—it is the rehabilitation of woman through the accomplishment of her defeat."[15] More ambivalently, advocates for the movement within the Christian thought of the late twentieth century that has come to be called "feminist theology" have also been striving— or, as one of them has put it, "desperately seeking"[16]—to come to terms with Mary as a symbol for "ultimate womanhood."[17] "The Mary myth," another of them has concluded, has "its roots and development in a male, clerical, and ascetic culture and theology. . . . The myth is a theology of woman, preached by men to women, and one that serves to deter women from becoming fully independent and whole human persons."[18] Conversely, Mary has also served advocates of Eastern Orthodoxy as a positive resource for the reinterpretation of the place of woman in Christian thought.[19]

One of the most important religious events of the twentieth century has been, and continues to be, the rise of the ecumenical movement. It began as a largely a Protestant phenomenon with the heirs of the Reformation reexamining the issues that had begun to drive them apart almost from the beginning. At that stage, the question of Mary did not play a prominent role, except for the disputes between liberalism and fundamentalism over the historical accuracy of the biblical accounts of the Virgin Birth.[20] But with the participation of Eastern Orthodox and then of Roman Catholic partners in the conversation, the question became unavoidable, and eventually it came to be seen in significant ways as epitomizing many general issues that divide the churches: What is the legitimate role of postbiblical tradition in Christian teaching? What is the role of the saints, and above all of this saint, in Christian worship and devotion? And who has the authority to decide matters of Christian teaching? Thus twentieth-century explorations have made the history of Mary a major issue also for the ecumenical encounter, and a careful and candid review of the issue and its implications from Roman Catholic, Eastern Orthodox, Protestant, and even Jewish perspectives has illumined not only the ecumenical problem but the problem of Mariology.[21]

In the chapters that follow I shall try to show historically what Mary has meant, by following a roughly chronological order to box the compass of some of the provinces of life and realms of reality in which she has been a prominent force at various periods in history. It has been a process, as Hans Urs von Balthasar has put it, "that oscillates (from the Virgin Bride to the Mother of the Church, from the answering person to the Source of the race)."[22]

Jan Van Eyck, *The Annunciation*, c. 1430, detail of the Angel Gabriel. Gemäldegalerie, Staatliche Kunstsammlungen, Dresden. (Alinari/Art Resource, N.Y.)

1 Miriam of Nazareth in the New Testament

*And in the sixth month the angel Gabriel was sent from God
unto a city of Galilee, named Nazareth, to a virgin
espoused to a man named Joseph, of the house of David;
and the virgin's name was Mary.*—Luke 1:26–27

B ecause this book is not an inquiry into who Mary was in the first
century but into what "through the centuries" she has been experienced
and understood to be, biblical materials dealing with her have an essentially retrospective function here. In light of the subsequent development
of devotion and doctrine, what did the Bible contribute to the portrait of
the Virgin? That perspective applies with particular force to the subject of
the next chapter, the allegorical and typological use of a Christianized Old
Testament for its bearing on the question of Mary, where the problem of
the original meaning of a passage, including the precise translation of the
Hebrew text, will have to be quite secondary to the meaning that the
passage acquired in Christian history through translation and exegesis.
But the New Testament, certainly no less than the Old, has continually
taken on new meanings in the course of the history of its interpretation,
meanings that have sometimes been the consequence of what it did not
say as much as of what it did. For to both Testaments we may apply the
sage comment of a scholar of the Hebrew Bible who has illumined some
special chapters in the history of its interpretation. "Just as a pearl results

from a stimulus in the shell of a mollusk," Louis Ginzberg observed, "so also a legend may arise from an irritant in the scripture."[1] Whether as stimulus or irritant or inspiration, Scripture has dominated attention to the Virgin Mary though it has not always controlled it.

Nevertheless, the account of Mary in the New Testament is tantalizingly brief, and anyone who comes to consider the biblical references to Mary from the study of later development of devotion to her and of doctrine about her, as this book is doing, must be surprised or even shocked to discover how sparse they are. One interpreter early in this century, who was intent on maximizing the evidence as far as permissible (and perhaps a little farther), was compelled to acknowledge that "the reader of the gospels is at first surprised to find so little about Mary."[2] Or, as the leading Greek-English lexicon of the New Testament put it in identifying the first of the seven women bearing the name Maria in the New Testament, "Little is known about the life of this Mary."[3] Depending on what one includes, it could all be printed out on a few pages. If that were all there were to go on, this book would be short indeed! In fact, the contrast between the biblical evidence and the traditional material is so striking that it has become a significant issue in the ecumenical encounter between denominations.[4] Out of that encounter has come a volume jointly written by Roman Catholic and Protestant scholars entitled Mary in the New Testament and devoted to a book-by-book and topic-by-topic analysis of the possible references to Mary in the New Testament. Although the work has all the disadvantages of a book that has been not only jointly written but subjected to a series of votes, it has assembled the material in a convenient form. Even more surprisingly, it reflects a remarkable consensus across confessional lines, especially in its adherence to the historical-critical method of studying the Bible but even in its conclusions about individual passages of the New Testament. Pointing out that "in the course of centuries mariology has had an enormous development" (which is the business of this book), the authors of Mary in the New Testament, because of their focus, paid little attention to that development.[5]

For biblical scholarship, the fact that "in the course of centuries mariology has had an enormous development" may be something of a problem. But for historical scholarship, that development is also an enormous resource. To be sure, Mariology was not the only doctrine to have undergone such a development; in fact, it would be impossible to identify a doctrine that has not done so. The most decisive instance of the development of doctrine, and the one by which the fundamental issues of what could by now be called "the doctrine of development" have been defined, is the dogma of the Trinity. For the doctrine of the Trinity was not as such a teaching of the New Testament, but it emerged from the life and worship, the reflection and controversy, of the church as, in the judgment of Christian orthodoxy, the only way the church could be faithful to the teaching of the New Testament. It did so after centuries of study and speculation, during which many solutions to the dilemma of the Three and the One had surfaced, each with some passage or theme of Scripture to commend it. The final normative formulation of the dogma of the Trinity by the first ecumenical council of the church, held at Nicaea in 325, took as its basic outline the biblical formula of the so-called great commission of Christ to the disciples just before his ascension: "All power is given unto me in heaven and in earth. Go ye therefore, and teach all nations, baptizing them in the name of the Father and of the Son and of the Holy Ghost."[6] But into the framework of that New Testament formula the Nicene Creed had packed many other biblical motifs, as well as the portentous and non-biblical technical term for which it became known, suggested apparently by Emperor Constantine: "one in being with the Father [homoousios tōi patri]."[7] With characteristic acuity, therefore, John Courtney Murray once formulated the implications of this for the ecumenical situation: "I consider that the parting of the ways between the two Christian communities takes place on the issue of development of doctrine. . . . I do not think that the first ecumenical question is, what think ye of the Church? Or even, what think ye of Christ? The dialogue would rise out of the current confusion if the first question raised were, what think ye of the Nicene homoousion?"[8] If the Protestant churches acknowledged the validity of the development of doctrine when it moved from the great commission of the Gospel of Matthew to produce the Nicene Creed, as all of the mainline Protestant churches did and do, on what grounds could they reject development as it had moved from other lapidary passages of the Bible to lead to other doctrines?

From the apparently simple statements "This is my body" and "This is my blood" in the words of institution of the Lord's Supper,[9] for example, had come not only the resplendent eucharistic liturgies of Eastern Orthodoxy and the Latin Mass with all its concomitants, including the reservation of the consecrated Host and devotion to it, but the long and complicated history of the development of the doctrine of the real presence of the body and blood of Christ in the Sacrament, leading in the Western church to the promulgation of the doctrine of transubstantiation at the Fourth Lateran Council in 1215 and its reaffirmation by the Council of Trent in 1551.[10] If the First Council of Nicaea was a legitimate development and the Fourth Council of the Lateran an illegitimate development, what were the criteria, biblical and doctrinal, for discerning the difference? As it stood, the statement of Christ to Peter in the New Testament, "Thou art Peter, and upon this rock I will build my church; and the gates of hell shall not prevail against it,"[11] left more questions unanswered than answered. But by the time the development of doctrine had done its work on the passage, it had come to mean, in the formula of Pope Boniface VIII, that "to every creature it is necessary for salvation to be subject to the Roman pontiff."[12] To reject this development of doctrine on the argument that it was a development and that development was in itself unacceptable made it difficult for the biblical exegesis of the Reformation and post-Reformation periods to contend with those on the left wing of the Reformation who, sharing the insistence of the "magisterial Reformers" on the sole authority of Scripture, rejected the reliance on the trinitarian doctrine of Nicaea as a necessary presupposition and method for reading biblical texts.

For having thus developed out of Scripture, the trinitarian perspective had in turn become a way—or, rather, the way—of interpreting

Scripture. As it was systematized at least for the West chiefly by Augustine, this method of biblical exegesis was cast in the form of a "canonical rule [*canonica regula*]."[13] The several passages of the Bible that appeared directly to substantiate the dogma of the Trinity, such as above all the baptismal formula at the close of the Gospel according to Matthew and the prologue about the divinity of the Logos at the opening of the Gospel according to John,[14] mutually reinforced each other to form the biblical proof for church doctrine. Conversely, however, any passages that, taken as they stood, appeared to contradict church doctrine were subject to the "canonical rule" and required careful handling. When, several chapters after the solemn prologue, "And the Word was God," the Gospel of John had Jesus say of himself, "My Father is greater than I,"[15] Augustine had to bring his heaviest weapons into action. If the Protestant Reformers and their descendants were willing to hold still for such a manipulation of New Testament passages in the interest of upholding a doctrinal development that had come only in later centuries—and they were—what stood in the way of such manipulation when the passage in question was "This is my body" or "Thou art Peter, and upon this rock I will build my church"?

Perhaps nowhere, however, was the challenge of this dilemma more dramatically unavoidable than in the relation between the development of the doctrine of Mary and its purported foundation in Scripture. For some components of that doctrine, the foundation seemed relatively straightforward. Both the Gospel of Matthew and the Gospel of Luke left it unambiguously clear that it was as a virgin that Mary had conceived her Son.[16] But further reflection did produce the puzzling discrepancy that the rest of the New Testament remained so silent on the subject, if indeed it was so unambiguous and so essential. The epistles of Paul, the other epistles of the New Testament, and the preaching of the apostles as recorded in the Book of Acts—none of these contained a hint of the virginal conception. Because Matthew and Luke did both contain it, the other two Gospels were of special interest. Mark's Gospel opened with the adult ministry of Jesus and conveyed no information about his conception, birth, and infancy. John's Gospel opened far earlier than that, "In the beginning" when there was only God and the Logos. Yet in its first chapter, just before the celebrated formula "And the Word was made flesh, and dwelt among us,"[17] it carried an intriguing textual variant that was relevant to this issue. "As many as received him," it promised, "to them gave he power to become the sons of God, even to them that believe on his name, which were born, not of blood, nor of the will of the flesh, nor of the will of man, but of God."[18] But in some early Latin witnesses who were not without authority on other textual questions, the plural phrase "which were born," referring to the regeneration of believers by grace, was replaced by the singular "who was born" or "who was begotten," apparently referring to the virgin birth of Christ; and according to the New Jerusalem Bible, "there are strong arguments for reading the verb in the singular, 'who was born,' in which case the v[erse] refers to Jesus' divine origin, not to the virgin birth."[19] Beyond this variant, however, is the question of the biblical support for the idea of "virgin birth" as such. For the uncontested proofs from the Gospels of Matthew and Luke asserted only, strictly speaking, the virginal conception, leaving unaddressed the question of the manner of his birth, not to mention the question of the virginity of Mary after the birth. A related question, the identity of the "brethren" of Jesus spoken of several times in the New Testament, will engage us, at least briefly, at a later point.[20] Early creeds passed over such distinctions when they simply confessed that he was "born of the Virgin Mary."[21]

To summarize the biblical materials and simultaneously to prepare the ground for the development that followed, this chapter and the next, then, will look at some of the major themes of later thought about Mary asking what the adumbrations of these were seen to have been within the text of the New and Old Testaments. This book is not the place for an extended exegesis of these texts, but only for an identification of what the subsequent tradition took to be the evidence from the Bible, including that portion of it which Christians came to call the "Old" Testament, for the themes to follow. Some of this material can be considered rather briefly; other texts and topics will require more detailed exegetical grounding. In these chapters, therefore, the themes that are woven into the titles of the remaining chapters provide, roughly in the order of their appearance, an opportunity to review some of the principal biblical texts. As epigraphs for the chapters in turn, these passages from the two testaments will be emblematic of the dominance of Scripture.

Ave Maria. "Hail Mary, full of grace: the Lord is with thee," was, according to the Vulgate, the salutation of the angel Gabriel to Mary.[22] In reaction against that translation, and against the meaning with which it had been freighted when "full of grace" was taken to mean that Mary had not only been the object and the recipient of divine grace, but, possessing that grace in its fullness, also had the right to act as its dispenser, the Authorized Version of the Bible translated the salutation to read: "Hail, thou that art highly favored." The Greek passive participle being rendered by these conflicting translations was *kecharitōmenē*, whose root, the noun *charis* and its cognates, meant "favor" in general and, particularly in the New Testament and other early Christian literature, referred to "grace," seen as the favor and unearned generosity of God.[23] In the immediate context of the account of the annunciation, it does seem to have been referring first of all to the primary initiative of God in selecting Mary as the one who was to become the mother of Jesus and thus in designating her as his chosen one. In Martin Luther's Christmas hymn "Vom Himmel hoch da komm' ich her [From heaven above to earth I come]," which was to become the leitmotiv in each successive cantata of Johann Sebastian Bach's *Christmas Oratorio* of 1734–35, another angel was presented as saying, to the shepherds of Bethlehem and through them to all the world, "Euch its ein Kindlein heut' geborn,/Von einer Jungfrau auserkoren [To you this day is born a Child, from an *elect Virgin*]." That was a Reformation formulation for this designation of Mary as the chosen one—"predestined one," it would not be unwarranted to say, as, among others, the Second Vatican Council would say in 1964[24]—through whom the plan of God for the salvation of the world was set into motion.

This historic interconfessional dispute over the full implications of kecharitōmenē should not obscure the far more massive role played by the opening salutation, *Ave*/Hail, through the centuries. It came to open the prayer that has, it seems safe to estimate, ranked second only to the Lord's Prayer in the number of times it has been spoken over those centuries in Western Christendom: "Hail Mary, full of grace, the Lord is with thee. Blessed art thou among women, and blessed is the fruit of thy womb, Jesus. Holy Mary, Mother of God, pray for us sinners, now and in the hour of our death. Amen. [*Ave Maria, gratia plena, Dominus tecum, benedicta tu in mulieribus, et benedictus fructus ventris tui, Jesus. Sancta Maria, Mater Dei, ora pro nobis peccatoribus, nunc et in hora mortis nostrae. Amen.*]"[25] Its first sentence, as punctuated here, combined two biblical salutations in the Vulgate version.[26] Its second sentence was a petition that combined the postbiblical title Theotokos with later Mariological doctrine, according to which the saints in heaven interceded for believers on earth, and a fortiori that the Mother of God, being "full of grace" and therefore the Mediatrix, was in a position to intercede for them, which they in turn had the right to request from her directly. In a striking way, therefore, the *Ave Maria* epitomized not only the irony of Mary's having become a major point of division among believers and between churches but the dichotomy between the sole authority of Scripture and the development of doctrine through tradition; for even those who affirmed the absolute supremacy of biblical authority would nevertheless refuse to pray the impeccably biblical words of its first sentence.

The Second Eve. Because the chronological sequence of the composition of the books of the New Testament does not correspond to the order in which they appear in our Bibles as a collection of canonical books, the oldest written reference to Mary (though not by name) that appeared in the New Testament was not in any of the Gospels but in Paul's Epistle to the Galatians: "When the fulness of the time was come, God sent forth his Son, *made of a woman*, made under the law, to redeem them that were under the law, that we might receive the adoption of sons."[27] Most New Testament scholars would agree that "made of a woman" did not mean or even imply "but not of a man" (although it also did not exclude the idea of the virgin birth), but rather that it was a

Semitic expression for "human being," as in the statement "Man that is born of woman is of few days, and full of trouble."[28] (For that matter, Macbeth was to discover that the prophecy of the witches, "None of woman born shall harm Macbeth," did not preclude a human father— but also that it did not include a caesarean section!)[29] Thus the phrase in Galatians was taken from early times as a way of speaking about Jesus Christ as truly human, in opposition to the widespread Christian tendency (considered in chapter 3) of supposing that the way to ensure that he be regarded as more than human was to describe him as less than human. But associated with this New Testament point was one of the devices employed by the apostle Paul to make this same point about the true humanity of Christ, which he did on the basis of a special interpretation of the Old Testament. It was expressed in the verse "As by one man's disobedience many were made sinners, so by the obedience of one shall many be made righteous."[30] From that typology of speaking about the First Adam and then about Christ as the Second Adam it was a short step, albeit a step that the New Testament did not take, to speak about Mary as the Second Eve, and thus to extrapolate from Paul's words to say as well, "As by one [woman's] disobedience many were made sinners, so by the obedience of one shall many be made righteous," through the One to whom she gave birth. I shall examine in chapter 2 how it was that because Mary, the Second Eve, was the heir of the history of Israel, the history of the First Eve could be—or, as the early Christians saw it, had to be—read as a biblical resource and a historical source for providing more information about her.

The Mother of God. Even in the Gospels as they have come down to us, the relation between Jesus and John the Baptist was a complicated one. The evangelists did divulge that the ministry of John the Baptist had caused "all men" among his contemporaries to "muse in their hearts of John, whether he were the Christ, or not."[31] Nevertheless they were at pains to explain that John himself had identified Jesus as "the Lamb of God, that taketh away the sin of the world" and that, when challenged, he explicitly subordinated his historic mission to that of Jesus—and his person to that of the one "whose shoe's latchet I am not worthy to unloose."[32] This tendency was carried over from the relation between John and Jesus to the relation between Elizabeth and Mary. For in the account of what came to be known as the visitation, not only had John the unborn "babe leaped in my womb for joy," but Elizabeth "spake out with a loud voice, and said, Blessed art thou among women, and blessed is the fruit of thy womb. And whence is this to me, that the mother of my Lord should come to me?"[33]

If this verbal exchange between Mary and her "cousin [*syngenis*]" Elizabeth[34] were to be interpreted as having taken place in Aramaic or even to have employed some Hebrew, the title attributed by Elizabeth to Mary, "the mother of my Lord," which was *hē mētēr tou kyriou mou* in Greek, could conceivably be taken as a reference to Jesus Christ as *Adōnai*, "my Lord," the term used as a substitute for the ineffable divine name, JHWH. That was, at any rate, how from early times Christian interpreters had seen the standard New Testament "Christological title of majesty"[35] *kyrios*, whether or not the Gospels or the apostle Paul had intended any such identification. And because, in the central affirmation of the faith of Israel, the Shema, "Hear, O Israel: the Lord our God is one Lord," repeated by Christ in the Gospels,[36] there already was the identification between "the Lord" and "our God" as one, the assembled bishops at the Council of Ephesus in 431 did not find it difficult to move from Elizabeth's formula of Mary as "the mother of my Lord" to Cyril's formula of Mary as Theotokos.

The Blessed Virgin. The chastity of Mary, in paradoxical combination with her maternity, was one of the elements held in common by the Gospel of Luke and the Gospel of Matthew. "And in the sixth month the angel Gabriel was sent from God unto a city of Galilee, named Nazareth, to a virgin espoused to a man named Joseph, of the house of David; and the virgin's name was Mary," *Maria* being one of the Greek forms of the Hebrew name Miryam, sister of Moses.[37] So began, in the first chapter of Luke's Gospel, the longest sustained account of Mary in the Bible.[38] In the next chapter, in the introduction to the story of the nativity, it was said that Joseph—and, according to many early Christian interpreters, Mary as well, though this was not made explicit[39]—was "of the house and lineage of David."[40] Although with fewer details, especially about Mary herself, Matthew's version paralleled that of Luke, also referring to her as a virgin and citing as evidence the prophecy of Isaiah that "a virgin [*parthenos*] shall be with child, and shall bring forth a son, and they shall call his name Emmanuel."[41]

It was Luke who in his first two chapters told the story of the exchange between Gabriel and Mary (the annunciation, from which the figure of Gabriel, as depicted by Jan Van Eyck, is shown here); of the exchange between Elizabeth, mother of John the Baptist, and Mary (the visitation), including the Magnificat, "My soul doth magnify the Lord" (which in some manuscripts was ascribed to Elizabeth rather than to Mary); of the coming of the shepherds (whereas Matthew uniquely had the coming of the Magi); and of the presentation of the infant Jesus in the temple, with Simeon's Nunc Dimittis, "Lord, now lettest thou thy servant depart in peace." So dominant was Mary's perspective in the way Luke narrated the story of the birth of Jesus that some early readers were driven to inquire where these details had come from, since they did not appear in other accounts. Luke's Gospel opened with words that some church fathers took as an explanation: "Forasmuch as many have taken in hand to set forth in order a declaration of those things which are most surely believed among us, even as they delivered them unto us *which from the beginning were eyewitnesses and ministers of the word; it* seemed good to me also *having had perfect understanding of all things from the very first,* to write unto thee in order."[42] Because it has usually been historians who have studied the structure and content of the Gospels, these introductory words have marked Luke as the historian among the evangelists.[43] He used about himself the Greek word *parēkolouthēkoti,* which meant that he had done historical research, more or less as his fellow historians did now. The sources on which he drew for that research were in part written, including the "many [who] have taken in hand to set forth in order a declaration of those things which are most surely believed among us," thus apparently including writers in addition to those who have been preserved in the pages of our New Testament. But the sources explicitly included the "eyewitnesses and ministers of the word," because Luke not only did not belong to the original twelve disciples and eyewitnesses but was not even a disciple of one of these; rather, according to tradition, he was a pupil and "the beloved physician" of the apostle Paul, who was "one born out of due time" in coming last to the band of the apostles.[44] When Luke undertook his research into the very beginnings of his narrative, as reflected in the first two chapters of his Gospel, who would have been the "eyewitnesses and ministers of the word" to whom he would have turned for what we today would call the "oral history" of those early events? The telling of the story in these chapters from the perspective of the Virgin Mary seemed to suggest her as primary among these original eyewitnesses and servants of the Gospel. In addition, although Luke, being a Gentile rather than a Jew, wrote, both in the main body of his Gospel and in the Book of Acts, a Greek that came closer to Attic standards than other parts of the New Testament and that sounded somewhat less like a translation, that quality was not present in these chapters, which in some respects did seem to be a translation from a Hebrew (or Aramaic) original. These considerations led early Christian writers to characterize the opening chapters of Luke's Gospel as the memoirs of the Virgin Mary—a characterization that has not commended itself to the historical-critical study of the Gospels. There even arose a tradition that Luke was the first painter of Christian icons, and the theme of Luke painting the icon of the Virgin became standard.[45]

The Mater Dolorosa. When the Apostles' Creed and the Nicene Creed, in their summary confessions about Jesus Christ as the Son of God, moved directly from his having been born of the Virgin Mary to his having suffered under Pontius Pilate without so much as mentioning his teachings or his miracles or his apostles, they were echoing, but also carrying at least one step further, the emphasis of the Gospels on his suffering and his crucifixion. Each Gospel, after its own fashion, shifted from the individual incidents and occasional glimpses of its previous narrative to a far more detailed preoccupation with the day-by-day and even hour-by-hour unfolding of the story of Christ's passion and death. From the perspective of the later history of interpretation the differences in their accounts of the passion were well illustrated by the compilation of "the seven words from the cross."[46]

Among these seven words, John provided the one most directly relevant here: "Woman, behold thy son! Behold thy mother!"[47] Homiletically if not theologically, "Behold thy mother" could easily become the charter for entrusting to the maternal care of Mary not only "the disciple whom Jesus loved," identified by the tradition though not by present-day scholarship as John the evangelist, but all the disciples whom Jesus loved in all periods of history, therefore the entire church past and present. As Origen of Alexandria had already put it in the first third of the third century, "No one can apprehend the meaning of [the Gospel of John] except he have lain on Jesus' breast and received from Jesus Mary to be his mother also. . . . Is it not the case that everyone who is perfect lives himself no longer, but Christ lives in him; and if Christ lives in him, then it is said of him to Mary, 'Behold thy son Christ.'"[48] But this scene also stirred the Christian imagination in more poignant ways; for, like the annunciation scene at the beginning of Christ's life, it seemed to provide a window into the inner life of the Virgin. From the beginning of Christ's life there also came the prophecy that would be seen as justification for such an exploration of the subjectivity of the Virgin when, as the Mater Dolorosa, she stood at the foot of the cross: "Yea, a sword shall pierce through thy own soul also."[49]

The Model of Faith in the Word of God. When the Epistle to the Hebrews, in its roll call of the saints throughout the history of Israel, rang the changes of those "of whom the world was not worthy," it introduced each name with the formula "By faith," after introducing this roster with its own definition: "Now faith is the substance of things hoped for, the evidence of things not seen."[50] And when the Epistle to the Romans defined that "faith cometh by hearing [*akoē*], and hearing by the word of God," and opened as well as closed its total message with the identification of "faith" as "obedience [*hypakoē*],"[51] it was summarizing a connection between obedience and faith, and between faith and the word of God, that had been especially prominent in the writings of the Hebrew prophets and in the teachings of Jesus. The differences between its declaration, so central to the Protestant Reformation, "that a man is justified by faith without the deeds of the law," and the declaration of the Epistle of James that "by works a man is justified, and not by faith only,"[52] would frustrate future attempts at harmonization, especially during the Reformation. But those differences did not detract from either the fundamental importance of faith to the entire New Testament message or the centrality of the doctrine of the word of God.

The one historical figure who played a major role in each of those New Testament pericopes—Hebrews, Romans, and James—was Abraham.[53] According to all three, he was what Romans called him, "the father of all them that believe."[54] But if there were to be a "mother of all them that believe," the prime candidate would have to be Mary, just as Eve was identified in the Book of Genesis as "the mother of all living."[55] The key statement by which Mary qualified for such a title was her response to the angel Gabriel, and through the angel to the God whose messenger Gabriel was: "Be it unto me according to thy word."[56] For without invoking the word "faith" explicitly, these words put into action the identification of faith with obedience, and by describing her obedience to the word of God made of her the model of faith. Indeed, beginning with Mary and moving backward through the history of Israel, it would be possible to devise a roll call of female saints—Eve and Sarah, Esther and Ruth, and many more—of whom she was an exemplar, just as it would be possible to begin with Mary and construct a similar roster of female saints since the New Testament era. And by its emphasis on faith such a roster could commend itself even to those heirs of the Protestant Reformation who have traditionally regarded with profound suspicion any such elitism among believers.

The Woman for All Seasons. Rosters of this kind would, of course, be a part, but only a small part, of all those who through the centuries have found in the Virgin Mary an object of devotion and a model of the godly life, for they shall occupy the balance of this book. As she was represented as predicting, "For, behold, from henceforth all generations shall call me blessed."[57] This was one of relatively few passages in the New Testament that seemed to envision a long period of many generations to come, along with the prophecy of Christ that "this gospel shall be preached in the whole world."[58] The content with which those successive generations would invest the title "blessed" would vary greatly through the centuries, but the striking quality would be the success with which, in all seasons, Mary's blessedness would be seen as relevant to men and woman in an equal variety of situations. And that has truly made her the Woman for All Seasons.

Marc Chagall, *The Pregnant Woman*, 1913. Stedelijk Museum, Amsterdam.

2 The Daughter of Zion and the Fulfillment of Prophecy

> He hath holpen his servant Israel, in remembrance of his mercy,
> as he spake to our fathers, to Abraham, and to his seed for ever.
> —Luke 1:54–55

In a real sense, our inquiry into the witness of the New Testament to the Virgin Mary has been begging the question—and, in light of subsequent history, begging it falsely. For with their belief in the unity of the Bible, where "the New Testament is hidden in the Old and the Old becomes visible in the New [Novum in Vetere latet, Vetus in Novo patet]," and with the consequent ability to toggle effortlessly from one Testament to the other and from fulfillment to prophecy and back again, biblical interpreters throughout most of Christian history have had available to them a vast body of supplementary material to make up for the embarrassing circumstance that, as quoted earlier, "the reader of the gospels is at first surprised to find so little about Mary."[1] For the reader of the four Gospels was not reading only the Gospels, nor even only the New Testament, for information about Mary. Indeed, before there were the four Gospels, much less the entire New Testament, there was a Scripture, which Christians eventually came to call "Old Testament" and which, because of the centrality of typology and allegory, and because of the concept of prophecy and fulfillment, we are obliged to call a "Christian

Scripture."[2] The authors of the volume cited earlier, *Mary in the New Testament*, could content themselves with the reminder that "in some Roman Catholic mariology, there is a study of how Mary's role was foreshadowed in certain OT [Old Testament] passages, on the principle that, just as God prepared the way for His Son in the history of Israel, so too He prepared the way for the mother of His Son."[3] As the history of the development of biblical interpretation in the early church makes evident, moreover, it was not only, as this comment suggests, "some Roman Catholic mariology" but the entire patristic tradition East and West, that carried on such study of the foreshadowing of Mary in the Old Testament. Many of the rubrics considered in chapter 1 about the witness of the New Testament could just as easily find a place here; and as in that chapter, the attention required by the biblical material varies widely.

For our purposes, therefore, the evidence of the Bible is important not because of its contrast with subsequent tradition but precisely because of its anticipation of that tradition. Or, to put it the other way around and more accurately, the biblical evidence is interesting in the light of the way the subsequent tradition used it—or, as some might say, misused it. The rationale for the distinctive characteristic of this biblical evidence is to be found in the phrase from the Christmas Gospel, "of the house and lineage of David."[4] As it stood in the Gospel, this referred to Joseph, not to Mary, whose lineage was not traced in the genealogies provided by the Gospels of Matthew and Luke.[5] But it was also those same two Gospels that made a point of the virginal conception of Jesus and therefore of the conclusion that Joseph was only "supposed"[6] by some— but clearly not by the evangelists—to have been the father of Jesus. If "son of David" was in the language of the Gospels a way of affirming the continuity of Jesus Christ with Israel and the continuity of his kingship with that of his celebrated forefather, then his descent from David had to be through his only human parent, Mary, who must then also have been "of the house and lineage of David." That reasoning has provided the justification for the practice of going far beyond and behind the New Testament, by searching through the ancient Scriptures of Israel for prophecies and parallels, topics and typologies, that would enrich and amplify the tiny sheaf of data from the Gospels: Miriam, sister of Moses, of course, because of her name, but also Mother Eve; and then all the female personifications, above all in the writings carrying the name of King Solomon, particularly the figure of Wisdom in the eighth chapter of the Book of Proverbs and, among the books called Apocryphal or Deuterocanonical, in the Wisdom of Solomon (the name *Wisdom* being feminine, as is *Chokmah* in Hebrew, *Sophia* in Greek, *Sapientia* in Latin, and *Premudrost* in Russian) and the Bride in the Song of Songs, which was the longest and the most lavish portrait of a woman anywhere in the Bible. The process of appropriating this material for the purposes of Marian devotion and doctrine, which may be described as a methodology of amplification, was, on one hand, part of the much larger process of allegorical and figurative interpretation of the Bible, to which we owe some of the most imaginative and beautiful commentaries, in words and in pictures, in all of Medieval and Byzantine culture. It was, on the other hand, and almost against the intention of those who practiced it, a powerful affirmation that because Mary was, according to the reasoning summarized earlier, "of the house and lineage of David," she represented the unbreakable link between Jewish and Christian history, between the First Covenant *within* which she was born and the Second Covenant *to* which she gave birth, so that even the most virulent of Christian anti-Semites could not deny that she, the most blessed among women, was a Jew. Without explicit connection to the Virgin Mary, Marc Chagall's portrait of a pregnant woman exalted to heaven cannot help but convey this reminder.

The Black Madonna. One of the most impressive results of the Mariological interpretation of the Old Testament being discussed in this chapter was the application of the lush imagery of the Song of Songs to Mary. "*Nigra sum sed formosa* [I am black but comely]" were almost the first words of the Bride in the Song.[7] From those words came the biblical justification for the many portraits of Mary that have shunned the conventional representation of her as Italian or North European in favor of the Black Madonna. As it stood, the statement seemed to bespeak an all too widespread sense of contradiction between blackness and comeliness. But in his definitive commentary on the Song of Songs, Marvin Pope has convincingly shown on linguistic grounds that "Black am I *and* beautiful," not "but beautiful," is the correct translation of the Hebrew of this verse, which has also been preserved in the Greek of the Septuagint: *Melaina eimi kai kalē.* The grammatical conjunction was, of course, less important than the substantive connection. If, as I am presupposing throughout this book, the history of the interpretation of the Bible has not been confined to commentaries and sermons but has been the subject of the arts and of daily life, the Black Madonnas of Częstochowa and Guadalupe ("La Morenita—Little Darkling")[8] have expressed for countless millions, more eloquently than books could have, the exegetical intuition that, regardless of the translation, the Virgin was indeed black *and* beautiful. That also made her a special ambassador to that vast majority of the human race who were not white.

The Woman of Valor. I have already mentioned that the early Christians searched in the Jewish Scriptures, and specifically in the early chapters of Genesis, for prophecies that were fulfilled in the gospel. The most notable—notable enough to have eventually earned the name of first gospel or protevangel—was the promise of God after the fall of Adam and Eve. It was addressed to the serpent (taken by common consent to be the devil): "And I will put enmity between thee and the woman, and between thy seed and her seed; it shall bruise thy head, and thou shalt bruise his heel."[9] Irenaeus of Lyons, writing in the second half of the second century, expounded this text at great length to prove that Jesus was the seed of the woman and the Son of God, who as the Second Adam had withstood the assault of the tempter, conquering where the First Adam had been conquered, and who on the cross had been "bruised" by the serpent but had crushed him in the process.[10] On the basis of the best manuscripts it is the general agreement of modern students of the Vulgate text that Jerome, who was one of the few scholars in the first several centuries of Christian history to know Hebrew as well as Greek and Latin, translated this in the same sense as the King James Version just quoted (as it appears in the best critical edition of the Vulgate, published in 1986): "*Inimicitias ponam inter te et mulierem, et semen tuum et semen illius; ipsum conteret caput tuum, et tu conteres calcaneum eius.*" But at some point in the transmission of the Latin text of the Vulgate, whether by mistake or by fraud or by pious reflection, that neuter "*ipsum*" corresponding to the neuter of "*semen* [seed]" was changed to a feminine: "*Inimicitias ponam inter te et mulierem, et semen tuum et semen illius; ipsa conteret caput tuum, et tu insidiaberis calcaneo eius.*"[11] In poems and works of art throughout the Latin West, this translation inspired images of the humble Virgin triumphing over the proud tempter.[12]

And, in keeping with the appropriation of Old Testament language in the interest of amplifying the New Testament, she came to be seen as the divinely given answer to the question of the final chapter of the Book of Proverbs, which the Authorized Version rendered with "Who can find a virtuous woman?": "*Mulierem fortem quis inveniet?* [The woman of valor, who will find?]"[13] Mary as the *Mulier Fortis* was an extension and expansion of Mary as the Second Eve, who had entered the lists of battle as the First Eve had done but who, being *fortis,* had defeated the devil, conquering the conqueror. By extension, therefore, she could become the patron of victory. Her blessing was invoked by armies going into battle, particularly against those who were perceived to be the enemies of the faith, such as the Muslims. Her images were carried on banners and on the person of the warrior. As Tolstoy had Princess Marya Bolkonskaya in *War and Peace* (a character modeled after his mother) say at the end of a letter to her friend Julie, lamenting "this unfortunate war into which we have been drawn, God knows how and why": "Farewell, dear, good friend. May our divine Savior and His most Holy Mother keep you in their holy and almighty care. Marya."[14] And "our divine Savior and His most Holy Mother" were able also to keep soldiers in their holy and almighty care during battle, because Christ as *Christus Victor* and his Mother as *Mulier Fortis* could be not only gentle and humble but fierce and victorious. This was, once again, a picture of Mary that was, on the basis of this method of biblical interpretation, more evident in the Old Testament than in the New but that then could on that basis be found in the New Testament as well. It could also provide women of the Middle Ages with some sense of what they might be—and of what, by the election of God, they could be. For the most sensational Medieval answer to the question of Proverbs about the Woman of Valor was Joan of Arc.

The Leader of the Heavenly Choir. In spite of the use of Eve and of various female figures from the Solomonic writings, in many respects the most obvious prototype of Mary anywhere in the Old Testament had to be Miriam, sister of Moses and Aaron, for whom the Virgin was almost certainly named. The Hebrew name *Miryam* for the sister of Moses was rendered into Greek in several slightly divergent forms: *Maria, Mareia, Mariam, Mariamē.*[15] Both the form *Maria* and the form *Mariam* appeared in the Gospels, with the first being employed initially by Matthew and the second being employed initially by Luke. Except for the name itself, however, it would seem to be vain to look within the pages of the New Testament for any typology involving the mother of Jesus and the sister of Moses. But once it had become legitimate, indeed imperative, for Christian interpreters to invoke what we have been calling here the methodology of amplification, an imaginative interpreter of the Bible such as Augustine was drawn to the text from the history of the victory of the children of Israel over the armies of Pharaoh at the Red Sea, as described in the Book of Exodus: "And Miriam the prophetess, the sister of Aaron, took a timbrel in her hand; and all the women went out after her with timbrels and with dances. And Miriam answered them, Sing ye to the Lord, for he hath triumphed gloriously; the horse and his rider hath he thrown into the sea."[16] The powerful impact of that scene was heightened still further, in a stroke of musical and dramatic genius, by George Frideric Handel in his *Israel in Egypt,* when he switched the order of these verses 20 and 21 in the fifteenth chapter of Exodus with verse 1 in such a way that Miriam became the *choregos,* like the leader of the chorus in Aeschylus or Sophocles. But Marian devotion had, in effect, done just that long before, by applying the implications of the title Daughter of Zion to the typology of Mary and Miriam.

Ever-Virgin [Semper Virgo]. Although neither the writings of the apostle Paul nor the earliest Gospel, that of Mark, contained any reference to the virgin birth, that same biblical resource and historical source of Jewish Scripture did; or at any rate, it did in the Greek translation of it that had been prepared by the Jews of Alexandria during the century or two before the rise of Christianity, the Septuagint. From that source it came to the Gospels of Matthew and Luke, with Matthew quoting as authority the Greek translation of the prophecy of Isaiah: "Therefore the Lord himself shall give you a sign; Behold, a virgin [*parthenos* in the Septuagint] shall conceive, and bear a son, and shall call his name Immanuel."[17] The Greek *parthenos* was the translation of a Hebrew word that meant "young woman," not specifically "virgin," and the word was so quoted in the Greek New Testament. Mary asked the angel of the annunciation: "How shall this be, seeing that I know not a man?"[18] Three of the Gospels— Matthew, Mark, and John, but not Luke—did speak in later chapters about "brethren" of Christ,[19] as did the apostle Paul.[20] The apparently obvious and natural conclusion from this would seem to have been that after the miraculous conception of Jesus by the power of the Holy Spirit, Mary and Joseph went on to have other children of their own.

But that was not the conclusion that the vast majority of early Christian teachers drew. Instead, they came to call Mary Ever-Virgin, *Aeiparthenos, Semper Virgo*. To do this in the light of biblical materials about the "brethren" of Jesus, they had to resort to some elaborate biblical arguments. The biblical support for calling Mary Ever-Virgin, however, came not chiefly from the New Testament but from the Song of Songs: "A garden inclosed is my sister, my spouse; a spring shut up, a fountain sealed [*Hortus conclusus, soror mea sponsa, hortus conclusus, fons signatus*]."[21] Thus Jerome, after stringing together a series of texts from the Song of Songs, came to this verse, which he took to be a reference to "the mother of our Lord, who was a mother and a Virgin. Hence it was that no one before or after our Savior was lain in his new tomb, hewn in the solid rock."[22] An interesting process of creative biblical interpretation was going on here. For according to the Gospels at the other end of the story of the earthly life of Jesus Christ, the grave of Jesus was "a new sepulchre," belonging to Joseph of Arimathea, where no one had ever been buried before.[23] The Gospels said nothing about the later history of the sepulcher, after the resurrection of Jesus, just as they said nothing about the later history of the womb of Mary. But on the strength of the "*hortus conclusus*" of the Song of Songs, Jerome, who was arguably the greatest biblical scholar in the history of the Western Church, felt justified in concluding both that there would never be another person buried in the sepulcher and that there was never another person born of the Virgin. It is amusing, though not important, to note that in both cases the auxiliary role in the story belonged to a man bearing the name of Joseph.

The Face That Most Resembles Christ's. In the language of the Old Testament, "face" became almost a technical term for "person." This usage had appeared already in the story of creation, where, according to the Greek translation, "God formed the man of dust of the earth, and breathed upon his face [prosōpon] the breath of life, and the man became a living soul."[24] Throughout biblical language, and beyond it even in modern languages, "face to face" was a way of saying "person to person."[25] The benediction that Aaron was instructed to pronounce upon the people of Israel applied the concept to God: "The Lord bless thee, and keep thee: The Lord make his face shine upon thee, and be gracious unto thee: The Lord lift up his countenance upon thee, and give thee peace."[26] For the God of Israel, unlike the idols of the heathen, had neither form nor face to "shine upon" anyone, and the anthropomorphic ascription of a "face" to God could refer only to the special relation cemented in the covenant. When the New Testament sought to affirm the continuity of that covenant but at the same time its extension beyond the borders of the people of Israel, it spoke of how "the God who commanded the light to shine out of darkness, hath shined in our hearts, to give the light of the knowledge of the glory of God in the face of Jesus Christ."[27] The face of Jesus Christ, therefore, was seen as the divinely given answer to the prayer of the psalm "When thou saidst, See ye my face; my heart said unto thee, Thy face, Lord, will I seek."[28] And so it seemed to be a valid extension of this concept, and an application to it of the identification of Mary as Mediatrix, for Bernard of Clairvaux and then Dante Alighieri to speak about the face of the Virgin Mary as the one through which to view the face of Jesus Christ, through which in turn the face of God was visible.

Visions of the Virgin Mary. It was from the prominence of visions in the religious experiences and personal revelations described in the Old Testament that the biblical warrant for the apparitions of the Virgin Mary in ancient and modern times came. By visions and revelations of the Almighty, Abraham received the promise as well as the awesome command to sacrifice his son Isaac—and then the command "Lay not thine hand upon the lad."[29] The vision of the "bush that burned with fire, and was not consumed" provided the setting for the "towering text"[30] of God's self-disclosure as "I am that I am."[31] Similarly, "in the day that king Uzziah died," as the prophet Isaiah had reported, "I saw the Lord sitting upon a throne, high and lifted up."[32] Other prophets of Israel, too, had been the recipients of such visions at their inauguration into office or later in their prophetic careers.[33] For Ezekiel and Daniel, the reception of visions and the communication of their content to the people or their rulers had become the central and defining quality of their prophetic apocalypticism.[34] All that might have been expected to end with the New Testament; for it emphasized the uniqueness and finality of the revelation in Jesus Christ, as a result of which the stock prophetic formula "And the word of the Lord came" to the prophet, still used for John the Baptist, was no longer appropriate, because the Word of the Lord had come in the flesh, and "all the prophets and the law prophesied until John."[35] Nevertheless, and perhaps somewhat surprisingly, the visions that had begun in the Old Testament did not cease in the New. In fact, the apostle Peter was described in the Book of Acts as having appropriated the prophecy of Joel, "And it shall come to pass in the last days, saith God, I will pour out my Spirit on all flesh: and your sons and your daughters shall prophesy, and your young men shall see visions, and your old men shall dream dreams," as being fulfilled now in his generation.[36] In the same book of the New Testament, Peter required a heavenly vision of unclean and forbidden foods to cure him of his subservience to kosher laws.[37] His apostolic colleague and sometime adversary, Paul, received a vision of Jesus Christ on the road to Damascus that threw him to the ground, blinded him, and converted him to the "way" of the Christians whom he had been persecuting, a vision that was followed by others; and, as he said, he "was not disobedient unto the heavenly vision."[38]

Jesus Christ himself had such heavenly visions, according to the

Gospels, for he "beheld Satan as lightning fall from heaven."[39] During his agony in the Garden of Gethsemane, "there appeared an angel unto him from heaven, strengthening him" for the passion and death he was about to undergo.[40] More directly relevant to our concerns here are the visions attendant upon the birth of Jesus Christ from the Virgin Mary. The most important of these was the annunciation, but the others are also of great interest. It was by a vision in a dream that Joseph was dissuaded from "putting her away privily" when he discovered that Mary was pregnant with the child Jesus, by another vision that he was warned of the plot of Herod against the threat of the child who was "born king of the Jews" so that he took the child and Mary his mother to Egypt, and by yet another vision that he was told when it was safe to return with Jesus and Mary from Egypt to Nazareth.[41]

But by far the most abundant collection of visions anywhere in the New Testament appeared in the book that now stands last in the canon, and that has often been regarded in the subsequent tradition, whether accurately or inaccurately is not important here, as the last to have been written: the Book of Revelation, the Apocalypse of Saint John the Divine, attributed to the evangelist John. By the time the panorama of its visions had closed, the seer of the Apocalypse had viewed not only "one like unto the Son of Man,"[42] but angels and beasts and heavenly cities, all marching in dramatic procession across the screen of his frenzied and ecstatic sight. At about the halfway point of the visions came the following: "And there appeared a great wonder in heaven; a woman clothed with the sun, and the moon under her feet, and upon her head a crown of twelve stars."[43] Whether or not this was originally intended as a reference to the Virgin Mary, it comported so well with the developing ways of speaking and thinking about her that in the early Middle Ages, from the seventh to the ninth century in both East and West, it became clear that this "symbol of the woman who is the mother of the Messiah might well lend itself to Marian interpretation, once Marian interest developed in the later Christian community. And eventually when Revelation was placed in the same canon of Scripture with the Gospel of Luke and the Fourth Gospel, the various images of the virgin, the woman at the cross, and the woman who gave birth to the Messiah would reinforce each other."[44] It is worth remembering that some centuries later, by a somewhat similar process, some descendants of the Protestant Reformation had no compunction about identifying the "angel having the everlasting gospel" in the Book of Revelation with the person and ministry of Martin Luther.[45]

The Immaculate Conception. The intricate connection between the interpretation of the Bible and the development of doctrine, as briefly identified in the preceding chapter, has worked in both directions simultaneously, no less for Mariology than for other branches of theology. A doctrine about her would take a particular form because, in addition to the devotion to her and the speculation concerning her that were such fertile gardens for the growth of doctrine, some passage of Scripture from either the Old or the New Testament required consideration for its bearing on Marian teaching. Conversely, the growth of Marian teaching out of these various sources made it necessary to bring the exegesis of one or another passage, as that exegesis may originally have evolved independently of such teaching, into harmony with what Mary had come to mean. For in the Middle Ages, particularly after Peter Abelard's *Sic et Non* [Yes and No] had called attention to seeming contradictions in the tradition, the harmonization of biblical or other authoritative texts became one of the most important assignments of scholastic theology.[46] As it was anticipated by Cyprian of Carthage and then formulated by Ambrose of Milan and Augustine of Hippo, the standard Western interpretation of the words of David in the psalm "Behold, I was shapen in iniquity; and in sin did my mother conceive me,"[47] had generalized the statement from David to apply it to all humanity. But that interpretation appeared to collide with the increasingly transcendent valuation that was being placed on the unique holiness of the Virgin Mary. It was out of the need to harmonize these two imperatives that the doctrine of the immaculate conception finally emerged in Roman Catholicism.

The Assumption of the Mater Gloriosa. Of all the major privileges and attributes attaching to the person of Mary, none would seem to be more extraneous to the biblical account of her in the New Testament than the assumption, which was promulgated as a dogma of the church, binding

on all believers, by Pope Pius XII on 1 November 1950, in the bull
Munificentissimus Deus. But that depended on how one went about establishing biblical warrant. For the status of Mary as daughter of Zion and heir of
the people of Israel meant that for her, just as for her divine Son, it was
permissible and even mandatory to ransack the pages of the Old Testament for additional information about her. After the resurrection, Christ
had appeared to the disciples at Emmaus, and "beginning at Moses and all
the prophets, he expounded unto them in all the scriptures the things
concerning himself,"[48] by a process that was taken to apply legitimately
also to Mary. Thus the absence of New Testament information about what
happened "when the course of her earthly life was run" was not a
sufficient deterrent. Therefore the saying of the prophet Isaiah that the
apostle Paul applied to the death and resurrection of Christ, "Death is
swallowed up in victory,"[49] could in *Munificentissimus Deus* be extended to
her. Part of what is being called here the methodology of amplification
was based on the premise that because of her unique and supreme
position among all humanity, as not only the highest of all women and
the highest of all human beings but the highest of all creatures, "higher
than the cherubim, more glorious than the seraphim," Mary came to be
regarded as not unworthy of any of the honors and privileges that had,
according to the Scriptures of both the Old and the New Testament, been
conferred on others.

In addition, as the Byzantine descriptions of her dormition made
clear,[50] two saints' lives of the Old Testament could, by following the
methodology of amplification, be taken to supply additional data about
how, when the course of an earthly life was run, someone could be and
had been "assumed *in body and soul* to heavenly glory." They were the brief
and enigmatic episode of Enoch in Genesis, and the dramatic episode of
Elijah in 2 Kings: "And Enoch walked with God: and he was not; for God
took him"; "And it came to pass . . . that, behold, there appeared a
chariot of fire, and horses of fire, and parted them both asunder; and
Elijah went up by a whirlwind into heaven. And Elisha saw it, and he
cried, My father, my father, the chariot of Israel, and the horsemen
thereof. And he saw him no more."[51] Jewish scholarship and devotion

had seized upon both of these and amplified them. In apocryphal and apocalyptic literature Enoch's later destiny became a topic for speculation.[52] The figure of Elijah likewise became the subject of lore and legend.[53] At the Seder meal for Passover an empty place is still set for Elijah; and according to the New Testament, Elijah appeared with Moses at the transfiguration of Jesus.[54]

Now if these two men of God already in the Old Testament were deemed worthy of the special privilege of being taken up into heaven, with a chariot of fire and horses of fire, did not that constitute a form of biblical evidence also about Mary, who, by an a fortiori argument, could be seen as having been eminently more worthy of such special treatment? For if this way to heaven had already, in at least these two cases, been opened up for mere mortals, was one to say that the very Mother of God was less deserving of it than they had been? The story of Mary and Martha, the sisters of Lazarus, which would eventually serve as the Gospel pericope for the Feast of the Assumption, closed with the words, "Mary hath chosen that good part, which shall not be taken away from her"; this referred, of course, to the sister of Martha and Lazarus, but it seemed to many to fit the mother of Jesus even better.[55] By a similar transposition of reference, an Old Testament text such as "When he ascended up on high, he led captivity captive, and gave gifts unto men," which had been applied to the ascension of Christ, also seemed to suit the assumption of Mary, through which gifts had been distributed to humanity.[56] Or when Christ promised, "If any man serve me, let him follow me; and where I am, there shall also my servant be," there was no "man," indeed, no one among mortals, who had served him in so special a way as Mary had; and therefore, in accordance with his promise to her before his ascension, she had also followed him into heaven.[57]

This celebration of the Virgin Mary and the elaboration of such praises in her name coincided chronologically with the heyday of this method of allegorical and typological biblical interpretation. Conversely, the rejection of both the Marian celebration and the allegory came together, first in the Reformation and then in the Enlightenment and its aftermath. Looking back at both developments, in the Middle Ages and in the Reformation and Enlightenment, it is difficult to avoid the tough questions of loss and gain. For the allegorical and typological method had saved the Hebrew Bible from its enemies and detractors in the early Christian movement, who read it literally and rejected it. They were also often the ones who opposed the direction in which the interpretation of the Virgin Mary was moving. The vindication of the Jewish Scriptures as part of the Christian Bible coincided not only chronologically but logically with this picture of Mary. Vastly different though they seemed to be in their approach to the Bible, therefore, a fundamentalist literalism and a modernist historicism both yielded a two-dimensional perspective in the reading of the Bible. At the same time they also led to an impoverishment in the attitude toward Mary. Whether these went together is an intriguing historical question, which we can only begin to answer through the study of art, literature, and thought in subsequent chapters. In what follows, these and other Old Testament texts and this methodology of amplification will figure prominently as the depository from which the development of doctrine and devotion would take the language it needed to speak about Mary.

Toni Zenz, door for Saint Alban's Church, Cologne, 1958. (Bildquelle: Rheinisches
Bildarchiv Köln)

3 The Second Eve and the Guarantee of Christ's True Humanity

As by one man's disobedience many were made sinners,
so by the obedience of one shall many be made righteous.
—Romans 5:19

In the second and third centuries after Christ, during the momentous age of cultural transition and spiritual-intellectual upheaval that historians call Late Antiquity, which falls somewhere between the Hellenistic age and the Byzantine and Medieval periods, the parallel between Mary and Eve was a primary focus for the consideration of two major issues of life and thought that continue to be perennial concerns in our era: the meaning (if any) of time and human history and the very definition of what it means to be human.[1]

A central contribution of the faith of Israel to the development of Western thought has been the interpretation of history. This is not to say that the question of the meaning of human history was absent from other cultures, for example from classical Greece. It was especially in the thought of Plato that this question received detailed attention. Book IV of Plato's *Laws* contains a profound analysis of the relative power of the several forces in history: "That God governs all things, and that chance [tychē] and opportunity [kairos] co-operate with Him in the governance of human affairs. There is, however, a third and less extreme view, that art [tech.nē] should be there also."[2] Serious reflection on the interrelation of those three forces, as Constantine Despotopoulos has pointed out, could become the foundation for a far-ranging philosophy of history.[3] It is also the case that the historians of ancient Athens—above all Thucydides in the Funeral Oration of Pericles, but also Herodotus—carried on serious reflection of this kind as they pondered Greek history.[4]

Nevertheless, the coming of the faith of Israel and of the Hebrew Bible into the Greco-Roman world, which took place first through its translation into Greek at Alexandria by Hellenistic Jews and then more massively and more decisively through the mission and expansion of Christianity across the entire Mediterranean world, challenged and eventually transformed the prevailing views of the nature and purpose of the historical process. To go on saying with Plato's *Laws* "that God governs all things" came to mean something radically different when the historical "opportunity," or *kairos*, at issue was the exodus of the children of Israel from Egypt and the giving of the law to Moses at Sinai, or the life, death, and resurrection of Jesus Christ. For in one sense, the belief that "God governs all things" was, if anything, intensified when the word "God" was taken to refer neither to the gods of Mount Olympus nor to the One of Platonic philosophy but to the God of Abraham, Isaac, and Jacob, or to Father, Son, and Holy Spirit. In spite of their profound and fundamentally irreconcilable differences, Judaism and Christianity both viewed human history as a process in which divine governance was a matter of divine initiative. Moses did not use his own ingenuity to discover God while tending Jethro's flocks on the plains of Midian; rather, it was God who chose him, sought him out, called to him from the burning bush, and imposed on him the task of telling Pharaoh "Let my people go!"[5] Similarly, the New Testament was not the account of how the upward tendency of human history had finally attained to the level of the divine, as though human flesh had become the Word of God; on the contrary, "In the beginning was the Word, and the Word was with God, and the Word was God. And the Word was made flesh, and dwelt among us."[6] In a radical and transforming sense, then, history was viewed *from above*, as the record of the actions of the living God. As the New Testament put it,

"Every good gift and every perfect gift is from above, and cometh down from the Father of lights, with whom is no variableness, neither shadow of turning."[7]

But that is only half the story, for at the same time the Jewish and Christian traditions viewed that same history also *from below*, as the record of authentically human actions for which human beings with free will were to be held morally accountable. Amid the historical changes and upheavals of the Mediterranean world during the second and third century, the sensitive spirits of Late Antiquity were pondering whether there was a discernible meaning in human history. One of the noblest of these sensitive spirits, Marcus Aurelius, who died in the year 180, put that question of the age this way in Book XII of his *Meditations*, writing not in Latin (though he was emperor of Rome) but in Greek: "There is a doom inexorable and a law inviolable, or there is a providence that can be merciful, or else there is a chaos that is purposeless and ungoverned. If a resistless fate, why try to struggle against it? If a providence willing to show mercy, do your best to deserve its divine succour. If a chaos undirected, give thanks that amid such stormy seas you have within you a mind at the helm."[8] To the consideration of those three alternatives, as outlined by the philosopher-emperor Marcus Aurelius, Judaism, and then Christianity, brought a view of history as an arena in which both "a providence that can be merciful" and a human activity that can be responsible were at work, so that neither could be thought of apart from the other. That was the deepest meaning of the Hebrew word *berith*, covenant, in which both parties engaged to do certain things, even if one of them was the Creator of heaven and earth and the other was a human creature; and for the Christian version of this authentically human side of the historical dialectic, Eve and Mary were key players.[9]

There does seem to have been a practice in early Christianity of reading the first three chapters of Genesis as anticipating the coming of Christ. Therefore they may have cast the story of the temptation of Christ by the devil as a kind of midrash on the story of the temptation of Adam and Eve. The tempter said to Eve: "In the day ye eat thereof . . . ye shall be as gods."[10] And the tempter said to Christ, who "had fasted forty days and forty nights [and] was afterward an hungered": "If thou be the son of God, command that these stones be made bread."[11] In the Epistle to the Romans, the apostle Paul had drawn the parallel: "As by one man [namely, Adam] sin entered into the world, and death by sin. . . . much more the grace of God, and the gift by grace, which is by one man, Jesus Christ, hath abounded unto many."[12] In 1 Corinthians he developed the parallel and the contrast in greater detail: "And so it is written, The first man Adam was made a living soul; the last Adam was made a quickening spirit. . . . The first man is of the earth, earthy: the second man is the Lord from heaven."[13] But for the category of history from below, as the record of authentically human actions for which human beings were to be held accountable, that contrasting parallel between the First Adam as "of the earth, earthy" and the Second Adam, Christ as "the Lord from heaven," which has had such an important career in the history of ideas, also raised serious problems, to some of which we shall return in the second half of this chapter.

For many of those problems the contrasting parallel between Eve and Mary provided profound insight and an important corrective. Thus Irenaeus, bishop of Lyons, who was born probably in Asia Minor about A.D. 130 and who died about A.D. 200, strikingly formulated this parallel in both of his surviving writings: in a passage from his treatise *Against Heresies* (written in Greek but preserved largely in a Latin translation), but also in a work that was long thought to have been permanently lost but that was discovered only in this century, and in an Armenian translation, the *Epideixis*, or *Proof of the Apostolic Preaching*. Playing off against each other various elements in Genesis and in the Gospels, such as the Garden of Eden versus the Garden of Gethsemane and the tree of the knowledge of good and evil versus the tree of the cross, Irenaeus then came to the most innovative and most breathtaking of the parallels:

> And just as it was through a virgin who disobeyed [namely, Eve] that mankind was stricken and fell and died, so too it was through the Virgin [Mary], who obeyed the word of God, that mankind, resuscitated by life, received life. For the Lord

[Christ] came to seek back the lost sheep, and it was mankind that was lost; and therefore He did not become some other formation, but He likewise, of her that was descended from Adam [namely, Mary], preserved the likeness of formation; for Adam had necessarily to be restored in Christ, that mortality be absorbed in immortality. *And Eve [had necessarily to be restored] in Mary, that a virgin, by becoming the advocate of a virgin, should undo and destroy virginal disobedience by virginal obedience.*[14]

Here was not only a parallel between the First Adam as "of the earth, earthy" and the Second Adam, Christ as "the Lord from heaven"—thus a contrast between the earthly and the heavenly—but a contrast between a calamitous disobedience by someone who was no more than human, Eve, and a saving obedience by someone who was no more than human, who was not "from heaven" but altogether "of the earth," Mary as the Second Eve. It was absolutely essential to the integrity of the two narratives that both the disobedience of Eve and the obedience of Mary be seen as actions of a free will, not as the consequences of coercion, whether by the devil in the case of Eve or by God in the case of Mary.

When it is suggested that for the development of the doctrine of Mary, such Christian writers as Irenaeus in a passage like this "are important witnesses for the state of the tradition in the late second century, if not earlier,"[15] that raises the interesting question of whether Irenaeus had invented the concept of Mary as the Second Eve here or was drawing on a deposit of tradition that had come to him from "earlier." It is difficult, in reading his *Against Heresies* and especially his *Proof of the Apostolic Preaching*, to avoid the impression that he cited the parallelism of Eve and Mary so matter-of-factly without arguing or having to defend the point because he could assume that his readers would willingly go along with it, or even that they were already familiar with it. One reason that this could be so might have been that, on this issue as on so many others, Irenaeus regarded himself as the guardian and the transmitter of a body of belief that had come to him from earlier generations, from the very apostles.[16] A modern reader does need to consider the possibility, perhaps even to concede the possibility, that in so regarding himself Irenaeus may just have been right and that therefore it may already have become natural in the second half of the second century to look at Eve, the "mother of all living,"[17] and Mary, the mother of Christ, together, understanding and interpreting each of the two most important women in human history on the basis of the other. With such moderns in mind, the parallelism was dramatically set forth by the German sculptor Toni Zanz in a metal door created in 1958 for the rebuilding of the Church of Sankt Alban in Cologne, which had been destroyed during World War II: in the lower left are Adam and Eve at the moment of the fall, in the upper right the Second Adam and the Second Eve at the moment of the crucifixion and redemption.

Once it was introduced into the vocabulary, this dialectic of Eve and Mary took on a life of its own. Because in Latin the name *Eva* spelled backwards became *Ave*, the greeting of the angel to Mary in the Vulgate as it was echoed by millions of souls in the prayer *Ave Maria*, there appeared to be a mystical Mariological significance in the very name. Less playfully and more profoundly, the elaborations upon the disobedience of Eve and the obedience of Mary produced extensive psychological comparisons between the two women. In those comparisons the negative interpretation of woman as embodied in Eve—vulnerable, irrational, emotional, erotic, living by the experience of the senses rather than by the mind and the reason, and thus an easy prey for the wily tempter—propagated the all-too-familiar stereotypes of misogynous slander that have so embedded themselves in the thought and language of so many nations, also but not only in the West. Modern polemical writers have combed the works of patristic and Medieval thinkers to find these stereotypes, and they have amassed a massive catalog that has by now passed from one book and article to another. It is not intended as a defense of the stereotypes, but it is intended as a necessary historical corrective, to point out that those same works of patristic and Medieval thinkers presented a counterpoise to the stereotypes, in their even more extensive interpretations of woman as embodied in Mary, the "Woman of Valor [*mulier fortis*]" who as the descendant and vindicator of the First Eve crushed the head of the serpent and vanquished the devil.[18] Historical justice requires that both poles of the dialectic be included. When, in *Paradise Lost*, John Milton, who was "an author unmistakably opposed to Catholicism and its veneration of Mary,"[19] nevertheless described how, in greeting Eve,

> . . . the Angel *Haile*
> Bestowed, the holy salutation us'd
> Long after to blest Marie, second Eve,[20]

he was quoting the angelic salutation "Ave Maria" and with it invoking the ancient parallel that is the theme of this chapter. But he did so, as a Puritan and Protestant, in a literary and theological context where the counterpoise of the Catholic portrait of Mary had largely been lost. Therefore Milton could have Adam, speaking after the fall, address an *Ave Maria* to the Virgin Mary in language that was clearly intended to make not only Eve but Mary know her proper place in the scheme of human history:

> . . . Virgin Mother, Haile,
> High in the love of Heav'n, yet from my Loines
> Thou shall proceed . . . .[21]

Milton's postmortem diagnosis of the psychology of the fall of Eve, step by painful step, is rightly celebrated as a flawed but brilliant character study. But when that autopsy of temptation is seen in the setting of the history of patristic and Medieval thought about the First and the Second Eve that had led up to Milton, it becomes clear that *Paradise Lost* emphasized one pole of the dialectic far more than the other. And the same has been true of many and lesser writers since Milton.

Returning to the categories of Marcus Aurelius and of Irenaeus (who were nearly contemporaries in the second century), the central theme of the thought of Irenaeus was, in the phrase of Marcus Aurelius, "a providence that can be merciful" and that had already proved itself to be merciful by bringing about a "recapitulation [*anakephalaiōsis*]" of human history, in which each successive stage of human sin had been restored by the successive stages of God's saving activity in Christ.[22] But the Stoic image of this "providence that can be merciful" often seemed to carry with it overtones of deterministic necessity, *anankē heimarmenē*, and to make free will problematical. That sort of deterministic necessity was by no means incompatible with profound insight into human motivation and psychology, as was evident not only from Marcus Aurelius but above all from Tolstoy.[23] In his famous second epilogue to *War and Peace*, Tolstoy attacked modern philosophies of history because of their lingering attachment to an untenable view of free will, concluding with the well-known axiom: "It is necessary to renounce a freedom that does not exist, and to recognize a dependence [that is, a determinism] of which we are not conscious."[24]

The theme of Mary as Second Eve likewise represented a critique of, and an alternative to, another view widely held in Antiquity and Late Antiquity: the cyclical theory of history, for which, as in the philosopher Porphyry, the metaphor of the wheel was the key. It was, in the formula of Charles N. Cochrane, a student of Herodotus, a "belief in the endless reiteration of 'typical' situations," to which, as for example in Augustine's *City of God*, the response was "the faith of Christians that, notwithstanding all appearances, human history does not consist of a series of repetitive patterns, but marks a sure, if unsteady, advance to an ultimate goal. As such, it has a beginning, a middle, and an end, *exortus, processus, et finis.*"[25] For according to Augustine, the cyclical theory was right in discerning "repetitive patterns," but these did not negate the particularity of unrepeatable events and persons, which happened uniquely, once and only once: Adam and Eve did not continue to be created over and over again, and did not yield to the seductions of the tempter over and over again, and were not driven out of the garden over and over again. But by the process Irenaeus called recapitulation, a Second Adam did appear in the person of Jesus Christ, once and for all, to repair the damage done by the First Adam; and a Second Eve did come in the person of the Virgin Mary, as Irenaeus put it, "that a virgin, by becoming the advocate of a virgin, should undo and destroy virginal disobedience by virginal obedience"[26]—not repetition but recapitulation.

Yet the words of 1 Corinthians quoted earlier, "The first man is of the earth, earthy: the second man is the Lord from heaven,"[27] identified a second concept of Late Antiquity to which the figure of Mary provided an answer: the notion of "the divine man [ho theios anēr]," which, when applied to the Christian understanding of the person of Jesus Christ, led almost inescapably to the danger that "the second man [who] is the Lord from heaven," because he was seen as *more* than merely human, would come to be seen as *less* than completely human. The tendency noted earlier that, in Louis Ginzberg's words, "just as a pearl results from a stimulus in the shell of a mollusk, so also a legend may arise from an irritant in the scripture,"[28] was at work already in the earliest stages of Christian thought about Jesus Christ—and about Mary. The most important evidence for that tendency was the apocryphal Gospel, the *Protevangel of James.*[29] Although it was an apocryphal Gospel,—one that did not achieve official status as part of the canon of the New Testament—it nevertheless "has dominated the development of the Marian legend, providing much of the basic material for Mary's biography."[30] Some of the legends about the Virgin contained in the *Protevangel of James* were the inviolate virginity of Mary not only in conception but in birth, as well as the related idea that she gave birth to Jesus without suffering birth pangs, and therefore the explanation that the "brothers of Jesus" spoken of in the Gospels must have been the children of Joseph the widower from his first marriage.[31] Although it is not clear, there are grounds to suppose that some of these legends about the Virgin Mary may implicitly have represented as well a hesitancy to ascribe total humanity to her divine Son, as that hesitancy was already being expressed in other sources nearly contemporary to the *Protevangel of James.* Irenaeus, to whom we owe the first large-scale exposition of the parallel between Eve and Mary, is likewise one of the sources from whom we learn that such a hesitancy among the followers of the Gnostic teacher Valentinus had led them to assert that Jesus had not been "born" of the Virgin Mary in the usual sense at all, but had "passed through Mary as water runs through a tube," not only without birth pangs but without the involvement of the mother except in a purely passive sense.[32] Christian art would eventually counter this tendency by its portrayals of the pregnant Mary.[33] It was likewise in response to this Gnostic threat to the true humanity of Jesus, as well as in defense of the unique position not only of Jesus but of Mary in the history of salvation, that Irenaeus found this decisive role for the Virgin.

The most important intellectual struggle of the first five centuries of Christian history—indeed the most important intellectual struggle in all of Christian history—took place in response to the question of whether the divine in Jesus Christ was identical with God the Creator.[34] For the answer to that challenge, too, was Mary, defined now as Theotokos and Mother of God.[35] Although that challenge to the full deity of the Son of God had been present from the earliest times of the Christian movement, as becomes clear from the iteration of the tempter's question "If thou be the Son of God"[36] by other doubters, the special challenge in the second and third centuries was the one that came from the opposite direction, questioning whether the divine man was truly "man" in the fullest sense of that word or whether in one way or another he needed to be shielded from the total implications of an authentic humanity. Many movements of Christian thought and devotion in the second and third century that were eventually lumped together and condemned as "Gnostic" shared this outlook, which came to be called "Docetism" from the Greek verb dokein, "to seem," meaning that the humanity was "merely apparent"; conversely, the earliest thinkers to be commended as "orthodox" were those who strove to vindicate, against these "Docetic" and "Gnostic" tendencies, the fully human dimension of the life and person of Jesus.

Although many individual incidents in the Gospels became battlegrounds for this conflict—for example, the very idea of his eating and drinking in a human fashion[37]—there were two junctures in his life on which both sides concentrated, the nativity and the crucifixion: in the words of the Apostles' Creed, "born of the Virgin Mary, suffered under Pontius Pilate." Wolfgang Amadeus Mozart, in the last sacred composition he completed before his death, and certainly one of the most exquisite and profoundly moving as well, set to music the affirmation that it had been these two events, "being truly born of the Virgin Mary [vere natum de Maria Virgine]" and "being truly sacrificed on the cross for mankind [(vere) immolatum in cruce pro homine]," that guaranteed both human salvation and the presence of "the true body [verum corpus]" in the Eucharist—and he did so by addressing another Ave to that "true body": Ave verum corpus.[38] The suffering and death on the cross was, to both sides, evidence of a nature that was, in Nietzsche's phrase, "human, all too human." Suffering was there regarded as unworthy of a truly divine nature; for by common consent (and, incidentally, without much explicit discussion), the divine nature was regarded as having the essential quality of being beyond the capacity for suffering or change, the quality defined by the Greek philosophical term apatheia, impassability, and incorporated into the Christian doctrine of God.[39] One of the leading Gnostic teachers, Basilides, was reported to have taken this revulsion at the idea of attributing suffering to the divine Christ so far that, on the basis of the report of the Gospels that on the way to Calvary the Roman soldiers "as they led [Christ] away, laid hold upon one Simon, a Cyrenian, coming out of the country, and on him they laid the cross, that he might bear it after Jesus,"[40] he claimed that Simon of Cyrene had been substituted for Jesus and crucified instead, sparing Christ the ignominy of the crucifixion and death.[41] Summarizing the response of an early Christian writer, Ignatius of Antioch, to such ideas, therefore, Virginia Corwin has said: "That the preaching of the cross and death of Christ continued to be a 'stumbling-block to unbelievers' (Eph. 18.1) need not surprise us, and Ignatius indicates why the docetic thinkers who were his opponents were repelled by it. In Ignatius' mind it was the final and incontrovertible proof that Christ truly became man and entered the scene of history."[42] It seems to have been at least partly with this controversy in view that so many versions of the early Christian creeds, including the Apostles' Creed and the Niceno-Constantinopolitan Creed, incorporated the phrase "under Pontius Pilate" into the recital of the sufferings of Christ, thereby identifying him as a truly human person and characterizing the suffering as a truly historical event that took place not in a mythical or Docetic "once upon a time" but at a particular place on the map and time in the history of the Roman empire.[43]

But Pontius Pilate was only one of the two dramatis personae mentioned in the creeds, and the second of them. The other, and the first mentioned, was the Virgin Mary; for the other decisive event on which the true humanity of Christ depended was that he was, as the Apostles' Creed said, "born of the Virgin Mary," a formula that appeared in various slightly differing permutations even more often than "under Pontius Pilate."[44] Here again, the Docetic campaign to shield him from the implications of being fully human had found various ingenious explanations, including the simile that at his birth he had passed through the body of Mary as water passes through a pipe, without affecting the medium and (more important) without being affected by the medium.[45] The response to this metaphor, and to the theory underlying it, was to emphasize his genuine birth from the Virgin Mary. For, as the founder of Christian Latin, Tertullian, put it, writing against Marcion, "All these illusions of an imaginary corporeality in [his version of Christ], Marcion adopted with this view, that his nativity also might not be furnished with any evidence from his human substance." To the contrary, Tertullian continued, "Since He was 'the truth,' He was flesh; since He was flesh, He was born. . . . He is no phantom."[46] The logic of the argument was clear, whether one accepted the substance of it or not: Salvation depended on the true and complete humanity of Christ in his life and death; that true and complete humanity depended in turn on his having been truly born; and his true birth in its turn depended on his having had a mother who was truly and completely human. And if, as the case argued by Irenaeus and others maintained, it was the voluntary and virginal obedience of Mary by which the voluntary and virginal disobedience of Eve was undone and set aright, Mary became, by that voluntary obedience, both the Second Eve and the principal guarantee of Christ's humanity.

As it was expounded in prose and especially in poetry, all of this frequently took the rhetorical form of saturation with dialectics and reveling in antithesis, as in the lines of a later British metaphysical poet

of the Baroque period, Richard Crashaw, a Puritan who converted to
Roman Catholicism:

> Welcome, all wonders in one sight!
> Eternity shut in a span!
> Summer in Winter, Day in Night!
> Heaven in earth, and God in man!
> Great little One! whose all-embracing birth
> Lifts Earth to Heaven, stoops Heaven to Earth—[47]

until the Virgin Mary could be seen as Our Lady of the Paradoxes:
Virgin but Mother, Human Mother but Mother of God.

As herself a creature, she was as well the one through whom the
Logos Creator had united himself to a created human nature.[48] In the
striking formula of Gregory of Nyssa, contrasting the First Adam with
the Second Adam, "the first time, [God the Logos] took dust from the
earth and formed man, [but] this time he took dust from the Virgin and
did not merely form man, but formed man around himself."[49] Although the Arianism that Athanasius combated is usually (and correctly) seen as the denial of the full and complete divinity of Christ,
many earlier heresies about Christ—and, at least according to the
charge of some interpreters,[50] Arianism itself—were guilty of denying
his full and complete humanity. Beginning already with the teachings
against which the later writers of the New Testament had directed their
emphasis on the visibility and the tangibility of the human "flesh" of
Christ, various early interpretations of the figure of Christ had striven to
exempt him from the loathsome concreteness that flesh is heir to. And
since nothing about human flesh was more concrete, and to many of
them nothing was more loathsome, than the processes of human pro-
creation and birth, they were especially intent on rescuing his humanity
from an involvement in those processes. This inevitably made Mary the
primary focus of their reinterpretations, as well as of the orthodox
replies. Not only had some of the Gnostics said that Christ "received
nothing from the Virgin,"[51] but (also according to the report of John of

Damascus, apparently quoting Irenaeus)[52] they had said that he passed through the body of Mary as "through a channel [*dia sōlēnos*]," that is, without being affected by the passive medium of his mother. This would appear to have been an exaggerated form of a notion, widespread in antiquity, that even in a normal conception and birth the mother functioned only as the "soil" for the child, which was produced by the "seed [*sperma*]" of the father.[53] In response to this Gnostic view of Mary, the earliest orthodox theologians had insisted that although Christ had been conceived in a supernatural manner without the agency of a human father, he was "truly [*alēthōs*] born," in the same manner as all other human beings are.[54] Even earlier, as has been noted in chapter 1, when the apostle Paul had wanted to assert that the Son of God, who had come "in the fulness of time," had participated in an authentic humanity, he said that he was "born of a woman,"[55] though apparently without implying thereby any explicit reference to the Virgin Birth or to the person of the Virgin Mary herself.

Having taken over the parallel from the Greeks, Western theologians were eventually able, as mentioned earlier, to take advantage of a verbal coincidence in the Latin language to play with the palindrome *Ave/Eva*. The First Eve had been, according to the etymology of the Book of Genesis, "the mother of all who live [*matēr pantōn tōn zōntōn*]," and therefore the Septuagint read: "And Adam called the name of his wife Life [*Zōē*]," rather than "Eve."[56] So the Second Eve, too, had become the new mother of all who believed and who lived through believing in her divine Son.

Epiphany and flight into Egypt, fifth-century mosaic. Santa Maria Maggiore, Rome. (Alinari / Art Resource, N.Y.)

4 The Theotokos, the Mother of God

And [Elisabeth] spake out with a loud voice, and said, . . .
And whence is this to me, that the mother of my Lord should come to me?
—Luke 1:42–43

Throughout history, and especially during the fourth and fifth centuries, the basic category for thinking about Mary was that of paradox: Virgin and Mother; Human Mother of One who is God, Theotokos.[1] For the most comprehensive—and, in the opinion of some, the most problematic—of all the terms invented for Mary by Eastern Christianity was certainly that title Theotokos. It did not mean simply "Mother of God," as it was usually rendered in Western languages (*Mater Dei* in Latin, and thence in the Romance languages, or *Mutter Gottes* in German), but more precisely and fully "the one who gave birth to the one who is God" (therefore *Bogorodica* and its cognates in Russian and other Slavic languages, and, more seldom but more precisely, *Deipara* even in Latin). Although the linguistic history of the title remains obscure, it does seem to have been a term of Christian coinage rather than, as might superficially seem to have been the case, an adaptation to Christian purposes of a name originally given to a pagan goddess.[2] The name appears in some manuscripts of the works of Athanasius.[3] Yet the textual evidence leaves ambiguous the question of how often Athanasius did use the title Theotokos for Mary.[4] In any event, it receives negative corroboration from its appearance, during the lifetime of Athanasius, in the attacks on the church by the emperor Julian "the Apostate," who criticized the superstition of the Christians for invoking the Theotokos.[5]

In the fifth century, the fear of mingling the divine and human natures in the person of Christ led Nestorius, patriarch of Constantinople, to stipulate that because it was only the human nature that had been born of her, Mary should be called not Theotokos, which gave the blasphemous impression that she had given birth to the divine nature itself and which therefore sounded like the title of the mother deities of paganism, but Christotokos, "the one who gave birth to Christ." In 431, slightly more than a century after the Christian religion had finally become a legal cult [religio licita] through the Edict of Milan, a council of Christian bishops met in the city of Ephesus—which had been the center of a flourishing devotion to the Greek goddess Artemis or Diana.[6] It was in Ephesus, in a scene graphically described in the Acts of the Apostles, that her devotees had rioted against Saint Paul and the other Christian apostles with the cry "Great is Diana of the Ephesians!"[7] There, assembled in the great double church of Mary, whose ruins can still be seen, they solemnly proclaimed that it was an obligation binding on all believers to call Mary Theotokos, making dogmatically official what the piety of orthodox believers had already affirmed, in the words of the first Anathematism of Cyril of Alexandria against Nestorius: "If anyone does not confess that Emmanuel is God in truth, and therefore that the holy virgin is the mother of God [Theotokos] (for she bore in a fleshly way the Word of God become flesh), let him be anathema."[8] It was, moreover, in honor of the definition by the Council of Ephesus of Mary as Theotokos that right after the council Pope Sixtus III built the most important shrine to Mary in the West, the Basilica of Santa Maria Maggiore in Rome; its celebrated mosaic of the annunciation and the epiphany gave artistic form to that definition.[9] A few centuries later John of Damascus would summarize the orthodox case for this special title: "Hence it is with justice and truth that we call holy Mary Theotokos. For this name embraces the whole mystery of the divine dispensation [to mystērion tēs *oikonomias*]. For if she who bore him is the Theotokos, assuredly he who was born of her is God and likewise also man. . . . The name [Theotokos] in truth signifies the one subsistence and the two natures and the two modes of generation of our Lord Jesus Christ."[10] And, as he argued elsewhere, that is what she was on the icons: Theotokos and therefore the orthodox and God-pleasing substitute for the pagan worship of demons.[11] At the same time, the defenders of the icons insisted that "when we worship her icon, we do not, in pagan fashion [*Hellēnikōs*], regard her as a goddess [*thean*] but as the Theotokos."[12]

That had come a long way even from the consideration of her as the Second Eve. It was probably the greatest quantum leap in the whole history of the language and thought about Mary, as we are considering it in this book. How and why could she have come so far so fast? At least three aspects of an answer to that historical question are suggested by the texts: the growth of the title Theotokos; in connection with the title, the rise of a liturgical observance called "the commemoration of Mary"; and, as a somewhat speculative explanation for both the title and the festival, the deepening perception that there was a need to identify some totally human person who was the crown of creation, once that was declared to be an inadequate identification for Jesus Christ as the eternal Son of God and Second Person of the Trinity.[13]

The origins of the title Mother of God are obscure. In spite of the diligence of Hugo Rahner and others,[14] there is no altogether incontestable evidence that it was used before the fourth century, despite Newman's categorical claim that "the title *Theotocos*, or Mother of God, was familiar to Christians from primitive times."[15] What is clear is that the first completely authenticated instances of the use of this title came from the city of Athanasius, Alexandria. Alexander, his patron and immediate predecessor as bishop there, referred to Mary as Theotokos in his encyclical of circa 319 about the heresy of Arius.[16] From various evidence, including the taunts of Julian the Apostate from a few decades later about the term Theotokos, cited earlier, it seems reasonable to conclude that the title already enjoyed widespread acceptance in the piety of the faithful at Alexandria and beyond. The history does not in any direct way corroborate the facile modern theories about the "mother goddesses" of Graeco-Roman paganism and their supposed significance for the development of Christian Mariology.[17] For the term Theotokos was apparently an original Christian creation that arose in the language of Christian devotion to her as the mother of the divine Savior and that eventually received its theological justification from the church's clarification of what was implied by the orthodox witness to him.

That justification was supplied by Athanasius, whose lifelong obsession it was to insist that to be the Mediator between Creator and creature Christ the Son of God had to be God in the full and unequivocal sense of the word: "through God alone can God be known," as the refrain of many orthodox church fathers put it. It did appear "inchoatively"[18] in his summary statement of "the scope and character of Holy Scripture," which "contains a double account [diplē epangelia] of the Savior: that he was God forever and is the Son, being Logos and Radiance and Wisdom of the Father; and that afterwards, taking flesh of a Virgin, Mary the Theotokos, for us, he was made man."[19] But the theological explanation of this "double account" went well beyond this summary statement of the creed. Most of the recent controversy about the theology of Athanasius has dealt with the question of whether he ascribed a human soul to Christ or whether he shared the "Logos-plus-flesh" schema of the incarnation, which came to be identified with the Apollinarist heresy.[20] That controversy has sometimes tended to obscure, however, his pioneering work in the elaboration of the "communication of the properties,"[21] the principle that, as a consequence of the incarnation and of the union of the divine and the human nature in the one person of Jesus Christ, it was legitimate to predicate human properties of the Logos and divine properties of the man Jesus, for example, to speak of "the blood of the Son of God" or "the blood of the Lord" or even (according to some manuscripts of the New Testament) "the blood of God."[22]

As Aloys Grillmeier has suggested, it was not until the debates over the term Theotokos in the first quarter of the fifth century "that the discussion of the so-called communicatio idiomatum in Christ began in earnest," even though language suggestive of it "had been employed since the apostolic age without further thought."[23] The place of Athanasius in its development seems, however, to be somewhat more important than Grillmeier made it. Grillmeier pointed to passages in which Athanasius "obviously regards the Logos as the real personal agent in those acts which are decisive for redemption, the passion and death of Christ," and he cited "expressions which describe the redemptive activity of the Logos according to the rules of the *communicatio idiomatum*." But in a long passage in his first *Oration Against the Arians*, Athanasius discussed in detail the question of the propriety of ascribing change and exaltation to the divine Logos, who could not be changed and did not need to be exalted. His answer was a paraphrase of the language of the New Testament about "Christ Jesus: who being in the form of God, . . . took upon him the form of a servant":[24] "As he, being the Logos and existing in the form of God, was always worshiped; so, being still the same though he became man and was called Jesus, he nevertheless has the whole creation under foot, and bending their knee to him in this name [Jesus], and confessing that the incarnation of the Logos and his undergoing death in the flesh has not happened against the glory of his Godhead, but 'to the glory of God the Father.'"[25]

Therefore when Athanasius spoke of the Logos "taking flesh of a Virgin, Mary the Theotokos,"[26] he was echoing the language of popular devotion; but he had already begun to provide the title with the very rationale that was to help defend it against attack half a century after his death. As Newman suggested in *The Arians of the Fourth Century*, the people were orthodox even when the bishops were not.[27] In his use of the Theotokos, as in his use of other titles and metaphors, Athanasius aligned himself with the orthodoxy of popular devotion and vindicated it. The idea of *lex orandi lex credendi*, that implicit in Christian worship there was a normative doctrinal content, which needed to be made explicit, seems to have been formulated shortly after the time of Athanasius,[28] but he evidently worked on the basis of some such idea.

The normative content of devotion also became evident in another context, when Athanasius used "the commemoration of Mary" to vindicate the orthodoxy of his doctrine. He did so in at least two of his writings. The more important of these is his epistle to Epictetus, which achieved wide circulation in Greek, Latin, Syriac, and Armenian in later centuries and was quoted in the decrees of both the Council of Ephesus in 431 and the Council of Chalcedon in 451.[29] It seems to have been called forth by the recrudescence, after the defeat of Arianism, of the ancient Docetic heresy, which denied the true and full humanity of Jesus or claimed that he did not have a genuinely human body.[30] Some were even going so far as to maintain that the body of Christ was of one essence [homoousion] with the Logos.[31] This new species of Docetism, about whose teachings scholars still do not agree, is often seen as a forerunner of the Apollinarist theology. In his response Athanasius argued on the basis of "the divine Scriptures" and of the decrees of "the fathers assembled at Nicaea" and accused the neo-Docetists of having outdone even the Arians: "You have gone further in impiety than any heresy. For if the Logos is of one essence with the body, that renders superfluous the commemoration and the office of Mary [peritte tēs Marias hē mnēmē kai hē chreia]."[32] And in his epistle to Maximus, combating the doctrine that the Logos had become man as a necessary consequence of his nature, Athanasius declared again: "If this were so, the commemoration of Mary would be superfluous."[33] Athanasius's theological point seems quite clear: Mary was again, as she had been to the anti-Gnostic fathers, the guarantee of the true humanity of Jesus Christ.[34]

What is less clear is the precise character of the "commemoration" to which Athanasius was referring. If the Greek word mnēmē meant no more than "memory," as it did in the New Testament and elsewhere,[35] then he would have been arguing that the remembrance of Mary, as enshrined for example in the creed or in memorial prayers, necessarily implied that the humanity of Christ took its beginning from her and had not preexisted from eternity. But mnēmē sometimes had a technical significance in the formation of the Christian calendar, referring to the anniversary of a saint or martyr.[36] Martin Jugie, in his early study of the first festivals devoted to Mary in both the East and the West, contended that the mnēmē of Mary referred to in early fifth-century documents was not the anniversary of her death or "dormition [koimēsis]"[37] but of her "nativity," which may have meant her entry into heaven.[38] In his later and massive study of the death and assumption of the Virgin he repeated, corrected, and amplified this argument.[39] For our purposes, however, this problem is secondary to the fundamental one. Is *tēs Marias hē mnēmē* a reference to some Mariological festival? There is some evidence to support the existence of a festival called the *mnēmē* of Mary and celebrated on the Sunday after Christmas,[40] but the evidence does not go back quite as far as Athanasius. Nevertheless, both that evidence and his language seem to make it plausible that such a commemoration of Mary was being kept already during his time and that his argument was based upon it.

He would then have been arguing that there was no justification for a festival commemorating the Virgin Mary the Theotokos if she had not played a part in the history of salvation. She belonged to the New Testament, not to the Old, and was not remembered, as the saints of ancient Israel were, as a prophet of the coming of Christ. Rather, she had a function or office, a *chreia*, as the chosen and commissioned one through whom alone the uncreated Logos received his created humanity. And that *chreia* or ministry was celebrated with grateful remembrance in the observance of the *mnēmē* or commemoration of Mary. The *chreia* was a given fact of the history of salvation, the *mnēmē* a given fact of Christian observance. Both the creed of the church and the calendar of the church, then, attested the doctrine that the human nature of Christ was a creature, just as they attested the doctrine that the divine nature of Christ was not a creature; and the sign of the bond between Christ the creature and mankind the creature was "the commemoration and the office of Mary," which would have been superfluous if the humanity of Christ had been some sort of component of his preexistence as the Logos of God. Although it is undeniable, from the evidence, that Athanasius never worked out as satisfactory a formula for the implications of the full and true humanity of the Lord as he did for those of his deity, it is equally clear that both aspects of the "double account"[41] were vouched for by the authority of the orthodox faith.

In the composition and identification of that authority, the worship and devotion of the church were seen as an important element of the definition of what Athanasius, in the conclusion of the Epistle to Epictetus, called "the confession of that faith which is both devout and orthodox [hē homologia tēs eusebous kai orthodoxous pisteōs]."[42] If Mary was Theotokos, as the language of Christian devotion declared she was, the relation between the divine and human in Jesus Christ had to be such as to justify this apparently incongruous term; hence the doctrine of the "communication of the properties." If Mary had the "office" of clothing the Logos in an authentic and therefore a created humanity, as in the "commemoration of Mary" the practice of Christian devotion declared she had, no aversion to flesh and blood could be permitted to vitiate the doctrine of the incarnation. To qualify as a dogma of the church, then, a doctrine had to conform not only to the apostolic tradition, as set down in Scripture and in such magisterial witnesses as the decrees of the Council of Nicaea, but also to the worship and devotion of the Catholic and apostolic church.

The creaturely status of Mary in relation to Christ indicated yet another line of development, the task of specifying more accurately the proper subject for predicates that had been misplaced by heresy. Most of the controversies in the fourth century dealt with the propriety of predications such as homoousios or Theotokos. But the literature of the controversies also suggested, or at least hinted at, a definition of heresy as misplaced predication, to which the eventual orthodox answer was a more precise specification of the subject. Only at the Council of Ephesus and beyond was this answer supplied, but by hindsight it may seen in an earlier stage of the development in the Arian controversy.

The Arian heresy, in the words of Henry Gwatkin, "degraded the Lord of Saints to the level of his creatures."[43] What it ascribed to Christ was more than it was willing to ascribe to any of the saints but less than it ascribed to the supreme Deity. The Arian doctrine concerning the saints is not easy to assemble from the fragments, though we know that the Thalia of Arius spoke of "the elect of God, the wise men of God, his holy sons."[44] There is some evidence that certain legends of the saints were handed down through Arian sources.[45] We are considerably better informed about the Arian view of the relation between Christ and the saints. According to the letter of the Arians to Alexander of Alexandria, the Logos was "a perfect creature of God, but not as one of the creatures,"[46] since he was the creature through whom God had made all the other creatures; therefore the "superiority" of this creature over all the other creatures was that he had been created directly whereas they had been created through him.[47] In his preexistence, then, the Logos was the perfect creature. But in his earthly career he *became* the perfect creature. Arianism seemed in its picture of the man Jesus Christ to have combined a denial of the presence of a human soul in him[48] with the doctrine of Paul of Samosata that he had made himself worthy of elevation to the status of "Son of God" by his "moral progress [*prokopē*]."[49] The Arians were reputed to have taught that God had elected him "because of his foreknowledge" that Christ would not rebel against him but would, "by his care and self-discipline [*dia epimeleian kai askēsin*]," triumph over his "mutable nature" and remain faithful.[50] Because the sonship of the Logos was a function of his perfect creaturehood and the sonship of the man Jesus was a consequence of his perfect obedience, the difference between his sonship and that of the saints was quantitative rather than qualitative, for by their own perfect obedience they could eventually attain to a participation in the same sonship.

Now this Arian doctrine of participation by the saints in the sonship of Christ had a counterpart in the Athanasian doctrine of participation through "divinization": "Because of our relationship to his body we, too, have become God's temple, and in consequence are made God's sons, in such a way that even in us the Lord is now being worshiped."[51] The sonship was due not in the first instance to the imitation of Christ by the saints but essentially to transformation by Christ, who, in the famous Athanasian formula, became human in order that the saints might become divine.[52] Athanasius contended that such a transformation and divinization was possible only because the Logos was Creator rather than creature. The Savior could mediate between God and humanity only because he himself was God. He was not promoted to a new status because he was the greatest of the saints but was restored to his eternal status after performing on earth the mission for which he had been sent into the flesh. Now the saints became sons of God, creatures in whom the Creator dwelt so fully that he could be worshiped in them. That status is what Arianism tried to make of Christ, a creature in whom the Creator dwelt so fully that God could be worshiped in him, the highest of the saints and therefore the mediator between God and humanity.

By drawing the line between Creator and creature and confessing that the Son of God belonged on God's side of that line, Nicene orthodoxy made possible and necessary a qualitative distinction between him and even the highest of saints, between his uncreated mediation and their created mediation.[53] Now that the subject of the Arian sentences was changed, what was to become of all the predicates? What we have seen so far in the Mariology of Athanasius would seem to indicate that, in a sense quite different from that implied by Harnack, "what the Arians had taught about Christ, the orthodox now taught about Mary,"[54] so that these creaturely predicates did not belong to Jesus Christ, the Son of God, but to the Virgin Mary, the Mother of God. The portrait of Mary in the Letter to the Virgins of Athanasius would fit the Arian description of the Son of God, who "was chosen because, though mutable by nature, his painstaking character suffered no deterioration." Athanasius spoke of her "progress-ing" and may even have been using here the word prokopē, moral progress, which the Arians had used of Christ.[55] Her progress, according to Athanasius, involved struggles with doubts and evil thoughts, but she tri-umphed over them and could thus become "the image" and "the model" of virginity for all those who strove for perfection, in short, the highest of the saints. The devotional language (Theotokos, "Mother of God") and the devotional practice (mnēmē, "commemoration") which, as we have noted earlier, lay behind the Mariology of Athanasius were the prime instance in all his thought of the doctrine that even a creature could become deserving of worship by virtue of the indwelling of the Creator. The hymn from which Athanasius may have been quoting the title Theo-tokos, the Greek original of the well-known Latin Sub tuum praesidium, was likewise the prime instance of such worship.[56]

It remained for further controversy to call forth further clarification of the doctrine, but in the light of that controversy we may see already in

Athanasius that it was a development by the specification of the subject. When the development did come, it came first and most fully in the Greek-speaking East, where the ascetical and devotional presuppositions of the doctrine of Mary were present long before they appeared in the West.

Rosemary Namuli, *Mary*, stone sculpture. East Africa. (Reprinted from Arno Lehmann, *Christian Art in Africa and Asia*, Concordia Publishing House, 1967)

5 The Heroine of the Qur'ān and the Black Madonna

Black am I and beautiful.
—Song of Songs 1:5 (translation by Marvin Pope)

One of the most profound and most persistent roles of the Virgin Mary in history has been her function as a bridge builder to other traditions, other cultures, and other religions. From the Latin word for "bridge builder" came the term pontifex, a priestly title in Roman paganism. In the form pontifex maximus it became one of the terms in the cult of the divine Roman emperor, and for that reason it was disavowed by Christian emperors already in the fourth century. Not long thereafter it was taken up by Christian bishops and archbishops, and it did not become an exclusive title for the bishop of Rome until considerably later.[1] But the concept of a pontifex, as distinct from the term, had far wider implications. Ultimately it applied to all those concepts and personalities whose fundamental message and significance could be expressed better by saying both/and than by saying either/or. One such was monasticism, which had appeared in several separate traditions and had manifested in them some striking similarities, as well as historic differences.[2] Efforts to cultivate exchange especially between Christian and Buddhist monasticism have made considerable headway in recent decades, and Thomas

Merton, Trappist monk and spiritual author, was engaged in such a "boundary journey" when he died in 1968.³ Whenever the antitheses of either/or at all levels have threatened to erupt into a holocaust, there has been a desperate need to identify and to cultivate such bridge-building concepts and personalities.

Perhaps no antithesis has been more far-reaching in its implications than the relation between the rest of the world and what has been called "Islamdom" (as a counterpart to "Christendom"), which now numbers nearly one billion believers. And therefore this general need for bridge builders has taken on a special urgency and poignancy in the attempt to understand the religion of the prophet Muhammad and the message of the Qur'ān, concerning which the fundamental ignorance of otherwise well-educated Westerners is not only abysmal but frightening. The foundation of the Islamic faith came in a series of incandescent divine self-disclosures, beginning in about the year 610 and continuing to near the end of the prophet's life in 632.⁴ These revelations are, to orthodox Muslim belief, the very voice of God. In them Muhammad was designated "a benevolence to the creatures of the world," whose message it was to say, "This is what has been revealed to me: 'Your God is one and only God.'"⁵ Muhammad memorized many of these sayings, as did a multitude of his followers; other sayings seem to have been written down right away, in whatever medium was at hand. The collecting of the Qur'ān is attributed to Abū Bakr, the first caliph, and the standard version to 'Uthmān, the third caliph, who established the textual tradition at Medina as the normative one and who also fixed the sequence of the 114 chapters, or sūrahs, more or less from the longest to the shortest. Many Western scholars tend to think that the Qur'ān in its present form began to be set down in about 650 but that the text was not definitively fixed until the tenth century; normative Muslim doctrine teaches that it was all written at once.

For Western readers first coming to the Qur'ān, one of the most surprising sections has often been the sūrah numbered 19 in the canonical collection, which bore the title "Maryam: Mary."⁶ For as the nineteenth of 114 sūrahs, this chapter was one of the longest in the Qur'ān. It was, moreover, the only sūrah to bear a woman's name, although sūrah 4 had the superscription "An-Nisā: The Women" and sūrah 60 was called "Al-Mumtahanah: The Woman Tried." But there was, for example, no sūrah named for Eve (who was, for Islam as for Judaism and Christianity, "the mother of all living"[7]), nor one named for Hagar, mother of Ishmael by Abraham and therefore in a real sense the founding mother of Islam. In the judgment of many scholars, sūrah 19 came from the Meccan period of the prophet's revelations, during which "references to Mary tend to emphasize the fact that she was the virgin mother of Jesus"; sūrah 3, by contrast, has often been assigned to the prophet's time in Medina, whose references to Mary "tend to focus on the negation of Jesus's divinity."[8] Sūrah 19 contained quotations, paraphrases, and adaptations from the Gospels of the New Testament, especially from the Gospel of Luke, which was, as mentioned earlier, the most detailed portrait of the Virgin Mary in the Christian Bible.[9] The parallels were important in their own right, but they became especially so when seen in connection with the differences between the Christian doctrine of Mary, as it had developed by the time of Muhammad in the early seventh century, and the Muslim portrait of her in the Qur'ān and in Islamic commentaries on the Holy Book.[10] For as Neal Robinson has pointed out, real parallels were being drawn not only between Muhammad and Jesus as part of the succession of prophets but between Muhammad and Mary as both bearers of the word of God.[11] As the Qur'ān says later, "And of Mary, daughter of 'Imran, who guarded her chastity, so that We breathed into her a life from Us, and she believed the words of her Lord and His Books, and was among the obedient."[12] In relation to the other materials about the history of Mary through the centuries and with the aid of commentators both Muslim and Western, then, what follows is a commentary on the portion of sūrah 19 dealing specifically with Mary.[13]

16. *Commemorate Mary in the Book.* These opening words followed upon a paraphrase of the account in the first chapter of the Gospel of Luke about the birth of John the Baptist, which seems to have been cast, as was the New Testament story, so as to emphasize the parallels between the birth of John the Baptist and the birth of Jesus: annunciation, miraculous divine

intervention, special mission for the about-to-be-born child.[14] But it is noteworthy that both in the New Testament and in the Qur'ān the annunciation of the miraculous birth of John was brought by the messenger of God to his father, Zechariah, whereas in Luke the annunciation by the angel of the birth of Jesus was addressed to his mother, Mary. In the Qur'ānic version, moreover, the name of Elizabeth, mother of John, did not even appear. Therefore, although the word of God to John the Baptist was "O John, hold fast to the Book,"[15] this section opened with the formula "Commemorate Mary in the Book," clearly assigning her a very special place in the historical plan of "Allah, most benevolent, most merciful." It may have been a reflection of postbiblical Christian Mariological spirituality and thought that the first narrative item in this commemoration of Mary was a report not contained in Luke or any of the other Gospels: "When she withdrew from her family to a place in the East and took cover from them." More likely, it would appear that at this point the commemoration of Mary brought echoes of the commemoration of Hagar, mother of Ishmael, in chapter 16 and again in chapter 21 of the Book of Genesis, the two accounts of her expulsion being rather difficult to harmonize; for Hagar did "take cover from" her family, that is, from Sarah and Abraham. It was to Ishmael, son of Abraham, that Islam looked as its founder, favored by God, who had promised about Ishmael, also in the Hebrew and Christian Scriptures and therefore both in the Jewish and in the Christian tradition, "I will make him a great nation."[16]

17. *We sent a spirit of Ours to her who appeared before her in the concrete form of a man. 18. "I seek refuge in the Merciful from you, if you fear Him," she said. He replied: "I am only a messenger from your Lord [sent] to bestow a good son on you."* And earlier: "The angels said: 'O Mary, indeed God has favoured you and made you immaculate, and chosen you from all the women of the world. So adore your Lord, O Mary, and pay homage and bow with those who bow in prayer.'"[17] This was the Qur'ān's version of the annunciation. In its basic outline it matched the account in the Gospel of Luke. There was an angelic messenger, identified in the New Testament as Gabriel but here less specifically as "the angels" or "a spirit of Ours." He identified himself as "only a messenger from your Lord." The content of the messenger's

announcement to her was, in the Qur'ān as in the Gospel, that she was to have a son. But here an interesting contrast asserts itself. In the Gospel, Gabriel said to Mary: "He shall be great, and shall be called the Son of the Highest: and the Lord God shall give unto him the throne of his father David: And he shall reign over the house of Jacob for ever; and of his kingdom there shall be no end."[18] Those words reflected, and formed a biblical foundation for, the Christian teaching that as "the Son of the Highest," Mary's Son occupied a unique position not only in human history but in the divine life itself, thus in the Holy Trinity. Because the single-minded concentration of the religion of the Qur'ān on the un-equivocal oneness of God excluded all such language about God's having a Son and therefore about there being a Trinity, that entire speech of Gabriel was encapsulated in the simple phrase "a good son." The angels said to Mary: "O Mary, God gives you news of a thing from Him, for rejoicing, (news of one) whose name will be Messiah, Jesus, son of Mary, illustrious in this world and the next, and one among the honoured, who will speak to the people when in the cradle and when in the prime of life, and will be among the upright and doers of good."[19] That was to say, the child to be born would be son of Mary, but not Son of God. The angelic message in Luke went on, moreover, to a prophecy that subsequent Christian interpreters were to find highly problematic, namely, that "the throne of his father David" would be his and that from that throne he would reign eternally. This prophecy and others like it in both the Old and the New Testaments figured prominently in the struggles during the second and third centuries over the question of whether Christ on his return would establish an earthly realm for a thousand years, struggles that have been reenacted repeatedly in Christian history, both at the end of the Middle Ages and in the twentieth century.[20] All of that, too, was absent from the Qur'ānic retelling, in which therefore Mary was not the Mother of the King and therefore would not be entitled, as she was in the Catholic tradition, to such a name as Queen.

20. *"How can I have a son,"* she said, *when no man has touched me, nor am I sinful?"* 21. *He said: "Thus will it be. Your Lord said: 'It is easy for Me,' and that: 'We shall make him a sign for men and a blessing from Us.' This is a thing already decreed."* Again, it is

important to note in the first instance the fidelity of the Qur'ān to the New Testament version of the account of Mary's words: "How shall this be, seeing I know not a man?"[21]—which followed the standard language of the Hebrew Bible, going back to the early chapters of Genesis, in using the verb "to know" as a euphemism for sexual intercourse.[22] Such fidelity to the New Testament means that for the Qur'ān and for its loyal adherents, no less than for the Gospel and its loyal adherents, Mary was correctly identified by the oxymoron Virgin Mother. That aspect of Muslim Mariology went on to create both admiration and consternation in the Christian responses to Islam, both in the Byzantine East and in the Medieval West. Similarly, the statements "Your Lord said: 'It is easy for Me,'" and "That is how God creates what He wills. When He decrees a thing, He says 'Be,' and it is,"[23] represented the counterpart to the word of Gabriel in Luke: "With God nothing shall be impossible."[24] But again the omissions were, if anything, even more interesting, and more relevant to the consideration of the portrait of Mary. For in the Gospel, Gabriel answered Mary's question by explaining, "The Holy Ghost shall come upon thee, and the power of the Highest shall overshadow thee: therefore also that holy thing which shall be born of thee shall be called the Son of God."[25] All of that explanation was conspicuously eliminated in the Qur'ān. The one to be born, the angelic messenger said here, would be "a good son"—a good son of Mary, that is—but would in no traditional Christian sense "be called the Son of God," for that would have implied the Trinity and, in Muslim eyes, have negated biblical monotheism. Probably for the same reason, the promise of Gabriel to Mary, "The Holy Ghost shall come upon thee, and the power of the Highest shall overshadow thee," had likewise disappeared; for there was no Trinity, and hence no "Holy Ghost" in the orthodox trinitarian sense of that title.

22. *When she conceived him she went away to a distant place. 23. The birth pangs led her to the trunk of a date-palm tree. "Would that I had died before this," she said, "and become a thing forgotten, unremembered." 24. Then [a voice] called to her from below: "Grieve not; your Lord has made a rivulet gush forth right below you. Shake the trunk of the date-palm tree, and it will drop ripe dates for you. 26. Eat and drink, and be at peace. If you*

see any man, tell him: 'I have verily vowed a fast to Ar-Rahman and cannot speak to any one this day.' " All of this was entirely new in relation to the New Testament. Even more explicit in these verses than at the beginning of this pericope, moreover, was the aforementioned typology between Mary, mother of Jesus, and Hagar, mother of Ishmael. In two separate chapters of Genesis, which may have represented distinct original traditions but which have both been incorporated into the book as we have it, Hagar went "to a distant place," the first time when her pregnancy aroused the jealousy of Sarah and the second time after the birth of Isaac.[26] Her despairing cry was answered by a miraculous intervention of God. Because the Qur'ān was, by definition, a new revelation that came all at once in a blinding series of moments of divine authority, we can only speculate about the earlier stages of this typology between Hagar and Mary. But it does not seem to stretch historical and literary probability to draw an analogy with the typology between Eve and Mary discussed earlier.[27] For Hagar, too, was a founding mother, as Eve was; and Ishmael was the eponymous beginning of the people known as Ishmaelites. This entire construct, therefore, may be seen to have been an Islamic way of celebrating the special place of the Virgin Mary in the history of the dealings of "Allah, most benevolent, ever-merciful," with the world. As the "good son" of Mary, his mother, Jesus stood in the succession of the called servants of God—after Abraham, father of Ishmael, and after Moses; and before Muhammad. Therefore the opening words of this section of the nineteenth sūrah, "Commemorate Mary in the Book," were followed in later sections by "Commemorate Abraham in the Book" and then by "Commemorate Moses in the Book," "the Book" being the standard term in the Qur'ān for the Hebrew Scriptures.[28]

The relation of Mary to that succession took a surprising turn in the following verses: 27. *Then she brought the child to her people. They exclaimed: "O Mary, you have done a most astonishing thing! 28. O sister of Aaron, your father was not a wicked person, nor your mother sinful!"* As it stood, the text identified Mary ("Maryam" in the superscription to this sūrah) with the "sister of Aaron" and sister of Moses, called "Miriam" in the Book of Exodus; in a similar way, the thirteenth-century Jewish polemic against Christianity, *Nizzahon*

Vetus, by means of the designation *Miriam m'gaddela nashaia*, conflated her with Mary Magdalene, perhaps with the intent of showing that, far from being the Holy Virgin Mother of God celebrated in Christian devotion and doctrine, Mary the mother of Jesus was a prostitute and a sinner.[29] Beginning already with Byzantine writers, Western critics of Islam and of the Qur'ān, who dismissed the prophet as an unlettered camel driver with delusions of grandeur, seized on this passage to prove just how confused he was, mixing up two women who lived well over a millennium apart simply because they had the same name. It became the standard explanation of this verse to say that Muhammad had heard Jews speak about Miriam and Christians speak about Mary—both of them, presumably, identified as "Maryam"—and in his ignorance had made the two women into one. As the editor and translator of the most widely circulated translation of the Qur'ān into English has explained, however, "Muslim commentators deny the charge that there is confusion here between Miriam, Aaron's sister, and Maryam (Mary), mother of Jesus. 'Sister of Aaron,' they argue, simply means 'virtuous woman' in this context."[30] But the typological use of Hagar in the retelling of the story of Moses in the Qur'ān could be taken to suggest that even without following the high doctrine of biblical inspiration of the Qur'ān taught by Muslim orthodoxy, it would be possible to see in this identification something other than a simple mistake. For there was, already in post-biblical Judaism, widespread speculation and expectation not only of the return of Elijah, for whom a place was therefore set at the Seder table, but of the subsequent historical role of Moses. Christianity had picked up on this speculation, both by contrasting Moses and Christ in such passages as the formula, "The law was given by Moses, but grace and truth came by Jesus Christ,"[31] and by coordinating Moses and Christ (and Elijah) on the Mount of Transfiguration, where the two Old Testament figures appeared on either side of Jesus as he was transfigured.[32] Because it was the basic insistence—and, as seen by Islam, the basic corrective—of the Qur'ān to restore Jesus to the prophetic succession, before Muhammad and after Moses, the parallelism between Moses and Jesus was a central emphasis. It would therefore appear to be at least a plausible alternative to the standard Western diminution of Muhammad to see this phrase "sister of Aaron," addressed to Mary mother of Jesus, as another documentation of that parallelism.

34. *This was Jesus, son of Mary: A true account they contend about. 35. It does not behove God to have a son. Too immaculate is He! When He decrees a thing He has only to say: "Be," and it is. 36. [Jesus only said] "Surely God is my Lord and your Lord, so worship Him. This is the straight path." 37. Yet the sectarians differed among themselves.* This summation was clearly polemical. It explicitly asserted a disjunction where orthodox Christianity had taught a conjunction: "This was Jesus, son of Mary"—"It does not behove God to have a son. Too immaculate is He!" By the time of the coming of the prophet Muhammad, more than five hundred years of post–New Testament theology had passed, during which, in the words of the Qur'ān, "the sectarians differed among themselves"—and mightily. Five ecumenical councils had met and passed dogmatic decrees: Nicaea in 325, Constantinople I in 381, Ephesus in 431, Chalcedon in 451, Constantinople II in 553. Thus there was by this time a massive body of material in the orthodox Christian "deposit of the faith [*depositum fidei*]." And because the relation between the divine nature and the human nature in the one person of Jesus Christ was the burden of so many of those dogmatic decrees, Mary had figured prominently in them, as the title Theotokos, the Mother of God, documented: Jesus Christ was Son of God *and* son of Mary, and the problem was how to express that distinction without creating a division. Therefore the Muslim reaction against the course that orthodox dogmatics had taken in the Christian church, specifically with regard to the person of Jesus Christ, also had to follow the Christian development by focusing serious attention on Mary, not as Theotokos, Mother of God, here, but as Mother of Jesus. In these verses of sūrah 19, therefore, the counterpoint was between the two opening affirmations: "This was Jesus, son of Mary"—"It does not behove God to have a son." And as for Christian orthodoxy, so in a directly antithetical way also for Muslim orthodoxy, the key to the correct understanding both of who Jesus was and of what he did was Mary, his mother.

The portrait of Mary the Virgin Mother of Jesus in the Qur'ān not only occupied an important place in the Qur'ān itself, and therefore in the faith of Islam, but it carried "bridge-building" implications in several directions. One of these was certainly the implications of Mary for the relation between Judaism and Islam. It may be difficult for some to believe, but the portrait of Judaism in the Qur'ān represented at heart a profound affirmation. "The People of the Book" was the honorific title with which it referred to the people of Israel throughout, and even some of the less than flattering language in sūrah 17, Bani Isrā'il, "The Children of Israel," was chiefly a repetition of what the Lord God had said about the people of Israel over and over in the Hebrew Bible. A case can be made for the thesis that the Qur'ān was a large-scale effort to redress the balance after six centuries of Christian anti-Judaism. That became evident in a special way through the reclaiming of Abraham as the common ancestor and father in faith, as he was celebrated in sūrah 14: "All praise be to God who bestowed on me Ishmael and Isaac in old age," Abraham prayed there,[33] linking the two sons of Abraham, and therefore the two peoples descended from those two sons, in coordination with each other, rather than in a subordination of Ishmael to Isaac. In the light of the subsequent importance of Egypt in Islamic culture and politics, it is amusing to note that the history of the patriarch Joseph, as elaborated in later rabbinical traditions, was retold in sūrah 12 from Israel's side, not from Egypt's side. And Moses emerged in the Qur'ān as the giver of the law and the predecessor of the prophet. But among these connections between Judaism and Islam, Mary occupied a special place. Because the Qur'ān could be read as the restoration of Jesus to the history of Israel, Mary had to be the decisive hinge in its campaign, for she was, also for Christians, the point of connection between Jesus and the history of Israel. And even in the negative language of the Qur'ān about Judaism she had to put in her appearance: "Cursed were disbelievers among the children of Israel by David and Jesus, son of Mary, because they rebelled and transgressed the bounds," God said through the prophet.[34]

Parallel to those implications of Mary for the relation between Judaism and Islam were the implications of Mary for the relation between Islam and Christianity. The portrait of the Virgin Mary in the Qur'ān was

one of its most surprising features even to the earliest authors of Christian responses to Islam. One writer of anti-Muslim treatises, Bartholomew of Edessa, probably in the ninth century, declared: "In the entire Qur'ān there do not occur any praises of Muhammad or of his mother Aminah, such as are found about our Lord Jesus Christ and about the Holy Virgin Mary, the Theotokos."[35] For, as Norman Daniel has said, "There is nothing else in all the Qur'ān to parallel the warmth with which Christ and His mother are spoken of. Christ is presented as a unique being, but His mother's personality appears more vividly. The Qur'ān inspires a devotion to Mary of which Muslims might have made more."[36] One can only add that Christians, too, might have made more of it than they did. The two principal objections of Islam to the Christian attitude toward Mary were to the concept and title Theotokos and to her portrayal in icons. Because of its dedication to the transcendence and otherness of God, Islam found the title Theotokos offensive—"It does not behove God to have a son. Too immaculate is he!"[37]—and at least some Muslim apologists claimed that Christians were including Mary the Mother of God in the Godhead. In spite of disclaimers of this in Christian responses, especially Byzantine responses, the Muslim critique may well have reflected kinds of confusion about Mary at the level of folk religion that were making her into a goddess, a confusion not without parallels in Christian history, as other chapters of this book suggest. The special standing of her image among Byzantine and Slavic icons[38] singled her out for special attention also from the Muslim spokesmen who attacked the worship of icons as idolatry. Nevertheless, as the Christian responses sought to make clear, Christian faith did not place her alongside the Deity but exalted her as the supreme exemplar of what human nature could become—and what it had become in her by the very sovereign will and decree of God of which the angelic messenger spoke when he said to Mary in the Qur'ān: "Your Lord said: 'We shall make him a sign for men and a blessing from Us.' This is a thing already decreed.'"[39] For Islam this meant, as an earlier sūrah had insisted, that "the Christ, son of Mary, was but an apostle, and many apostles had [come and] gone before him; and his mother was a woman of truth."[40]

But even beyond all of these implications were the implications of the picture of Mary in the Qur'ān for multicultural Christian understanding with Islam and beyond. The urgent need to find symbols and concepts in our several cultural traditions that can perform the function of a *pontifex*, the function of priestly mediation and bridge-building, suggests that there has probably been no symbol or concept in Christendom that has carried out this "pontifical" vocation of mediation with more success and more amplitude than Mary.[41] And a primary proof for that thesis was the picture of Mary in the Qur'ān, in which, according to the interpretation quoted from Daniel, her "personality appears more vividly" even than that of her son or of the prophet. But with apologies to Muslim iconoclasm, this thesis would have to be extended chiefly through attention to the sacred pictures of Mary in a variety of cultures.[42] It would apply as well to the feasts and festivals devoted to her and to the shrines that have sprung up in her honor at such places as Lourdes, Fátima, Marpingen, and Guadalupe.[43] And here an important contribution to what might be called the "multicultural Mary" came from a source discussed earlier, the words of the Bride from the Song of Songs: "Black am I and beautiful,"[44] together with the portraits of the Virgin Mary that have been grouped as "Black Madonnas."[45] As part of the same commentary in which he corrected the usual translation of those words, Marvin Pope, citing the most important art-historical monograph on the subject,[46] presented several hypotheses to explain the Black Madonnas, concluding that an origin in Asia Minor seemed "highly probable" and drawing significant parallels with the Black Demeter, Isis, and other black deities of paganism.[47] The early history of the veneration of the Virgin Mary in Africa anticipated these later developments.[48]

The title "Black Madonna" acquired special significance when it came to be applied to the celebrated icon of Mary at Jasna Góra in the Polish city of Częstochowa, attributed to Saint Luke the icon painter, which is the most revered sacred image in Central Europe and the object of countless pilgrimages (see p. viii, above).[49] Prince Ladislaus Opolszyk brought it to Częstochowa in 1382, and Prince Jagiełło built the church for the shrine of the icon after his marriage to Queen Jadwiga of Poland

and his coronation in 1386. Out of a lifetime spent in the Polish culture of which she was the primary symbol, Henryk Górecki in 1976 composed his Opus 36, *Symfonia pieśni żałosnych* [Symphony of songs of complaint], which stands with Benjamin Britten's *War Requiem* and the *Leningrad Symphony* of Dmitry Shostakovich as a memorial to the victims of the Second World War. But it also stands as the expression, especially in its soprano arias, of what the Polish tradition has seen in the face of the Black Madonna of Częstochowa.[50] The blackened face of the Virgin in that icon was the result of smoke, but it has nevertheless had the salutary effect of stimulating and sanctioning the process of what Pope John Paul II, a special devotee of the Virgin of Częstochowa, has called "acculturation," particularly liturgical and artistic acculturation. Yet by an irony that is not without many historical parallels, the most forceful statement ever made of the case for these multicultural images came from a source that denounced all images, the Holy Qur'ān of Islam.

Johannes Vermeer, *Allegory of Faith*, c. 1671–74. The Metropolitan Museum of Art, New York, The Friedsam Collection, Bequest of Michael Friedsam, 1931.

6 The Handmaid of the Lord
and the Woman of Valor

And Mary said,
Behold the handmaid of the Lord.
—Luke 1:38

A woman of valor who will find?
—Proverbs 31:10

If historians of art or of the church were to follow the example of
their colleagues in the natural sciences by compiling a "citation index,"
not of the articles, papers, and books of other scholars as scientists do, but
of the themes that have captured the attention of painters and sculptors
throughout history, and especially if they were to prepare such an index
together, it seems clear that among all the scenes in the life of the Virgin
Mary that have engaged the piety of the devout and the creativity of the
artists, the annunciation has been predominant. The annunciation has
been so prevalent, in fact, that the number of references to it in such an
index would probably exceed the number of references to all other
Marian themes combined. Each theme and chapter in this book could in
one way or another have been illustrated by an artistic rendering of the
annunciation.[1]

Depending on how one interprets them, at least three works of early
Christian art in the Roman catacombs appear to have portrayed the an-
nunciation: one from the Catacomba di Santa Priscilla, another from the
Catacomba di Santi Marcellino e Pietro, and a third from the Catacomba

di Via Latina, discovered only in 1956.[2] The annunciation became a theme for altarpieces and other paintings in the Western Middle Ages, becoming especially frequent in the later Middle Ages, as David Robb has shown.[3] In the Byzantine East, the annunciation constituted one of the twelve feasts of the church year. Eventually the annunciation became the subject of many icons in the East, including two Byzantine cameos that have been dated by some art historians to as early as the sixth century; these are preserved in the collections of the Hermitage Museum in Saint Petersburg.[4] More grandly, the annunciation often appeared on the "royal portal" of the iconostasis in a Byzantine church. At the "great entrance" of the priest through the iconostasis in the course of the *Byzantine Liturgy of Saint Basil*, he recited the several "comings" of God and Christ in the course of the history of salvation, including above all the coming that took place through the incarnation at the event of the annunciation to Mary.[5] So also the annunciation painted on that portal represented the supreme coming of God the Logos in the flesh that he received from the Virgin Mary.

As these artistic representations suggest, the primary importance of the annunciation was believed to lie in the miracle of the incarnation.[6] In the dramaturgic structure of the first chapter of the Gospel of Luke, the annunciation constituted the narrative counterpart to the climax of the first chapter of the Gospel of John: "And the Word was made flesh."[7] It was the central meaning of the annunciation, and of Christian faith and teaching about the doctrine of the incarnation, that, as these words of John's Gospel confessed (which were recited as part of the Angelus), "*Verbum caro factum est*, The Word was made flesh,"[8] and that this had happened when, in the words of the Epistle of Paul to the Galatians, "God sent forth his Son, made of a woman."[9] Throughout history the attention to the person of Jesus Christ was, as in the words just quoted, closely linked with attention to his Mother. What the Gospel of John stated in the language of theology and of Hellenistic philosophy when it said "The Word [Logos] was made flesh," the Gospel of Luke described in the language of drama and dialogue, in the form of an exchange between Mary as the chosen one of God and the angel Gabriel as the emissary of

God. This annunciation, as well as the earlier one to Zechariah, father of John the Baptist, followed a set outline and stylized form.[10]

At the same time, the annunciation represented for Christian thought the supreme example and paradigm for pondering the mysterious question that had occupied so much attention in both the history of philosophy and the history of theology and that had engaged the major attention of thinkers not only in the Christian tradition but in the Jewish and Muslim traditions as well: the relation between necessity and free will or between divine sovereignty and human freedom. This was one of the most difficult of all Christian controversies to explain to Jewish thinkers, who saw no need of choosing between the freedom of God and the freedom of the human will. Throughout history Mary was seen as, on one hand, the "handmaid of the Lord," as she called herself in Luke,[11] the one who became the instrument of the divine plan. In every century she served as the model of patience, indeed of quietistic passivity and unquestioning obedience. When the prophet Isaiah asked, "Shall the clay say to him that fashioned it, What makest thou?" and again affirmed, "We are the clay, and thou our potter"; or when the apostle Paul, echoing these words of the Hebrew Bible, asked, "Hath not the potter power over the clay, of the same lump to make one vessel unto honor, and another unto dishonor?"[12]—that was an affirmation of the unknowable and unquestionable authority of God, in relation to which the human race and the individual person had to be viewed as submissive, even as inert matter. The word of the angel of the annunciation, "With God shall nothing be impossible," became the basis for seeing Mary, by her own self-designation of Handmaid (*Ancilla* in the Vulgate), as proof that when the sovereign authority and almighty will of God prevailed, as they always had and always would eventually, the outcome was one that had to be be acknowledged as good and wise altogether, even though it had been veiled in obscurity for the eyes of mortals at the time. It added to this definition of Mary the Handmaid that she was a woman and was therefore supposedly cast, by a deadly combination of nature and creation and fall, in the role of the passive and submissive one, the vessel that received. Therefore she could be held up to women as a model of how they ought to behave, in submissive obedience to God, to their husbands, and to the clergy and hierarchy of the church.

But throughout most of the history of reflection on the events of the annunciation and on the participation of the person of Mary in those events, this portrait was only half the picture. For it has often been noted that an obedience that is open to the future should be defined as supreme activity, not passivity. On closer inspection, therefore, the title Handmaid of the Lord was significantly more complex than many of its interpreters had supposed. The Greek term was doulē kyriou, literally, woman slave of the Lord. It was the feminine form of the much more familiar and more frequent phrase in the masculine, doulos Iēsou Christou, slave of Jesus Christ,[13] which became, in the New Testament, almost a technical term for the apostles. It went on to become the more elaborate and more complete title "slave of the slaves of God [servus servorum Dei]": Augustine, for example, had styled himself "slave of Christ and slave of the slaves of Christ [servus Christi servorumque Christi]," but beginning with Pope Gregory the Great servus servorum Dei was added to the panoply of the standard titles of the bishop of Rome.[14] It would be difficult, on the basis of studying the pontificate of Gregory I, to conclude that the term servus provided a justification for passivity or quietism. At its foundation, the term was a reference to the paradox of Christ as being both in "the form of God [morphē theou]" and in the "form of a slave [morphē doulou]."[15] The masculine title doulos and the feminine title doulē appeared together in the New Testament only once, in a quotation from the Greek of the Septuagint in the second chapter of the Book of Acts: "And on my servants and on my handmaidens [epi tous doulous mou kai epi tas doulas mou] I will pour out in those days my Spirit." And then the quotation added the portentous promise: "and they shall prophesy."[16] In the case of the male slaves, the douloi, the fulfillment of that promise was the history of the apostolic church as described in the following twenty-six chapters of the Book of the Acts of the Apostles and its continuation through the ages. But for the fulfillment of the promise of the prophet Joel in the case of the female slaves, the first and the preeminent place to look, as her association with the apostles in the first chapter of the Book of Acts suggested,[17] was the one who had

Vault of the Cubiculum of the Annunciation, fresco, fourth century. Catacomb of Priscilla, Rome. (Scala / Art Resource, N.Y.)

Annunciation and Visitation, Coptic Christian textile, sixth century. Victoria & Albert Museum, London. (Victoria & Albert Museum / Art Resource, N.Y.)

Annunciation and Visitation, ivory sculpture book cover, late eighth century. Musées Royaux d'Art et d'Histoire, Brussels.

Annunciation from an Armenian manuscript of the Gospels, c. 1280. Yerevan, Armenia.
(© Edimedia)

Simone Martini, *The Annunciation*, detail, 1333. Galleria degli Uffizi, Florence. (Eric Lessing / Art Resource, N.Y.)

Annunciation at the Fountain, tapestry, early fourteenth century. Ikonenmuseum, Museen der Stadt Recklinghausen. (© Giraudon)

Andrea della Robbia, *Annunciation*, glazed terracotta, sixteenth century. La Verna, Santuario. (Scala/Art Resource, N.Y.)

Facing page: Fra Angelico, *The Annunciation*, illuminated initial from Missal, c. 1430. MS 558, f.33v., Museo di San Marco, Florence. (Nicolo Orsi Battaglini/Art Resource, N.Y.)

Carlo di Giovanni Braccesco, *Annunciation*, late fifteenth century. Musée du Louvre. (Erich Lessing / Art Resource, N.Y.)

Previous page: Carlo Crivelli, *The Annunciation, with Saint Emidius*, 1486. National Gallery, London.

El Greco, *The Annunciation*. Museum of Fine Arts (Szepmuveszeti Muzeum), Budapest. (Erich Lessing / Art Resource, N.Y.)

Previous page: Matthias Grünewald, *Annunciation*, detail, Isenheim Altarpiece, c. 1510–15. Musée Unterlinden, Colmar. (Giraudon / Art Resource, N.Y.)

Pierre-Auguste Pichon, *The Annunciation*, 1859. Basilique Notre-Dame, Clery-Saint-André. (Giraudon / Art Resource, N.Y.)

Orazio Gentileschi, *Annunciation*, c. 1623. Galleria Sabauda, Turin. (Scala / Art Resource, N.Y.)

Annunciation from an Ethiopian wood-carved box with panel paintings, eighteenth or nineteenth century. Musées Royaux d'Art et d'Histoire, Brussels.

Dante Gabriel Rossetti, *Ecce Ancilla Domini!* (*The Annunciation*), 1849–50. Tate Gallery, London. (Tate Gallery, London/Art Resource, N.Y.)

Henry Ossawa Turner, *Annunciation*, 1898. Philadelphia Museum of Art, The W. P. Wilstach Collection.

Salvador Dali, *The Annunciation*, 1947. Private collection. (Edimedia © ADAGP 1996)

identified herself in the story of the annunciation as *doulē kyriou;* and the content of her first prophesying was to be found in her responses to Gabriel, and then in the revolutionary cadences of the Magnificat. That certainly did not sound very "passive" or quietistic.

For, as the dual title of this chapter suggests, she was throughout the centuries the Handmaid of the Lord and the Woman of Valor, and neither of these without the other. Thus in a time far later than the subject matter of the present chapter, the period of slavery in the United States, "masters taught their slaves Christianity in order to inculcate obedience, but spirituals like 'Oh, Mary,' 'Go Down, Moses,' and others indicate that some slaves identified with those Biblical heroes who had challenged slavery in ancient times."[18] The Greek word for annunciation was *euangelismos,* which indicated the function of the annunciation story as the prime exemplar of "evangelization," as this was depicted in the icons of the event and as it was expounded in the commentaries of the Greek Christian tradition on the narrative. That function became evident in the formulations of the fourth-century philosophical theologian Gregory of Nyssa, as he commented on the words of the annunciation from the Gospel of Luke:

> At once, with the coming upon her of the Holy Spirit and with her being overshadowed by the power of the Most High, the human nature in Mary (where Wisdom built her house) [Prov. 9:1], though naturally part of our sensuous compound [of flesh and spirit], became that which that overshadowing power in essence was; for "without contradiction the less is blessed of the better" [Heb. 7:7]. Seeing, then, that the power of the Godhead is an immense and immeasurable thing, while man is a weak atom, at the moment when the Holy Spirit came upon the Virgin and the power of the Most High overshadowed her, the tabernacle formed by such an impulse was not clothed with anything of human corruption; but, just as it was first constituted, so it remained, even though it was man, spirit nevertheless, and grace, and power. And the special attri-

butes of our humanity derived luster from this abundance of divine power.[19]

For in spite of the extraordinary, indeed unique, character of the event of the incarnation of the Logos in the man Jesus Christ, these thinkers took it also as a model of how the "gospel [*euangelion*]" functioned everywhere and at all times, and therefore it was as well for them the defining example of the full meaning of human freedom. It was, they maintained, a narrow and crabbed conception of freedom to equate it with anarchy and permissiveness and thus to define it as having the right to do whatever one pleased, no matter how destructive to self or to others; for in its fullest and deepest sense it included supremely, as the twentieth-century French man of letters Paul Claudel said and described it, the "liberty to obey."[20] For if the human creature, having been endowed by the Creator with free will as well as with the inalienable right to employ that freedom, was to employ freedom to attain authentic selfhood and authentic humanity, such a liberty to obey implied, as Hans Urs von Balthasar said, that "no finite freedom can be freer from restrictions than when giving its consent to infinite freedom."[21] And the supreme illustration for von Balthasar, as for such Greek theologians as Maximus Confessor whom von Balthasar had interpreted so brilliantly, was the consent of the "finite freedom" of the Virgin Mary to the "infinite freedom" of God in the annunciation.

In the annunciation to Mary, the word of God was communicated through a created messenger (and "angel" originally meant "messenger" in Greek, as the equivalent term had in Hebrew), the angel Gabriel. But unlike the "angel of the Lord" who in one night had slain 185,000 Assyrian soldiers from the armies of Sennacherib,[22] Gabriel brought the word of God to Mary in order to evoke a response from her that was free and unconstrained. In Greek Christian thought, Mary was predestined to be the Mother of Christ; she was the chosen one of the Almighty. And the will of the Almighty was law, for, once again in a formula of Gregory of Nyssa, "the power of the divine will is a sufficient cause for the things that are and for their coming into existence out of nothing."[23] Yet these Greek

Christian thinkers insisted at the same time that it was only when Mary said, and of her own free will, "Behold, the handmaid of the Lord: be it done to me according to thy word,"[24] that the will of the Almighty was carried out. And, they argued, if that was true of the most shattering intervention into human life and history ever launched by God, it had to be true of how the grace of God always operated, respecting human freedom and integrity and therefore, as in the defining case of Adam and Eve, risking disobedience.

As Irenaeus had put it, in the contrast between Eve and Mary discussed earlier,[25] "just as the former was led astray by the word of an angel, so that she fled from God when she had transgressed His word; so did the latter, by an angelic communication, receive the glad tidings that she should be the bearer of [portaret] God, being obedient to His word. And if the former did disobey God, yet the latter was persuaded [suasa est] to be obedient to God, in order that the Virgin Mary might become the patroness [advocata] of the virgin Eve."[26] She was "persuaded," not coerced, to yield an obedience that was no less voluntary in its affirmation than the disobedience of Eve had been in its negation. As free will could not be taken away from Eve in order to say that she was not accountable for her actions, so it could not be taken away from Mary either, in a misguided attempt to make the grace of God seem greater by minimizing or denying human free will. It was a differentiating characteristic of Byzantine philosophy and theology, and one that often provoked puzzlement or exasperation in the West, that in its views of the relation of grace and free will it did not work with the alternatives developed in the time of Augustine. When Pelagius, Augustine's arch-opponent in the controversy on grace, free will, and predestination, was summoned in 415 to a gathering of Greek theologians and bishops at Lydda-Diospolis in Palestine, he explained his teaching about the relation between grace and free will to the synod in such a way that he was pronounced orthodox— much to Augustine's consternation.[27] Augustine's defensive account of these proceedings, On the Proceedings of Pelagius, was one of the few works of his to be translated into Greek, perhaps during his lifetime, and was included in the Bibliotheca of the ninth-century scholar and patriarch of

Constantinople Photius. From a comparison of the decree, Augustine's reaction, and Photius's treatment, it is evident that for Eastern Christian thought the Augustinian formulation of the antithesis of grace and freedom, or even of nature and grace, represented a wrong question, to which any answer would have to be wrong.

In the West, the supreme paradigm for the relation between nature and grace, and hence between freedom and grace, was the apostle Paul. His experience of the violent intervention of God when he was thrown to the ground and blinded on the road to Damascus, which was recounted three separate times in the Book of Acts and rather differently in his self-defense at the beginning of the Epistle to the Galatians, was an experience of radical discontinuity between what he had been and what he became.[28] This radical discontinuity compelled him to look for continuity; hence, in the ninth, tenth, and eleventh chapters of the Epistle to the Romans he affirmed both his identification with his past and his drastic break with that past.[29] That Pauline model of conversion was at work in the thought of Augustine. When, in the famous scene in the garden, Augustine heard the voice saying "Tolle, lege [Pick it up, read it]," what he read was a passage from Paul on the theme of discontinuity with the past.[30] Paul had admonished the Romans, and was now admonishing Augustine: "Not in rioting and drunkenness, not in chambering and wantonness, not in strife and envying. But put ye on the Lord Jesus Christ, and make not provision for the flesh to fulfil the lusts thereof."[31] And, as Augustine had said somewhat earlier, "with great eagerness, then, I fastened upon the venerable writings of thy Spirit and principally upon the apostle Paul."[32] Again in the thought of Martin Luther, Paul and a passage from his Epistle to the Romans set the pattern: "The justice of God is revealed in the gospel from faith to faith [Iustitia enim Dei in eo revelatur ex fide in fidem]."[33] As he described in the autobiographical foreword to his collected Latin works, an apologia pro vita sua written in 1545, the year before his death, Luther as a monk and novice exegete had struggled over the meaning of this passage because he assumed that "the justice of God" referred, as he thought it did throughout Scripture, to the quality of the divine nature by which God was just and by which therefore God condemned sin. All of that changed, and as he said "I felt that I . . . had entered paradise itself through open gates," when he perceived that Paul was speaking instead about the justice with which God endowed the sinner in justification. It came, not as the consummation of the human quest, but as the intervention of the divine initiative.[34] Luther's doctrine of nature and grace, then, while significantly different from Augustine's, did emphasize discontinuity. And when, in 1525, he carried on his famous controversy with Erasmus and wrote *The Bondage of the Will*, he believed himself to be expounding the teaching of Paul as he denied to the human will before conversion any positive functioning toward the grace of God and as he put the whole action on the sovereign will of God.

Thinkers of the Eastern tradition, in contrast, characteristically substituted a complementarity for this antithesis. This does not mean that they in the slightest diminished the miracle of the grace of God, which they extolled in prose and poetry, praying as though everything depended on divine grace but acting as though everything depended on human works. But they interpreted grace simultaneously as a totally unearned divine gift and as an affirmation of continuity with nature and creation—and therefore with freedom. In the paradoxical formula of a leading seventh-century Byzantine thinker, Maximus Confessor, God "grants a *reward* as a *gift* to those who have believed him, namely, eternal deification."[35] Apparently "reward" and "gift" were not mutually exclusive but complementary concepts that together produced salvation as "deification."[36] One scholar pointed out, in commenting on such passages as this, that it was "possible for Maximus to say, on the one hand, that there is no power inherent in human nature which is able to deify man, and yet, on the other, that God becomes man *insofar* as man has deified himself."[37]

That characteristically Eastern emphasis on continuity came to voice in a highly personal letter written by Basil of Caesarea, probably in the year 375:

> The teaching about God which I had received as a boy from
> my blessed mother and my grandmother Macrina, I have ever

held with increased conviction. On my coming to ripe years of reason I did not shift my opinions from one to another, but carried out the principles delivered to me by my parents. Just as the seed when it grows is first tiny and then gets bigger but *always preserves its identity, not changed in kind though gradually perfected in growth*, so I reckon the same doctrine to have grown in my case through gradually advancing stages. What I hold now has not replaced what I held at the beginning.[38]

Significantly, what Basil said there about the continuity of his maturation in the context of Christian nurture he even applied, with significant and appropriate modifications, to the relation between Christianity and Classical culture, especially in his famous letter-essay, known in English as *Exhortation to Youths as to How They Shall Best Profit by the Writings of Pagan Authors*, in which he urged his nephews to plumb the depths of the classical Greek tradition and to learn from it lessons for their Christian faith and life.[39] And in the thought of his brother, Gregory of Nyssa, quoted earlier, that affirmation of continuity and that insistence on freedom even in relation to divine grace came to new depths of insight.[40]

But in support of that characteristically Byzantine emphasis on the active role of free will as it accepted the word and grace freely given by God, the active response of the Mother of God in the annunciation as she accepted the word and grace of God was a key incident. As the Eastern thinkers interpreted it, when she became the paradigm, the incarnation both in all its novelty and in its profound continuity with everything that she had been until then could be affirmed. Therefore she was "full of grace [*kecharitōmenē*]," as the angel Gabriel had said in saluting her.[41] For "the entire treasure of grace" dwelt in her,[42] but even though it was the grace of the Almighty, it dwelt in her by her own free will. Her free response to the will and grace of God made her, in a unique sense, a co-laborer with God—as the apostle Paul said to the Corinthians, "We, then, as workers together [*synergoi*] with him"[43]—and therefore also an exemplar of freedom. In many of the centuries of thought and reflection about Mary, that role as exemplar may have been overshadowed by a cramped rendition of her words "Behold the handmaid of the Lord," so that the full dynamism was lost. But repeatedly the power of the annunciation narrative managed to reassert itself in all its vigor: "For he hath regarded the low estate of his handmaiden: for, behold, from henceforth all generations shall call me blessed."[44]

As if to refute, or at least to counterbalance by a preemptive linguistic strike, the quietistic interpretation that would be imposed on this portrait of Mary as, in her own words, *Ancilla Domini*, the Handmaid of the Lord, the Medieval portrayal of the Virgin also applied to her the words: "A woman of valor who will find?"[45] celebrating her as *Mulier Fortis*, the Woman of Valor. Whatever the original Hebrew term ḥāyil may have meant in the context of the closing chapter of the Book of Proverbs—several modern translations of the Bible into English seem to agree on the rendering "capable" here—the Hebrew vocable did allow for the meaning "valor"; and both the Greek translation in the Septuagint, *andreia* (this being the word for the classical virtue of "fortitude"), and the Latin translation in the Vulgate, *fortis*, understood it that way. Woman of Valor thus became a striking formula for the motif and metaphor of Mary as warrior and champion, as conqueror and leader.

The most influential expression of that motif, at any rate in Western Christendom, was the eventual Latin translation of the words of punishment addressed by God to the serpent after the fall of Adam and Eve, to read: "I shall put enmity between you and the woman, and between your seed and her seed; she will crush your head, and you will bruise her heel [*Inimicitias ponam inter te et mulierem, et semen tuum et semen illius; ipsa conteret caput tuum, et tu insidiaberis calcaneo eius*]."[46] There is clear evidence that this was not how Jerome translated the text; for as a Hebrew scholar, he knew that the pronoun should not be rendered with "she," and one of the earliest manuscripts of his translation, as well as an early use of it by Pope Leo I, carried the reading *ipse*, not *ipsa*.[47] Nevertheless, the reading eventually became *ipsa*, for reasons that are not clear. Yet even when it did, early interpreters of the feminine pronoun applied it to the church as the one who had crushed, and was continuing to crush, the head of Satan.[48] In his commentary on Genesis the Venerable Bede, in whose Anglo-Saxon

England the cult of Mary was flourishing,[49] quoted the passage with the feminine pronoun but declared that "the woman crushes the head of the serpent when the holy church dispels the snares and venomous lures of the devil";[50] and another eighth-century monk, Ambrosius Autpertus, celebrating "the daily victory of Christ in the church," saw this victory prefigured in the words spoken to the serpent in Paradise, that ipsa, the woman, would crush his head.[51] But it was already standard practice to identify the church with Mary, as the first one to have believed in the incarnation and, between Good Friday and Easter, the only one to have believed in the resurrection. By far the dominant Medieval interpretation of the feminine pronoun in this passage, therefore, was the Mariological one.[52] Having already applied to Mary the first half of the statement to the serpent, "I shall put enmity between you and the woman," Bernard of Clairvaux continued, "And if you still doubt that he has spoken of Mary, listen to what follows: 'She will crush your head.' For whom was this victory reserved except for Mary? Beyond doubt it was she who crushed the venomous head."[53]

Both biographically and iconographically, there would appear to be some possibility of connecting this first so-called messianic prophecy with the complex symbolism in Johannes Vermeer's late painting of circa 1671–74, Allegory of [the] Faith. "Only in Allegory of Faith," writes Arthur K. Wheelock, Jr., "does he explicitly incorporate abstract theological concepts into a visual vocabulary similar to his other paintings."[54] Vermeer was an adult convert to Roman Catholicism.[55] His conversion was reflected in a number of his paintings, including Christ in the House of Mary and Martha, which is often read as a depiction of the Medieval interpretation of the two sisters as representative of the relation between the contemplative and the active life. Scholars have identified the female figure in his Woman Holding a Balance as the Virgin Mary, the Mediatrix standing between the human race and divine judgment.[56] That judgment was depicted not only by the balance on which, as the words of Isaiah had said, "the nations are as a drop of a bucket, and are counted as the small dust of the balance,"[57] but by the painting of the last judgment on the wall behind her.

Because, as the Second Vatican Council was to put it in its decree Lumen Gentium, "Mary in a certain way unites and mirrors within herself the central truths of the faith [maxima fidei placita in se quodammodo unit et reverberat],"[58] a painting bearing the title Allegory of Faith (or Allegory of the Faith) could well concentrate on her. In the foreground, in a direct allusion to the narrative of the fall of Adam and Eve and the words of Genesis, was the bleeding carcass of a serpent, its head crushed by a stone, and next to it an apple; over it stood the victorious form of a woman, with her foot on a globe of the world. The painting on the wall, which as in Woman Holding a Balance seems to have been intended as a commentary on the action in the painting, portrayed the crucifixion, where the serpent did bruise the heel of the Mother and of the Son but was himself vanquished; in addition, as if to make sure that the viewer did not miss the point, there was a crucifix on the wall. There does not seem to be any way, even with a magnifying glass, to identify the title of the open book, much less its specific words. If it was a Bible, in Dutch or perhaps more likely in Latin, the text seems to have been near the end. Could that perhaps have been the vision of the Woman Clothed with the Sun from the Book of Revelation?[59] Or would it be completely far-fetched to speculate that the book might have been a Hebrew Bible, which was easily available in seventeenth-century Holland, and therefore have been open near the beginning rather than near the end—and specifically at the words of the Lord to the serpent, but interpreted in accordance with the accepted Latin translation and graphically documented by that venomous but now harmless serpent's head?

Another of the ways in which Mary showed herself to be the woman of valor spoken of in Proverbs was her role as lodestar and guide of mariners, "Mary, the star of the sea [Maria maris stella]," a name that was said to have been given her from on high.[60] The name was thought to have been prophesied in the oracle, "A star shall come forth out of Jacob."[61] Because "this class of [nautical] metaphor is extraordinarily widespread throughout the Middle Ages,"[62] the image of Mary as the star guiding the ship of faith was especially attractive, even though it depended at least in part on a trick of language. Its origins seem to lie in

Jerome's etymology for the name "Mary" as "a drop of water from the sea [stilla maris]," which he preferred to other explanations. This etymology was taken over by Isidore of Seville, but in the process "drop [stilla]" had become "star [stella]." On that basis, apparently in the ninth century, an unknown poet composed an influential hymn, hailing Mary as the Star of the Sea, the nourishing Mother of God, the Ever-Virgin, the Gate of Heaven:

> Ave, maris stella,
> Dei mater alma
> atque semper virgo,
> felix caeli porta.[65]

Soon the title became a part of the homiletical language about the Virgin, as well as of theological literature; but it was especially in poetry that the symbol of the courageous Mary as the lodestar of voyagers through life found expression. As Lodestar, she was seen as continuing to overcome the enemies and the storms, and therefore as continuing to be the Woman of Valor who was the Handmaid of the Lord.

Icon of the Virgin, Egypt, Byzantine period, sixth century. © The Cleveland Museum of Art, 1996, Leonard C. Hanna, Jr., Bequest 1967.144.

7 The Adornment of Worship
and the Leader of the Heavenly Choir

And Miriam the prophetess, the sister of Aaron, took a timbrel in her hand;
and all the women went out after her with timbrels and with dances.
And Miriam answered them, Sing ye to the Lord, for he hath triumphed gloriously;
the horse and his rider hath he thrown into the sea.
—Exodus 15:20–21

The identification of Mary, mother of Jesus, with Miriam, sister of Moses, was not only a theme of the Qur'ān[1] but had long before been a theme of Christian typology. Commenting on the words of the psalm "Among them were the damsels playing with timbrels [*in medio iuvenculae tympanistriae*],"[2] Augustine identified the Virgin Mary as "*nostra tympanistria*," because, like Miriam before the children of Israel, she led the people of God and the angels of heaven in the praise of the Almighty.[3] And thousands of English-speaking Protestant congregations in this century—most of them without realizing that they were carrying on this typology of Miriam and Mary, and many without realizing that they were addressing Mary at all—have attributed to her a role as the adornment of worship and leader of the heavenly choir, in the words of John A. L. Riley's hymn of 1906, "Ye Watchers and Ye Holy Ones":

O higher than the cherubim,
More glorious than the seraphim,
Lead their praises, Alleluia!

Thou Bearer of th' eternal Word,

Most gracious, magnify the Lord, Alleluia!

which was to say that when the angels of heaven, the cherubim and seraphim, praised God, they were led by one whom the Archangel Gabriel had hailed as "most gracious" and who had begun her own hymn with the words "My soul doth magnify the Lord," the one who, being the Theotokos, was the Bearer of the eternal Word of God, the Logos-made-flesh. Such sentiments about her, of course, would probably have been harder to voice from the pulpits of such congregations than from the hymnals in their pews.

Even in congregations where the association of the Virgin Mary with worship came naturally, moreover, she figured much more prominently outside the official public liturgy than within it. In the liturgy, the prayers of the Eastern *Liturgy of Saint Basil* and *Liturgy of Saint John Chrysostom* invariably invoked her intercessions.[4] Above all, the hymn *Akathistos* (whose title meant "not sitting down")[5] multiplied its celebration of her as "unwed bride" and object of the church's praises, and it was in turn reflected in the visual arts.[6] In the Western liturgy of the Mass, too, the recitation of the saints above who were joined with the church on earth in petition, praise, and thanksgiving accorded her pride of place. Nevertheless, two of the most widespread and popular devotions to Mary in the Western tradition were nonliturgical in character. The first was usually associated in its origins with the Dominican Order and the second with the Franciscan Order, although both of them became well-nigh universal throughout Roman Catholicism. The practice of the rosary was probably not originated by Saint Dominic, as conventional wisdom supposed on the basis of the unsubstantiated legends recounted by Alan de la Roche in his narrative of revelations. Nevertheless, the rosary did have special ties with the Order of Preachers.[7] Following a devotional practice that appeared also outside Christianity, for example in Hinduism, Buddhism, and Islam, the rosary was a string of beads to be used as a mnemonic device for the recitation of prayers. In fact, the very word *bead* in English came from the universal Germanic word for "to pray," as in the modern German *beten* and the modern English word bid; and, as the Oxford English Dictionary explained, "the name was transferred from 'prayer' to the small globular bodies used for 'telling beads,' i.e., counting prayers said, from which the other senses naturally followed."[8] With some variations from one tradition of observance to another, the prayers of the rosary consisted of 15 recitations of the Pater Noster, 15 sets of 10 recitations of the Ave Maria, and 15 recitations of the Gloria Patri, each of the sets of fifteen prayers being concentrated on one of the mysteries of the redemption; thus a full cycle of the rosary included 150 prayings of the Ave Maria.[9]

The Angelus, by contrast, was connected with the admonition issued in 1269 by Bonaventure, as minister general of the Order of Friars Minor, that Franciscan friars imitate Francis of Assisi by reciting Ave Marias in response to the ringing of the evening bell for prayer. This was expanded, apparently during the fourteenth century, into an Angelus in the morning (first noted at Parma in 1317–18), at noon (Prague in 1386), and in the evening (Rome in 1327, elsewhere even earlier).[10] It also achieved wide circulation among the laity; and it was, for example, incorporated into the first act of Puccini's Tosca, in the prayer of the sacristan, as was the Te Deum Laudamus into the mighty chords of the closing scene of that act. The Angelus took its name from the words of the Gospel of Luke: "Angelus Domini ad Mariam, Ave gratia plena, . . ."[11] Through these two extraliturgical forms of worship as well as through various components of the liturgy itself, the history of Mary embedded itself in the language and the spirituality of countless believers throughout the Western world.

But the area of worship in which Mary performed as leader most effectively was in the adornment of icons.[12] For in the eighth, ninth, and tenth centuries the political, religious, and artistic future of the Byzantine empire and of Byzantine culture was at stake in a struggle for its very identity, during the several successive attacks of Iconoclasm on the use of images in Christian worship. The argument against images, and eventually the argument for them as well, came to be based on the question of whether one could portray the divine-human person of Christ in an icon. But the argument also involved in a special way the person of the Virgin, just as the founding of Byzantium had.[13] According to their opponents, the Iconoclasts attacked not only the worship of icons generally but the orthodox devotion to Mary specifically.[14] They were also reported to have rejected the orthodox belief in the special intercession of Mary on behalf of the church.[15]

In response to such attacks, orthodox theologians—such as John of Damascus, who argued that "the honor paid to an image was meant not for the depiction but for the person depicted"[16]—felt compelled to define how the various forms of "worship [*proskynēsis*]" that Christians were permitted to render to creatures were to be differentiated from the "adoration [*latreia*]" that could be addressed only to God the Creator, not to any creature.[17] If paid to idols, such worship was (in the original term) "idololatry [*eidōlolatreia*],"[18] although the Iconodules insisted that this term did not apply at all to their worship of icons. But by "God the Creator" orthodox theology since the Council of Nicaea and even much earlier had meant God the Holy Trinity, Father, Son, and Holy Spirit, to each of whom it was legitimate to pay a "worship [*proskynēsis*]" that was "adoration [*latreia*]," exclusively restricted to the true God. Such "adoration [*latreia*]," moreover, was addressed, as it had been since the New Testament, to the person of Jesus Christ: whereas Christ had said on the cross, according to Luke, "Father, into thy hands I commend my spirit,"[19] Stephen, the first Christian martyr, had, also according to Luke, called out "Lord Jesus, receive my spirit,"[20] thus moving with evident ease from a prayer that had been addressed to the Father to the same prayer that was now addressed to the Son. For "at the name of Jesus," the apostle Paul declared, "every knee should bow, of things in heaven, and things in earth, and things under the earth, and every tongue should confess that Jesus Christ is Lord, to the glory of God the Father."[21] To Christian orthodoxy, this "bowing the knee" and "worship [*proskynēsis*]" was genuine and complete "adoration [*latreia*]," and it included as its proper object the entire person of the Son of God incarnate—not his divine nature alone, since his divine nature was not alone after the incarnation but was united, permanently and "inseparably [*achōristōs*]" (as the Council of Chalcedon had declared in 451),[22] to the human nature, which could not be the object of "adoration [*latreia*]" in and of itself, being a creature, but which could and should be adored in the undivided person of the God-man.

All other orthodox "worship [*proskynēsis*]," by contrast, was simple "reverence [*douleia*]," hence not a violation of the First Commandment. In at least some passages of his works, John of Damascus did distinguish between "adoration [*latreia*]" and "reverence [*douleia*]."[23] But by a curious turn of linguistic history, the best available documentation for this distinction was not in his writings, nor in those of any other Greek patristic or Byzantine thinkers at all, but in Latin Christian authors, above all Augustine of Hippo. Augustine wrote in his *City of God*:

> For this is the worship which is due to the Divinity, or, to speak more accurately, to the Deity; and to express this worship in a single word, as there does not occur to me any Latin term sufficiently exact, I shall avail myself, wherever necessary, of a Greek word. *Latreia*, whenever it occurs in Scripture, is rendered by the word "service." But that service which is due to men, and in reference to which the apostle writes that servants must be subject to their own masters [Eph. 6:5], is usually designated by another word in Greek [*douleia*], whereas the service which is paid to God alone by worship, is always, or almost always, called *latreia* in the usage of those who wrote from the divine oracles.[24]

This passage was among the first witnesses—or, at any rate, among the earliest preserved witnesses—to make the distinction specific.[25] It must be added that for Augustine to occupy that position in the history of Greek was somewhat ironic, in view of his repeated admissions about his unreliable knowledge of Greek: he had developed an intense dislike for the Greek language, even for the reading of Homer, as a schoolboy,[26] and then as a Catholic bishop defending the Nicene doctrine of the Trinity he had to confess that he did not fully grasp the terminological subtleties in the fundamental trinitarian distinctions made by Greek theologians during the preceding several generations.[27]

As Theotokos, Mary—and that included the Mary of the icons—
was the legitimate object of orthodox Christian "worship [*proskynēsis*]."
Such distinctions were all the more necessary because of the many
postures and gestures of respect toward many persons that were prescribed not only by Byzantine piety but by Byzantine social custom.
Already in classical Greek usage, all of these expressions of respect at all
levels could come under the category of "worship [*proskynēsis*]," which
therefore not only meant to "make obeisance to the gods or their
images, fall down and worship" but pertained especially to "the Oriental fashion of prostrating oneself before kings and superiors."[28] That
fashion was exaggerated still further by what Charles Diehl called "the
thousand refinements of the precise and somewhat childish etiquette
which regulated every act of the imperial life" in Constantinople.[29] In
this profusion of acts of "worship,"[30] there needed to be a special way
of speaking about the worship of God and about the worship of the
saints, and particularly about the worship of the Virgin Mary. Therefore
Medieval Latin theology, illustrated for example by Thomas Aquinas
(who used the Greek terms in their Latin form), found that the simple
distinction between "adoration [*latreia*]" and "reverence [*douleia*]," as it
been drawn by John of Damascus, did not do full justice to the special
position of the Theotokos. For she was certainly less than God, but just
as certainly she was more than an ordinary human being and more than
any other saint; therefore she was not entitled to *latria*, yet she was
entitled to more than *dulia*.[31] For her cultus, then, the appropriate term
was *hyperdulia*.[32] After the Middle Ages, the Latin church was to find the
distinction between *latria* and *dulia* (including *hyperdulia*) additionally
useful when, in the aftermath of the Reformation, Protestant polemics
was regularly accusing the church of "Mariolatry."[33] "Mario-latry"
would have to be defined as a form of *latria* paid to Mary; and extravagant though the language of prayers and hymns addressed to her did
undoubtedly become also in the West, this distinction was intended to
stand as a barrier against "Mariolatry"—albeit a barrier that may sometimes have been all but invisible to the piety of ordinary believers,
whether Western or Eastern, in their prayers to her and to her icon.[34] As

even the defenders of the icons had to acknowledge, the relation between technical theology and the piety of ordinary believers was difficult to handle.[35]

Perhaps the most dramatic of all the traditional portrayals of the
Virgin Mary in Byzantine art was the so-called Deesis (from the Greek
word deēsis, entreaty or intercession).[36] This was the word regularly used
in classical Greek for an "entreaty" of one kind or another.[37] In Byzantine Greek it was employed for various secular petitions and supplica-
tions, such as those addressed to the emperor by his subjects.[38] But it
also became the standard term in patristic Greek, and then in Byzantine
Greek, for intercessory prayers: for those addressed by the church "not
only to God but also to holy men, though not to others"; for the prayer
which Christ as the eternal Mediator presented to the Father; and also
for the prayers that the saints, and especially the Mother of God, as
created mediators presented to Christ and to the Father on behalf of the
church.[39] The Deesis as an art form was divided into three sections or
panels. At the center was the figure of Christ as Lord. On either side of
Christ were, pleading with Christ on behalf of sinners, the Mother of
God and John the Baptist (often identified as "the Forerunner [ho Pro-
dromos]").[40] The Deesis could be presented in artistic creations of various sizes. On one tiny eleventh-century Byzantine reliquary, which is
just over three inches square when folded, the Deesis appears in cloi-
sonné, its two panels of Mary and John folding over the panel of the
central figure. By contrast, the uncovering of the mosaic of the Deesis
on a wall in Hagia Sophia in Istanbul shows this Byzantine motif on a
very large scale.

Historians of Byzantine art and architecture have exploited the significance of the Deesis with sensitivity and skill,[41] establishing the term
Deesis in English usage. Unfortunately, historians of Byzantine spirituality
and theology have not investigated the Deesis with equal thoroughness,
despite the profound and suggestive way it presented several of the
central motifs in the Eastern Christian understanding of the entire "dispensation [oikonomia]" of the history of salvation. The juxtaposition of
Mary and John the Baptist in the Deesis was a way of identifying the

two figures who, according to the Christian understanding of the history of salvation, stood on the border between the Old Testament and the New. According to the saying of Christ in the Gospel, the line of the Old Testament prophets had come only as far as John the Baptist.[42] This was taken by Justin Martyr in the second century to prove that after John there would no longer be any prophets among the people of Israel.[43] Zechariah, the Baptist's father, was a priest of the "tribe of Levi," who continued the sacerdotal mediation between God and the people going back to Aaron. John's parents were the recipients of an "annunciation [euangelismos]" by the angel Gabriel, analogous to that which came a few months later to the Virgin Mary, cousin of John's mother, Elizabeth.[44] According to Gregory of Nyssa, "the gift in him was pronounced by him who sees the secrets of a man to be greater than any prophet's."[45] For Christ himself had said about John the Baptist: "Never has there appeared on earth a mother's son greater than John the Baptist."[46]

No mother's *son* was greater than John the Baptist, but one mother's *daughter* was greater than any mother's son or daughter, namely, Mary the Mother of God, whom Gregory of Nyssa earlier in the same treatise called "Mary without stain [amiantos]."[47] Not only iconographically but theologically, she occupied a unique place in Eastern Christendom, which was, as we have seen, where both the devotion to her and the speculation about her had been concentrated throughout the early centuries of Christian history. The devotion to Mary had found its supreme expression in the Byzantine liturgy. From its sources in the Greek church fathers and in Byzantine Christianity, Eastern Mariology went on to exert a decisive influence on Western interpretations of Mary throughout the patristic and early Medieval periods, with church fathers like Ambrose of Milan functioning as transmitters of Greek Mariology to the Latin church.[48]

Behind the differences between the Latin and the Greek traditions lay an even more profound difference, identified by the teaching of Greek Christian theology that salvation conferred on its recipients nothing less than a transformation of their very humanity, by which they partake of the reality of the Divine. Anders Nygren saw the idea that "the human is raised up to the Divine" as one that the Greek church father Irenaeus shared "with Hellenistic piety generally."[49] And there were clear echoes of Hellenism in the Christian version of the doctrine.[50] But this idea of salvation as deification or theōsis[51] was not exclusively Greek; it appeared in various of the Latin fathers, including Augustine, and, as Nygren acknowledged, it was even occasionally echoed in the writings of the Protestant Reformers and their followers.[52] At almost the same time as the tapestry *Icon of the Virgin*, which illustrates this chapter, was created, a Latin Christian writer incorporated the idea of divinization into a work of philosophical reflection that achieved wide circulation in the Middle Ages: "Since that men are made blessed by the obtaining of blessedness, and blessedness is nothing else but divinity, it is manifest that men are made blessed by the obtaining of divinity. And as men are made just by the obtaining of justice, and wise by the obtaining of wisdom, so they who obtain divinity must needs in like manner become gods. Wherefore everyone that is blessed is a god, but by nature there is only one God; but there may be many by participation."[53] The idea could, moreover, lay claim to explicit biblical grounding. As it stood, "I have said, Ye are gods," was a mysterious Old Testament statement in the Book of Psalms, addressed to the rulers of this world.[54] But as quoted by Christ in the New Testament, this statement became proof that "he called them gods, unto whom the word of God came, and the scripture cannot be broken."[55] Because believers in Christ were preeminently "those unto whom the word of God came," and among them this was preeminently true of Mary, it followed, according to the Greek Christian tradition, that they—and above all she—were also preeminently those who should be called "gods." For this, too, was a "scripture that cannot be broken."

The Scripture that provided justification for the idea, and that therefore became the locus classicus cited in support of it especially in Byzantine theology, was the arresting New Testament formula: "Whereby are given unto us exceeding great and precious promises: that by these ye might be partakers of the divine nature [*theias koinōnoi* physeōs], having escaped the corruption that is in the world through lust."[56] Both the negative emphasis of the Greek church fathers on salvation as escape from "transiency, corruption [phthora]" and their positive emphasis on salvation as participation in the divine nature were articulated in this one New Testament passage. Thus the Greek word theōsis, deification or divinization, came to stand for a distinctive view of the meaning of salvation, summarized in the Eastern patristic formula, current already in the second and third centuries: "God became human so that man might become divine." This view had then been fundamental to the development of the doctrine of the Trinity; as Athanasius had put it, "By the participation of the Spirit, we are knit into the Godhead."[57] While striving to protect the biblical formula of participation in the divine nature from any trace of pantheism by emphasizing the inviolable transcendence of a God beyond language or thought or even being, the Greek fathers and their Byzantine pupils strove no less assiduously to give concrete content to its promise of a humanity made divine through the incarnation of the Logos of God in the person of Jesus Christ.

That concrete content found its supreme exemplar in the person of Mary the Theotokos, also in Russian Orthodox art.[58] The painters of the icons seem to have manifested no hesitation in portraying Mary as "divine," and the defenders of the icons often seemed to be almost insouciant in their manner of speaking about her "divine" qualities; for "divine" was indeed the right word for her as Theotokos. In its ultimate significance, salvation as deification, like every heavenly promise, was eschatological and could not be fully achieved by anyone here in this present life on earth. But Mary was proof positive that it could be achieved, truly though not fully, and in this world; her portrayal in icons was evidence of this fact, as was the Magnificat, which was sung as part of the Orthros, or Morning Office of the Greek church.[59]

Icons of Christ simultaneously presented both "the form of God" and "the form of a servant"[60] as they had been inseparably united in his person through the incarnation. Although his "divine nature" had not always been perceptible to his contemporaries behind "the nature of a slave," which they did see, in the transfiguration it had become visible already in this world and even before his resurrection. This was expressed in the earliest preserved mosaic of the transfiguration, whose iconographic interpretation William Loerke has skillfully connected to Maximus Confessor's theological interpretation of the event:

> About seventy-five to eighty years after the mosaic was set, Maximus the Confessor gave the Transfiguration an imaginative and profound interpretation. He saw Christ in this vision as a symbol of himself, a manifestation of the hidden in the visible, in which the luminous garments at once clothe the human nature and reveal the divine. The event was not a fixed image, but an unfolding drama. The brilliant garments of Christ, the changing tones of blue in the aureole, and the transparencies in the rays of light coming from the aureole, suggest a hidden force coming into view—the visual analogue of Maximus' interpretation.[61]

And the historical analogue for it, a reality that was at once the anticipation and the result of the miracle of the transfiguration of Christ, was Mary the Mother of God. She did not have a pre-existent divine nature, as Christ did, but was completely human in her origin, like all other human beings. Yet because she had been chosen by God to be the Theotokos, her completely human nature had been transfigured; and already in this earthly existence she had in a special way become a "partaker of the divine nature," as the Second Epistle of Peter had promised that all who believed in her divine Son would.

The ground for "deification" as a distinctively Eastern depiction of salvation was a distinctively Eastern depiction of the atonement. It was, according to Byzantine theology, necessary but not sufficient to speak of human salvation as the forgiveness of sins. The interpretation of the passion and crucifixion of Christ as the sacrifice for sin—an interpretation that came from Scripture and was therefore common to East and West—had a corollary image of *Christus Victor* as the distinctive way for the Christian East to speak about the mystery of the redemption. By his victory Christ as Second Adam had conquered sin and death, and through his transfiguration he had given humanity a glimpse of its eventual destiny; Mary as Second Eve had also manifested this destiny, because of her Son and because of the divine life that he had conferred—first on her, and then on all. Such a view of the human condition and of salvation sometimes came dangerously close to defining the sin of Adam and Eve as the consequence not of their having transgressed the commandments of God but merely of their being temporal and finite; such a definition of sin would then seem to have manifested greater affinities to Neoplatonism than to the New Testament. But the very concentration on Mary the Theotokos as the historical fulfillment of this promise of humanity made divine prevented this view from falling completely into the Neoplatonic teaching.

As the battle over iconizing Christ provided the grounds for defending the practice of iconizing his Mother, so her icon supplied the justification for the icons of all the other saints. The tapestry *Icon of the Virgin* offered striking documentation of that connection between Mary and the other saints: surrounding the imposing figures of the Theotokos and the archangels Michael and Gabriel were medallions of apostles and saints. Conversely, the defense of portraying the divine-human Christ led to a defense of portraying the human Mary who, through him and because she was chosen to give birth to him, had been made divine. And since the concept of deification was also the fundamental constituent of the Byzantine definition of sainthood, it was an obvious extrapolation from these Mariological discussions to affirm that the saints, too, were to be iconized. How, the Iconodules asked, was it possible to portray the supreme commander without portraying his troops?[62] For the life of Christ depicted in the icons was not merely the life he had lived while on earth during the first century. The resurrected Christ lived on in the life of his church—and in the lives of his saints. It would, they argued, be a disastrous foreshortening of perspective on his image if the portrayal of that life did not include portrayals of those in whom it had continued, and was continuing, to make sacred history. Yet the theology of icons could not stop even there. The Logos whose

incarnate form it was legitimate to iconize was himself the living image
of God and the one through whom heaven and earth and all that is
therein had been created. The Mother of God whom it was permissible
to depict on an icon was the Queen of Heaven. The saints whose lives
were celebrated on the iconostasis and on individual icons were now in
the presence of God in heaven. And standing by, not as recipients of
salvation but nevertheless as participants in the drama, were the angels,
who in the upper zone of this icon attended the exalted Christ and who
in the lower zone stood on either side of his Mother. All of these images
stood in relation to one another, in what Byzantine theology makes it
necessary to call a "great chain of images."

Iconographically as well as theologically, the supreme person represented on this tapestry *Icon of the Virgin* was not the Virgin Mary but
Christ. As Christ enthroned in glory, he occupied the higher of the two
zones, which, though smaller, was certainly preeminent. In the lower
zone, moreover, the Christ Child was still Christ the Lord, as he grasped
the top of a scroll, probably the scroll of the law. Yet the most prominent figure in size, and in many ways the most striking in style, was the
portrait of Mary the Mother of God seated on her throne, with an
archangel on either side:

> On our tapestry the Virgin sits on an elaborately jewelled
> throne of Byzantine type with an enormous red cushion. She
> is clad in a simple purple *palla* and tunic and black shoes.
> One end of the *palla*—or *mataphorion*, to use its Greek name—
> is draped over her head as a veil; beneath it her hair is con-
> cealed by a little white cap on which is an "embroidered"
> gold cross. Her head is framed by a large yellow nimbus.
> The Christ Child, without a nimbus, is seated in her lap at
> the left. He is dressed in a golden-yellow tunic and *pallium*;
> purple *clavi* decorate the shoulders of the tunic. . . . The Vir-
> gin's costume is that of a woman of the ordinary classes in
> late antiquity. This is the costume in which she is universally
> represented on all pre-Iconoclastic Byzantine monuments. Al-

though never represented in the elaborate costume of an empress, as was frequently done in contemporary Roman art,
her simple garments are nevertheless consistently purple, the
color reserved for Byzantine royalty.[63]

Although the *Icon of the Virgin* is a tapestry rather than a painting, it does appear iconographically necessary to associate its distinctive treatment of the figure of Mary the Mother of God, including the throne, with the history of the Byzantine liturgical and theological definition of Mary as Theotokos, which would thereafter influence the way she was later portrayed in the Christian art of the West no less than in that of the East.[64]

Giotto di Bondone, *Marriage of the Virgin*, between 1304 and 1313. Scrovegni Chapel, Padua. (Alinari / Art Resource, N.Y.)

8 The Paragon of Chastity
and the Blessed Mother

How shall this be, seeing I know not a man?
—Luke 1:34

T he paradox of Mary as Virgin Mother not only effectively illustrated but decisively shaped the fundamental paradox of the Orthodox and Catholic view of sexuality, which was epitomized by the glorification of virginity over matrimony—and by the celebration of matrimony, but not of virginity, as a sacrament. For as Virgin she served as the unique and sublime paragon of chastity. At the same time as Mother she was uniquely "blessed among women," as Elizabeth called her and as the words of the *Ave Maria* saluted her, not because she was Virgin but specifically because she was, as Elizabeth went on to say, "the Mother of my Lord."[1] The tensions represented by that paradox ran through much of subsequent Christian history, and especially through the history of the effort to define the meaning of morality and the Christian life. For this history, too, the person of Mary was a major force.

Christian asceticism certainly predated Christianity. The world early Christianity entered was experiencing a series of vigorous movements dedicated to the denial of the claims of the physical life and to the cultivation of the disciplines of self-restraint in relation to food, drink, bodily comfort, and above all sexuality.[2] The classical Greek word *askēsis,* which referred in general to practice and discipline, came to be applied specifically to these practices of self-restraint and self-denial.[3] The language of military discipline and of athletic training was applied to the moral realm to explain the need for abstinence in the interest of some greater goal, in this life or in the life to come. As Marcus Aurelius said, applying the military metaphor, "life a warfare, a brief sojourning in an alien land; and after repute, oblivion. Where, then, can man find the power to guide and guard his steps? In one thing and one alone— Philosophy. To be a philosopher is to keep unsullied and unscathed the divine spirit within him, so that it may transcend all pleasure and all pain."[4] The writings bearing the name of the apostle Paul also invoked military language to describe Christian discipline.[5] But Paul's most vivid metaphor for ascetic discipline came from athletics, as practiced in the Hellenistic world: "Know ye not that they which run in a race run all, but one receiveth the prize? So run, that ye may obtain. And every man that striveth for the mastery is temperate in all things. Now they do it to obtain a corruptible crown; but we an incorruptible [one]. I therefore so run, not as uncertainly; so fight I, not as one that beateth the air. But I keep my body and bring it into subjection: lest that by any means, when I have preached to others, I myself should be a castaway."[6] Keeping the body and bringing it under subjection, which clearly was a duty incumbent on all Christians, eventually became the special province of the professional ascetic.

Sometimes, though not necessarily, the ascetic impulse was rooted in a metaphysical dualism, whether or not it was Platonic in origin, a view of the world and of human nature according to which human appetites, and above all sexual desire, having come from a lower source in their creation and being shared with the lower animals, were in conflict with the imperatives of the spirit and of the higher nature in human beings, so that the only way to liberate the mind and spirit was to overcome these appetites through denial. Though not directly connected with such speculation, the institution of the vestal virgins in Rome obliged them to preserve their virginity for the duration of their service, normally five years but sometimes much longer, and subjected them to entombment alive if they violated it.[7]

It seems evident that at least in part the celebration of virginity and the cultivation of asceticism came about in revulsion against what were taken to be the excesses of sexual self-indulgence in Late Antiquity. Later moralists have been fond of quoting Roman satirists like Tacitus, Juvenal, and Martial on these excesses; even Edward Gibbon, with his ill-concealed scorn for monasticism and asceticism, followed Tacitus's "honest pleasure in the contrast of barbarian [German] virtue with the dissolute conduct of the Roman ladies," noting that "the most dangerous enemy [of chastity] is the softness of the mind."[8] As Peter Brown has shown, there was a widespread sense in the society of Late Antiquity that human life needed to be rescued from its tendency to allow the senses unfettered reign and that true holiness could be found in rejecting what Gibbon called "the softness of the mind" in favor of restraint.[9] And as this was true of the individual, so it could be true of society, which therefore needed within it the presence of full-time and permanent ascetics who could be a challenge and an example to those who lived an ordinary life of the appetites and the senses.

So pervasive was the ascetic impulse in Late Antiquity that even Judaism came under its spell in some places. In the institution of the Nazarites, described in the Book of Numbers, Israel had had a group who bound themselves by sacred vows to live in self-denial, "to separate themselves unto the Lord."[10] The best-known example was Samson, who at the annunciation by the angel of the Lord to his father, Manoah, was designated "a Nazarite unto God from the womb."[11] But the Jewish philosopher and theologian Philo of Alexandria, a contemporary of Jesus and Paul, in a treatise entitled On the Contemplative Life, described a further elaboration of Jewish asceticism in group he called "Therapeutae," men and women who lived in a monastic community in the Egyptian desert near Alexandria. Among these, Philo said, "the women also share . . . , the greater part of whom, though old, are virgins in respect of their purity (not indeed through necessity, as some of the priestesses among the Greeks are, who have been compelled to preserve their chastity more than they would have done of their own accord), but out of an admiration for and love of wisdom, with which they are desirous to pass their lives, on account of which they are indifferent to the pleasures of the body, desiring not a mortal but an immortal offspring."[12] The striking similarities between this community of Therapeutae in Hellenistic Judaism and early Christian monasticism persuaded Eusebius, the first historian of Christianity, that Philo had in fact been describing a Christian group; quoting this passage, he took such evidence to be "more striking examples, which are to be found nowhere else than in the evangelical religion of the Christians."[13] As the comments of Eusebius indicated, asceticism and monasticism were beginning to take firm hold in the church by the fourth century. The most important documentation of this comes from *The Life of Saint Antony* by Athanasius of Alexandria, once more the biography of a monk in the Egyptian desert, but this time of a Christian monk, who learned to "fortify his body with faith, prayers, and fasting" even when "the devil took upon himself the shape of a woman and imitated all her acts simply to beguile Antony."[14] Significantly, it was from a Latin translation of the life of Antony, perhaps prepared during Athanasius's lifetime on one of his Western exiles, that Augustine learned about Christian asceticism.[15]

As might have been expected, the apologists for Christian asceticism fixed on the Virgin Mary as a model of the life of virginity and self-denial. Athanasius did so in his *Letter to Virgins*, in which he described Mary in language intended to motivate the female ascetics to whom he was writing.[16] Also notable among such apologists for the monastic life was Jerome, whose influence reached many of his contemporaries. For example, his "long drawn out correspondence" with Augustine on a variety of subjects, Peter Brown has said, "is a unique document in the Early Church. For it shows two highly-civilized men conducting with studied courtesy, a singular rancorous correspondence."[17] Jerome's greatest importance in history is certainly his translation of the Bible into Latin, but he made other major contributions. Among these, two of the most far-reaching were his monastic foundations and his doctrine of Mary. Early in life, before his ordination into the priesthood, Jerome lived as a hermit in the Syrian desert at Chalcis, devoting himself to ascetic practices and to scholarly study, including the study of Hebrew, which was to stand him in such good stead as commentator and translator of the Jewish Scriptures. A public career followed, at Constantinople and then at Rome as secretary to Pope Damasus; but even then he was a vigorous proponent of the ascetic life, persuading a number of Roman aristocratic women, including Paula and her daughter, Eustochium, as well as Marcella and Melania, to give up their lives of privilege and position in the fashionable society of Rome and to enter monastic communities.

These communities were in Palestine, to which in 386 Jerome himself emigrated and established a monastery in Bethlehem. Observing that "in those days no highborn lady at Rome had made profession of the monastic life, or had ventured—so strange and ignominious did it then seem—publicly to call herself a nun," he credited Athanasius's *Life of Antony* for having inspired Marcella and other women to the ascetic life.[18] In a letter to Eustochium on her mother's death, which he "spent the labor of two nights in dictating"[19] and which amounted to a miniature biography, Jerome described Paula's asceticism and the monastic community of consecrated women that she had headed. "So strictly did Paula separate them from men," he explained, "that she would not allow even eunuchs to approach them, lest she should give occasion to slanderous tongues (always ready to cavil at the religious) to console themselves for their own misdoing."[20] In another letter, addressed to Gaudentius, which contained some of his most moving statements about the sack of Rome in 410,[21] he spoke about the vocation of virginity. Clearly specifying, "What I say I do not say as universally applicable," he nevertheless asked Gaudentius: "Are you a virgin? Why then do you find pleasure in the society of a woman?" And concerning a small girl whom her father had dedicated to a life of virginity from her infancy, he prescribed that she "should associate only with girls, she should know nothing of boys and should dread even playing with them."[22]

Jerome was at the same time one of the most influential interpreters in the early church of the life and person of the Virgin Mary. Writing against Jovinian, who though himself a monk had attacked what he regarded as an exaggerated view of virginity, Jerome composed a sharp polemic in which, as the standard English manual on early Christian literature has put it, "the exegesis proposed for 1 Cor. 7 along with the picturesque expressions drawn from pagan antifeminist literature provoked resentment."[23] His treatise *Against Helvidius*, written in 383, was a defense of the perpetual virginity of Mary, "to show that the mother of the Son [of God], who was a mother before she was a bride, continued a Virgin after her son was born."[24] He took advantage of his formidable rhetorical skills as a controversialist and his outstanding skills as a biblical scholar to prove that the references in the New Testament to Jesus as Mary's first-born son did not necessarily mean that there were any sons of Mary after him, because "every only-begotten son is a first-born son, but not every first-born is an only-begotten."[25] He also devoted lengthy and careful argumentation to the problem arising from the references in the Gospels that spoke of the "brethren" of Jesus.[26] To resolve the problem, Jerome maintained "that the sons of Mary, the sister of our Lord's mother, who though not formerly believers afterwards did believe, can be called brethren of the Lord."[27] Jerome's defense of the perpetual virginity of Mary set down the standard arguments, which went on being used by subsequent expositors of this doctrine, even including Martin Luther. But after completing the portion of his treatise devoted to Mary, Jerome appended a discussion of the relative merits of virginity and matrimony, an issue that had been part of the treatise of Helvidius to which Jerome was writing an answer. "Are virgins better than Abraham, Isaac, and Jacob, who were married men?" Helvidius had argued. "Are not infants daily fashioned by the hands of God in the wombs of their mothers?" which seemed to Helvidius to imply necessarily that matrimony was at least as holy as virginity.[28]

Jerome's reply was to present himself as continuing the argumentation of the apostle Paul: "It is good for a man not to touch a woman. Nevertheless, to avoid fornication, let every man have his own wife, and let every woman have her own husband. So then he that giveth [a virgin] in matrimony doeth well; but he that giveth her not in matrimony doeth better."[29] This did not say that matrimony was evil: it was good, but the preservation of virginity was even better. On the basis of this New Testament authority Jerome felt qualified to say: "I beseech my readers not to suppose that in praising virginity I have in the least disparaged matrimony, and separated the saints of the Old Testament from those of the New, that is to say, those who had wives and those who altogether refrained from the embraces of women."[30] Nevertheless, Jerome did in fact go on to disparage matrimony—and women in general—as in the following vivid description, for which he summoned a rhetorical skill that had been honed on the writings of Cicero:

> The virgin's aim is to appear less comely; she will wrong herself so as to hide her natural attractions. The married woman has the paint laid on before her mirror, and, to the insult of her Maker, strives to acquire something more than her natural beauty. Then comes the prattling of infants, the noisy household, children watching for her word and waiting for her kiss, the reckoning up of expenses, the preparation to meet the outlay. . . . Meanwhile a message is delivered that the husband and his friends have arrived. The wife, like a swallow, flies all over the house. She has to see to everything. "Is the sofa smooth? Is the pavement swept? Are the flowers in the cups? Is the dinner ready?" Tell me, pray, where amid all this is there room for the thought of God? Are these happy homes?[31]

And in a sense, the best argument he could summon against the clear impression that such a description conveyed was to protest: "We do not condemn matrimony, for virginity itself is the fruit of matrimony."[32]

Missing in Jerome's presentations were, first, a more detailed consideration of Mary not only as Virgin but at the same time as Mother, and, second, a clearer statement of the sacramental definition of matrimony. The first of these was supplied by another of Augustine's associates, the man who brought him to the Christian gospel, Ambrose of Milan, who was, more than Augustine, a genuine *Doctor Marianus*, at least partly because of his strong dependence on the Greek Christian tradition.

Ambrose led the way in positing a "causal connection between the

virginal conception and the sinlessness of Christ . . . , the combination of
the ideas of the propagation of original sin through sexual union and of
the sinlessness of Christ as a consequence of his virginal conception";[33]
this would eventually force the Western Church to define the doctrine of
the immaculate conception of Mary.[34] No less than Jerome, Ambrose
insisted on the perpetual virginity of Mary, who, he said, "did not seek
the consolation of being able to bear another son."[35] He also followed the
words of Paul just quoted in recognizing that virginity was on a higher
plane than matrimony, strongly rejecting those who claimed "that there
is no merit in abstinence, no grace in a frugal life, none in virginity, that
all are valued at one price."[36] Like Jerome, Ambrose devoted several
writings to the theme of virginity, including the treatise Concerning Virgins.
As the manual of early Christian literature quoted earlier on Jerome put it
in speaking of Ambrose, "This composition, which is held to be the first
organic treatise of spirituality and theology on the theme of virginity in
Latin, maintains a balanced and positive judgment on matrimony."[37] In
Book II of this treatise, having set forth for his sister, Marcellina, a description and commendation of the virginal estate, he drew the connection
with Mary: "Let, then, the life of Mary be as it were virginity itself, set
forth in a likeness, from which, as from a mirror, the appearance of
chastity and the form of virtue is reflected. From this you may take your
pattern of life, showing, as an example, the clear rules of virtue: what you
have to correct, to effect, and to hold fast."[38]

Holding her up as a model of the Christian life, Ambrose described
all kinds of virtues as having shone forth in Mary the Virgin, and specifically six virtues: "The secret of modesty, the banner of faith, the secret of
devotion, the Virgin within the house, the companion for the ministry
[of Christ], the Mother at the temple."[39] But the second of these two
triads of virtue, "the Virgin within the house, the companion for the
ministry [of Christ], the Mother at the temple," enabled Ambrose to go
beyond the first triad, "the secret of modesty, the banner of faith, the
secret of devotion," and thus to deepen his portrait well beyond Jerome's.
The first triad characterized the Virgin in the privacy of her heart and in
the mystery of her relation to God, whereas the second moved outward

to her historic mission as the Mother of Christ. For "the Virgin within the house" was also "the Mother at the temple," and because she was not only Virgin but Mother she could be "the companion for the ministry of Christ." This put many of the stories in the Gospels into a new light, but it also tended to place even her virginity into the context of her divine maternity, as W. J. Dooley has made clear.[40] "Whatever she did was a lesson," Ambrose inferred from the Gospel story; for she "attended to everything as though she were warned by many, and fulfilled every obligation of virtue as though she were teaching rather than learning."[41] Therefore Ambrose also emphasized Mary's "abundance of services" and her being both "busy in private at home" and "accompanied by others abroad"[42]—which included being "busy" in the very ways that Jerome caricatured.

The metaphysical dualism mentioned earlier as a frequent corollary of asceticism in Late Antiquity did not disappear with the coming of Christianity but took up a place also in Christian thought, above all in the thought of those many Christian theologians who combined their Christianity with Neo-Platonism. When that happened, Christian asceticism expressed itself in a rejection of the body that appeared to deny that God had created it, and therefore in a revulsion at sexuality that equated it with immorality. Because most writers on the subject were men, and unmarried men at that, the revulsion easily became a misogynous contempt for women as the devil's snare to corrupt the *vita angelica* of the ascetic or celibate man. A second need, therefore, was the identification of matrimony as a sacrament of the church, which was a lengthy and complex process. Curiously, matrimony was the only one of the eventual list of seven sacraments to be identified in the New Testament as a *mystērion* or *sacramentum*.[43] Although these words were not originally used in Greek and Latin in the technical sense of the word *sacrament*. they contributed to the definition of matrimony as a sacrament.[44]

The role of the doctrine of Mary in this development of the doctrine of matrimony was somewhat obscure, as became evident, for example, in Giotto's painting *The Marriage of the Virgin*, in the Arena Chapel in Padua, by which John Ruskin was so captivated.[45] Superficially this might be taken to be just another depiction of a wedding, with the bride and groom dressed in finery and the guests supporting them with love and prayers. But there was something unique about this wedding and about this couple, specifically about the bride, who, having taken a prior vow of chastity, was and yet was not involved in the proceedings. In viewing this painting, one cannot but be reminded of the portrayal of *Saint Francis Being Married to Poverty*, celebrated also in Canto XI of Dante's *Paradiso*, in which the Franciscan renunciation of worldly goods was consecrated in an allegorical ceremony that was ordinarily the occasion for conferring worldly goods.[46] Here, too, the wedding was authentic, yet it had a singular quality because of the Bride. She was, as the Greek hymn *Akathistos* had called her, "the unwed Bride [*nymphos anymphētos*]."

For on one hand, both theologians and canon lawyers defended the thesis that the matrimony of Mary and Joseph was a true marriage even though it was not sexually consummated, on the basis of the principle that "it is consent, not sexual intercourse, that makes a marriage [*consensus, non concubitus, facit connubium*]." Therefore "a marriage in which both spouses voluntarily and for supernatural motives follow the precedent of Mary and Joseph in practicing total abstinence, either from the beginning or only later" is identified as a *Josephsehe* and has standing as a valid union.[47] But on the other hand, it proved to be difficult to deduce, on the basis of the mystical view of Mary as archetype of the church, and of the church in turn as the spouse of Christ, clear implications for the sacramental nature of human matrimony, which was not instituted by Christ during his ministry on earth (not even at the wedding in Cana of Galilee)[48] but by the Creator of Adam and Eve in the Garden of Eden before the fall into sin. Nevertheless, as the portrait of Mary as the Virgin combatted the perceived excesses of sexuality in Late Antiquity, so the portrait of Mary as the Mother likewise combatted the perceived excesses of asceticism. And the truth was seen to lie in the paradox.

Michelangelo Buonarroti, *Pietà*, 1498–99/1500. Saint Peter's Basilica, Vatican State. (Alinari/Art Resource, N.Y.)

9   The Mater Dolorosa
and the Mediatrix

Yea, a sword shall pierce through thy own soul also.
—Luke 2:35

During the High Middle Ages of the twelfth and thirteenth centuries, which in a special way combined what Ernst Robert Curtius has called "the essential message of medieval thought," defined by him as "the spirit in which it restated tradition,"[1] with what Charles Homer Haskins has called a genuine "Renaissance of the twelfth century,"[2] that combination of tradition and innovation was nowhere more dramatically in evidence than in its portrayal of Mary as the Mater Dolorosa, Mother of Sorrows, and its correlative doctrine of Mary as the Mediatrix. The sheer number of references to her in poetry and prose, together with her ever-deepening prominence in the visual arts, would make it difficult not to agree with Otto von Simson's judgment that "the age was indeed the age of the Virgin."[3] In the Czech art of the Gothic period, for example, she was a dominant figure.[4]

If the systematic clarification of the title Mediatrix was the principal objective expression of Mariology and the chief theological contribution to the Christian teaching about Mary during this period, this must be seen also in creative tension with the growth of its most important subjective expression, the literary form and devotional motif of the Mater Dolorosa: Mary had simultaneously lamented the death of Christ because he was her Son and welcomed it because he was her Savior and the Savior of the world. The prophecy of Simeon in the Gospel, that "a sword will pierce your own soul also [*et tuam ipsius animam pertransiet gladius*],"[5] had long been taken as a reference to the experience through which Mary would have to pass as simultaneously the most important and the most involved spectator at the crucifixion, as well as a reference to her own death.[6] The description accompanying the third word from the cross, "Woman, behold thy son!" and "Behold thy mother!"—that "there stood by the cross of Jesus, his mother"[7]—although it came from the Gospel of John, seemed clearly to be the fulfillment of Simeon's warning in the Gospel of Luke. The combination of these two pictures, the Mother standing at the foot of the cross and the Mother with her groaning, sorrowing, and grieving soul pierced by a sword, produced the evocative verses of the *Stabat Mater Dolorosa*:

> Stabat mater dolorosa
> iuxta crucem lacrimosa
> dum pendebat filius;
> cuius animam gementem
> contristantem et dolentem
> pertransivit gladius.[8]

This anonymous poem may have been set to music soon after it was composed or may even have been written to be sung; but it remained an attractive text for composers until the nineteenth and twentieth centuries, drawing the attention of such widely different masters as Giovanni Pierluigi Palestrina, Franz Joseph Haydn, Giovanni Pergolesi, Franz Schubert, Giuseppe Verdi, and Krzysztof Penderecki.[9] The contrast between the renderings of the poem by Gioacchino Rossini and his younger contemporary Antonín Dvořák is instructive for understanding not only the differences between these two composers but the range of subjective emotion that could be expressed in the *Stabat Mater*. Dvořák's reading was meditative, looking inward into the anguished soul of the Virgin and then into the anguished soul of the pious believer and pondering the meaning of the awesome event on the cross. Rossini's, by contrast, was irresistibly operatic, at times almost exuberant, as in his dramatic setting for solo tenor voice of the words from Simeon's prophecy, "Cujus animam gementem pertransivit gladius." It was a free adaptation in German of the Latin text of the *Stabat Mater* when Johann Wolfgang von Goethe in his *Faust* had Gretchen in her hour of crisis pray to the Mater Dolorosa, "Incline thy countenance graciously to my need, thou who art abounding in pain. With the sword in thy heart and with a thousand pains thou dost look up at the death of thy Son. Thou dost look to the Father and send sighs upward for [thy Son's] trial and for thine own,"[10] thus giving sublime poetic expression to authentic folk piety toward the Virgin Mary—and, more important for his eventual poetic purpose, preparing the way for the supreme exaltation of the Mater Gloriosa.[11] Similarly paraphrasing the words of the *Stabat Mater* without quoting them, the Symphony no. 3 of Henryk Górecki used an exchange between Christ and his Mother to expand the scope of the sorrows of the Mater Dolorosa by embracing all the suffering and the fallen of the Second World War:

> Where has he gone,
> My dearest Son?
> Perhaps during the uprising
> The cruel enemy killed him.
> [*Kajze mi sie podzioł*
> *mój synocek miły?*
> *Pewnie go w powstaniu*
> *złe wrogi zabiły*].[12]

But those were relatively restrained versions of the *planctus Mariae* or *Marienklagen*, the poetry of the complaints of Mary in this and later periods.[13] As those titles for the genre in Latin and German suggest, the Mater Dolorosa became a well-known Marian theme particularly in the Western church. But thanks to recent studies by Margaret Alexiou and Gregory W. Dobrov, it is now possible to draw the lines of development back from this Western version to the Byzantine poetry of the Lamenting Virgin, and back even from that to the classical threnody of the lamenting woman.[14] Thus in the *Kontakion* of Romanos Melodos, Mary complained:

> I am vanquished by loving grief, child, vanquished
> And cannot bear the thought of being in my chambers while you
>   are on the cross;
> I, at home while you are in the tomb.
> Let me come with you! The sight of you soothes my pain.

To which Christ replied:

> Lay aside your grief, mother, lay it aside.
> Lamentation does not befit you who have been called "Blessed."
> Do not obscure your calling with weeping.
> Do not liken yourself to those who lack understanding, all-wise
>   maiden.
> You are in the midst of my bridal chamber.

As Dobrov has put it, "This, of course, alludes to the Virgin's exalted status whereby she, as second in rank only to the Godhead, absorbs much of Christ's function as intermediary between God and man."[15]

What the poetry of the Middle Ages in both West and East was describing in its moving verses, the visual arts in both West and East also portrayed.[16] It would be possible for this purpose to examine the many statues, altarpieces, and woodcuts in which the Virgin was being pierced by the sword. But Michelangelo's *Pietà* was certainly the best-known attempt, in statuary or in painting, to capture the depth of the Virgin's grief as she held the broken body of her crucified Son.[17] It only added to the poignancy that, as has often been noted, Michelangelo presented Mary as a young woman who, because of her unique position as the Virgin full of grace, had not been subject to the ravages of age, just as in death her body would not be subject to the ravages of corruption.[18] On her face, for all its youthful beauty, sorrow and serenity are mingled: these, her most tragic hours, in which her Son had cried, "My God, my God, why hast thou forsaken me?"[19] were at the same time the hours of her fulfillment, and of the fulfillment of the words of the Lord concerning her in the vision to Joseph: "And she shall bring forth a son, and thou shalt call his name Jesus: for he shall save his people from their sins."[20]

This theme—that, in the words of one of the most profound of twentieth-century Roman Catholic theologians, Hans Urs von Balthasar, "She suffers along with her Son, and in her spirit, she experiences His death"[21]—was by no means restricted to art, poetry, and sacred song. Repeatedly during the Middle Ages, the Mater Dolorosa provided the content of Marian visions,[22] in various periods and in places as widely separated as Sweden and Spain. Thus in the first book of the *Revelations* of Saint Birgitta of Sweden, Jesus said to his mother: "You are like the precious gold that has been beaten on the iron anvil, for you have been tried with countless tribulations. Through my suffering, you have suffered more than anyone else."[23] Elsewhere Birgitta paraphrased the account of the crucifixion in the Gospels as Mary might have narrated it (in the antique language of a non-Latin manuscript of Birgitta's visions): "I, his moest sorowful moder . . . for sorrow y myght unneth stonde. And my sonne, seying me and his frendis weping without comffort from the jntret of his breat . . . weping and crying out unto the fader, he said: 'Fader and my Godde, why haest thou for-saken me?' as yf he had said: 'There is none that must haue mercy on me but thou fader.' . . . for he said it more mevid out of my compassion than his owne."[24] And at the other end of the north-south axis of Medieval Europe, Saint Teresa of Avila, whom Pope Paul VI in 1970 decorated with the title Doctor of the Church, described a vision in which "the Lord . . . laid Himself in my arms in the way depicted in the 'Fifth Anguish' of Our Lady. . . . 'Be not afraid of this,' He said to me, 'for the union of My Father with thy soul is incomparably greater than this.' " As the editor of Teresa notes, the "Fifth Anguish (more properly the Sixth) represents Mary with the dead body of her Son in Her arms."[25]

The author of the most influential theological treatise ever written about Christ as Mediator, *Why God Became Man*, Anselm of Canterbury at the end of the eleventh century, also wrote a treatise *On the Virginal Conception and on Original Sin*, as well as fervent prayers addressed to the Virgin as Mediatrix.[26] As Anselm himself pointed out, the two treatises were closely connected, because consideration of Christ the Mediator provoked the question of "how it was that God assumed a man from the sinful mass of the human race without sin," which was also a question about Mary.[27] In Christian iconography as well as in Christian literature, there was a new attention to the significance of Mary: a painting of Ildefonsus of Toledo in the seventh century, who had been celebrated for his devotion to her, constituted "one of the oldest expressions of the cult of the Virgin, which was then beginning to pervade Christian piety."[28] Mary was also seen as the woman who conquered worldly wisdom through the miracle of the virgin birth, as well as the one who conquered the false teachings of the heretics and resisted the incursions of the barbarians.

Her uniqueness was the subject of titles that were bestowed on her. As in the East so also in the West, poets and theologians vied with one another in elaborating distinctive appellations for the Virgin. For she was "the standard-bearer of piety,"[29] whose life of prayer the faithful imitated in their own. She was a model to them because she was "courageous in her resolution, temperate in her silence, prudent in her questioning and righteous in her confession."[30] As "the Queen of Angels, the ruling Lady of the world, and the Mother of him who purifies the world," she could acquire such titles as these: Mother of Truth; Mother and Daughter of Humility; Mother of Christians; Mother of Peace; My Most Merciful Lady. She was also called, in a term reminiscent of Augustine, the City of God. The paradox that a creature had become the mother of her Creator justified such names as "the fountain from which the living fountain flows, the origin of the beginning." Therefore she was "the woman who uniquely deserves to be venerated, the one to be admired more than all other women," in fact, "the radiant glory of the world, the purest maid of earth." Thus she excelled all others, "more beautiful than all of them, more lovable than all of them, supersplendid, supergracious, super-glorious." The glory of her name had filled the world.

Most of this could have been—and had been—said centuries earlier. What set the devotion and thought of this period apart from what preceded it was the growing emphasis on the office of Mary as Mediatrix. The title itself seems to have appeared first in Eastern theology, where she was addressed as "the Mediatrix of law and of grace." Whether from such Eastern sources or from Western reflection, the term came into Latin usage, apparently near the end of the eighth century. It was, however, in the eleventh and twelfth centuries that it achieved widespread acceptance. The title was a means of summarizing what had come to be seen as her twofold function: she was "the way by which the Savior came" to humanity in the incarnation and the redemption, and she was also the one "through whom we ascend to him who descended through her to us . . . , through [whom] we have access to the Son . . . , so that through [her] he who through [her] was given to us might take us up to himself." The term Mediatrix referred to both of these aspects of Mary's mediatorial position.

In the first instance, it was a way of speaking about her active role in the incarnation and the redemption. There seemed to be a direct and irrefutable inference from the universally accepted thesis that "it would have been impossible for the redemption of the human race to take place unless the Son of God had been born of a Virgin" to the corollary thesis that "it was likewise necessary that the Virgin, of whom the Logos was to be made flesh, should herself have been born." Thus she had become "the gate of Paradise, which restored God to the world and opened heaven to us." By her participation in redemption she had filled heaven with the saved and had emptied hell of those who would have been condemned except for her. Her assent to the word and will of God had made the incarnation and therefore the redemption possible. "O woman marvelously unique and uniquely marvelous," Anselm prayed, "through whom the elements are renewed, hell is redeemed, the demons are trampled under foot, humanity is saved, and angels are restored!" The reference to Mary's restoration of the angels was an allusion to the idea that the number of the elect would make up for the number of the angels who had fallen; Mary was seen as the one through whom "not only a life once lost is returned to humanity, but also the beatitude of angelic sublimity is increased," because through her participation in salvation the hosts of angels regained their full strength. In the same sense she wrought reparation for what Adam and Eve had done, and she brought life to all their posterity. Through her, then, the royal priesthood spoken of in the New Testament[31] had truly come into being in the Christian church. All of this made her "the minister and cooperator of this dispensation, who gave us the salvation of the world."

Mary's cooperation in the plan of salvation helped to explain the puzzling circumstance in the Gospel narratives, that after his resurrection Christ had not appeared first to his mother: "Why should he have appeared to her when she undoubtedly knew about the resurrection even before he suffered and rose?" She was the virginal human being of whom was born the divine human being who was to save the sinful human being. She was "the sanctuary of the universal propitiation, the cause of the general reconciliation, the vessel and the temple of the life and the salvation of all." Such praises as these by Anselm of the Virgin's place in the history of salvation, voiced in the setting of prayers, as so much of the language about her was, could only mean, in the words of Bernard of Clairvaux, that "she is our Mediatrix, she is the one through whom we have received thy mercy, O God, she is the one through whom we, too, have welcomed the Lord Jesus into our homes." Or, as Thomas Aquinas put it in the thirteenth century, "She was so full of grace that it overflows on to all mankind. It is indeed, a great thing that any one saint has so much grace that it conduces the salvation of many; but most wondrous is it to have so much as to suffice for the salvation of all mankind; and thus it is in Christ and in the Blessed Virgin. Thus in every danger thou canst find a refuge in this same glorious Virgin. . . . [Mary says] 'In me is all hope of life and of virtue.'"[32]

This title Mediatrix, however, applied not only to Mary's place in the history of salvation but also to her continuing position as intercessor between Christ and humanity, as the one whose "virginity we praise and whose humility we admire; but thy mercy tastes even sweeter, and it is thy mercy that we embrace even more fondly, think of even more often, and invoke even more frequently." The remembrance of Mary's "ancient mercies" aroused in a believer the hope and confidence to "return to thee [Mary], and through thee to God the Father and to thy only Son," so that it was possible to "demand salvation of thee [Mary]." The consummation of the believer's glory was the awareness that Mary stood as the Mediatrix between him and her Son; in fact, God had chosen her for the specific task of pleading the cause of humanity before her Son. And so she was "the Mother of the kingdom of heaven, Mary, the Mother of God, my only refuge in every need." Mary was addressed as the one who could bring cleansing and healing to the sinner and as the one who would give succor against the temptations of the devil; but she did this by mediating between Christ and humanity. "By thy pious prayer, make thy Son propitious to us," one could plead; or again: "Our Lady, Our Mediatrix, Our Advocate, reconcile us to thy Son, commend us to thy Son, represent us to thy Son. Do this, O Blessed One, through the grace that thou hast found [before God], through the prerogative that thou hast merited, through the mercy to which thou hast given birth."

"As we make a practice of rejoicing in the nativity of Christ," one preacher exhorted, "so we should rejoice no less at the nativity of the mother of Christ." For it was a basic rule that "whatever we set forth in praise of the Mother pertains to the Son, and on the other hand when we honor the Son we are not drawing back from our glory to the Mother." Christ was pleased when praise was offered to the Virgin Mary; conversely, an offense against either the Son or the Mother was an offense against the other as well. It was particularly the intercessory implication of the title Mediatrix that could be interpreted as taking something away from Christ, who was "the High Priest so that he might offer the vows of the people to God." The countervailing force against what the Protestant Reformation was to construe as Mariolatry and as a diminution of the glory of Christ, the sole Mediator,[33] was the recognition that she had been "exalted through thy omnipotent Son, for the sake of thy glorious Son, by thy blessed Son," as Anselm put it in one of his prayers. It was, moreover, a consensus that Mary had been saved by Christ, a consensus that had a decisive effect on the eventual formulation of the Western doctrine that by her immaculate conception she had been the great exception to the universality of original sin.[34] Extravagances of devotion and rhetoric were curbed by the principle that "the royal Virgin has no need of any false honor."

It was perceived as an appropriate honor and an authentic expression of her position in the divine order when Mary was acclaimed as second in dignity only to God himself, who had taken up habitation in her. The ground of this dignity was the part she had taken in the redemption, more important than that of any other ordinary human being. Through her Son she had been exalted "above all creatures" and was worthy of their veneration. This applied to all earthly creatures, but it included all other creatures as well, so that "there is nothing in heaven that is not subject to the Virgin through her Son." Echoing the language of the *Te Deum* about the praise of God, as other Marian hymns were to do later in the Middle Ages, a poem of Peter Damian proclaimed: "The blessed chorus of angels, the order of prophets and apostles affirm thee to be exalted over them and second only to the Deity." For none of them— "neither the chorus of the patriarchs for all their excellence, nor the company of the prophets for all their powers of foretelling the future, nor the senate of the apostles for all their judicial authority"—deserved to be compared with the Virgin. Because she was the one who held first place among the entire celestial host, whether human or angelic, she, next to God himself, should receive the praises of the whole world. There was, in short, "nothing equal to Mary and nothing but God greater than Mary." As the greatness of God could be defined in the famous formula of Anselm's ontological argument for the existence of God as "that than which nothing greater can be thought," so the purity of the Virgin could be defined, again by Anselm, as "that than which, under God, nothing greater can be thought." Among all that could be called holy, save God, Mary possessed a holiness that was unique.

Therefore it was also fitting that veneration and prayer should be addressed to her. Although there had long been such worship of the Virgin, as we have seen in previous chapters, various leaders of the church during these centuries systematically encouraged and nourished her cult. In a revealing autobiographical memoir, one Benedictine abbot, Guibert of Nogent, described how, when his mother was in great pain at his birth, "this vow was made . . . that if a male child should be born, he would be given over to the service of God and . . . offered to her who is

Queen of all next to God." Another Benedictine abbot, Bernard of Reichenau, made it a practice to refer to himself as "the slave of the Mother
of God." And yet another Benedictine abbot, Anselm, who went on to
become archbishop of Canterbury, commonly addressed prayers simultaneously to "my good Lord and my good Lady," saying to them: "I
appeal to you both, devoted Son and devoted Mother." What has been
called "the glowing reverence for Mary" in Bernard of Reichenau was
characteristic of the age. Prayers to Mary were cited as support for admo-
nitions and arguments on behalf of her cult, and it was urged that such
prayers would gain the succor of "the Mother of the Judge in the day of
need." The very day of the Sabbath was said to have been dedicated to
Mary, and those who appealed to her as "the Gate of Heaven, the Window
of Paradise" when they were plagued by the guilt of their sins received
full absolution.

It was no exaggeration of the importance of Mary in the devotion and
worship of the church when the festival of her nativity, said to have been
announced to her mother by an angel just as the nativity of Christ from
her was to be announced to her (although the New Testament was silent
about the first of these annunciations), was celebrated and asserted to be
"the beginning of all the festivals of the New Testament . . . , the origin of
all the other festivals." As was inevitable with any saint, and a fortiori
with her, it became a standard expression of piety to attribute to Mary the
performance of various miracles. A few of these may have taken place
during her earthly life, but others were continuing to take place long
afterward, up to the very present; moreover, the number of such miracles
ascribed to Mary would increase after the Middle Ages, reaching something of an apex in the nineteenth and twentieth centuries.[35] A special
form of the devotion to her miracles was the cultivation of her relics. In
her case this was made much more complicated than in that of any other
saint by the widely held belief that no parts of her body had remained on
earth, because at her death she had been assumed bodily into heaven, a
belief that was finally promulgated as a dogma by Pope Pius XII in
1950.[36] At Chartres, for example, according to one writer, "the name
and the relics of the Mother of God are venerated through almost all the

Latin world"; he was referring above all to her "sacred tunic." Yet when a particular church claimed to possess such relics, the same writer responded that if "she, through the same Spirit by whom she conceived, knew that he to whom she gave birth by faith was to fill the entire world," she would not have kept such mementos of his childhood as his baby teeth or her own mother's milk. A more appropriate way of celebrating her memory was the commemoration of her nativity or the recitation of the *Ave Maria*, whose cultic repetition became characteristic of piety during this period and whose exposition eventually provided a basis for the articulation of her special place in the history of salvation. Clearly there was a close correlation between the subjectivity of the devotion to Mary as the Mater Dolorosa and the objectivity of the doctrine of Mary as the Mediatrix. It was not the correlation of paradox, as was the celebration of her under the rubrics of the Paragon of Chastity and the Blessed Mother,[37] but the correlation of complementarity, at least until, in the modern era, the denial of her objective transcendence by many would deprive her of the title of Mediatrix even though the simultaneous rise of subjectivism would continue to find symbolic, if sometimes sentimental, expression in the Mater Dolorosa.

Quinten Massys, *The Virgin and Child Enthroned, with Four Angels*, c. 1490–95. National Gallery, London.

10 The Face That Most Resembles Christ's

Behold thy mother!
—John 19:27

One of the most sublime moments in the history of devotion to Mary came in the closing cantos of Dante's *Divine Comedy*, in which Bernard of Clairvaux gives praise to the Blessed Virgin Mary.[1] These praises were in great measure derived from Bernard's many writings about Mary.[2] For, as Steven Botterill has said, Bernard was "helped by the fact that his thinking is not on the cutting edge of academic theology: his writings about Mary are filled with an intense and intensely personal devotion to the Virgin, and aim as much to stir his audience's hearts as to provoke activity in their minds."[3] As Bernard instructed Dante, pointing to a family resemblance that has been caught, for example, by the Antwerp painter Massys (d. 1530):

> Look now upon the face that is most like
> the face of Christ, for only through its brightness
> can you prepare your vision to see Him.[4]

The privilege of beholding Mary, which had been granted in special measure to Bernard and which then Dante proceeded to share with

Bernard, was a transforming vision and quite literally an indescribable one. Yet this vision prepared for an infinitely grander one and pointed beyond itself to the vision of Christ as "the exalted Son of God and of Mary,"[5] and to the beatific vision of God. This "canto of apotheosis,"[6] beginning with the paradox, "Virgin mother, daughter of your Son,/more humble and sublime than any creature,"[7] stood as a summation and as a goal of the entire Divine Comedy—and of the entire history described in the preceding chapters of this book—as well as an anticipation of much of the history that was to follow. For it was Mary, as the "Gentle Lady" in heaven, by whose intercession the "stern judgment up above is shattered," who, near the beginning of the poem, commanded Beatrice to go to the assistance of the poet, "who loves you so/that—for your sake—he's left the vulgar crowd," thus setting the whole itinerary of Dante the pilgrim in motion.[8] And at the conclusion of the poem, Mary was to Dante not only "Our Lady [nostra donna]"[9] but "Our Queen [nostra regina],"[10] "the Queen of Heaven,"[11] and "the Empress [Agusta],"[12] the fulfillment of the promise of Paradise and the archetype of all who were saved. For "by virtue of being closer to the human plane, she is more approachable by those who have reason to fear, or who cannot comprehend, the ineffable mystery of God or the stern authority of Christ."[13]

It would be easy for the reader to be caught up by the rhapsodic, almost dithyrambic ecstasy of Bernard's poem and by the vision of a transcendent Virgin Mary that it celebrated, and in the process to forget that for Dante and for Bernard of Clairvaux, as for the entire Medieval tradition, Mary stood in continuity with the human race, the same human race to which the poet and his readers belonged. Therefore the glory with which she was crowned was a special form—different in degree, but finally not different in kind—of the glory in which all the saved participated, a glory that was communicated to her, as to them, by the grace and merit of Christ. She was, in the paradox of the incarnation, the Daughter of her Son, who had redeemed her, an emphasis that was, already among the Franciscans of Dante's time, an important component of the developing doctrine of the immaculate conception.[14] Early in the

Paradiso, in response to Dante's unspoken question about the relative degrees of merit and hence of salvation, Beatrice had to explain:

> Neither the Seraph closest unto God,
> nor Moses, Samuel, nor either John—
> whichever one you will—not *Mary* has,
> I say, their place in any other heaven
> than that which houses those souls you just saw,
> nor will their blessedness last any longer.[15]

Degrees of salvation there were, and therefore circles of Paradise, "in ways diverse" and "from stage to stage," as Beatrice had explained even earlier;[16] and Mary occupied the highest of these. Without such degrees of salvation there would not be perfect justice on the basis of merit, which varied from one to another and which therefore had to be rewarded by differing degrees of glory; and, for that matter, without these degrees of salvation and of damnation there would have been no *Divine Comedy*. The justice of God was a mystery that remained "past understanding,"[17] also when it brought about the damnation of pagans who had never had the opportunity to hear the gospel. Nevertheless, those who were destined to dwell eternally in the lower degrees of Paradise affirmed that "in His will is our peace"; for "every place/in heaven is in Paradise, though grace/does not rain equally from the High Good,"[18] because these were all degrees of the same heaven and of the one Paradise, as Mary was the culminating point of the one humanity, still in the one heaven.

As the culminating point, Mary was the new "Mother of all living," as Eve had been, according to the Bible, "mother of all living."[19] Mary therefore stood in a typological relation to Eve.[20] This relation of Eve and Mary, which I described in chapter 3 on the basis of Irenaeus of Lyons, was, significantly, the theme with which Bernard began his discourse about the Virgin Mary in the canto preceding his apostrophe to her:

> The wound that Mary closed and then
> anointed was the wound that Eve—so lovely
> at Mary's feet—had opened and had pierced.[21]

And now, in Bernard's explanation and Dante's vision, Mother Eve was seated at the feet of Mother Mary—and in a higher place than Rachel or even Beatrice.[22] None of this would have comported with the scheme of salvation as Dante was expounding it unless Mary as the Second Eve had been genuinely and completely a member of the human race. When Cacciaguida in Paradise spoke of how his mother invoked Mary "in pains of birth";[23] or when Buoconte still in Purgatory described having lapsed into a coma after being wounded in battle, just as he "had finished uttering the name of Mary [nel nome di Maria fini]";[24] or when Piccarda Donati, after recounting her quite remarkable life story,

> began to sing "Ave
> Maria" and, while singing, vanished as
> a weighty thing will vanish in deep water—[25]

the one whom all three were invoking in extremis was one who, though their Mediatrix, was also their fellow human being, who in fact could not have been truly their Mediatrix unless she had been their fellow human being.

She was at the same time the personal embodiment of the supreme virtues of which humanity was made capable through the gift of grace: in her, as Bernard said, "is every goodness found in any creature."[26] Yet in this connection there was a curious circumstance in the Divine Comedy, and one whose explanation is by no means obvious: much of the most explicit consideration of the specific virtues of Mary appeared in the Purgatorio rather than in the Paradiso. The hymn of Bernard in the Paradiso did laud her as "the noonday torch of charity" for those already in heaven and as "a living spring of hope" for those still on earth.[27] Therefore she not only manifested great faith, which was implicit throughout,[28] but she was likewise the exemplar of both hope and charity. In short, she embodied all three virtues celebrated in 1 Corinthians 13: "faith, hope, charity, these three."[29] It was on these three virtues that, in Cantos XXIV–XXVI, Dante was examined by the three apostles, or "doves,"[30] Peter, James, and John, a trio who had already been anticipated in the closing cantos of the Purgatorio[31] and who formed the inner circle of the twelve apostles.[32] Yet the virtues that stood out were the ones for which Mary was being singled out in the *Purgatorio*, rather than those that were identified with her in the *Paradiso*. Perhaps part of the reason was that the souls in Paradise were already enjoying the fruits of virtue, which they shared (though in lesser measure) with Mary, whereas those in Purgatory, who still had to attain to Paradise, stood in need of the grace that was merited and communicated through the virtues of Mary, which therefore needed a more complete description.

The attack on "arrogant Christians" in Canto X of the *Purgatorio* thus had as its foil the humility of the Virgin Mary, who at the annunciation had called herself "the handmaid of God."[33] Similarly, when the pilgrim came to the place where "the sin of envy / is scourged within this circle," what he heard arising from those who were being cleansed of such envy was "the cry of, 'Mary pray for us.'"[34] Further on, as he saw "people whom the fire of wrath / had kindled," they were contrasted with "the gentle manner" of the Virgin's reproof to her twelve-year-old son when she found him in the temple at Jerusalem: "Son, why hast thou thus dealt with us? behold, thy father and I have sought thee sorrowing."[35] The terrace of those who had been guilty of "sloth and negligence" was one where it was no longer Mary's "gentle manner" but her "haste" and her zeal that were being celebrated.[36] The sin of avarice, whose "hungering is deep and never-ending," caused its victims here in Purgatory to lament "Sweet Mary [*Dolce Maria*]!"[37] Those "whose appetite was gluttonous" stood in the sharpest possible contrast with Mary, who while on earth had not concerned herself with satisfying her own hunger.[38] And those who were in Purgatory to burn away the fires of lust had to cry aloud the words of the Virgin Mary in her chastity.[39] The tour through Purgatory thereby became at the same time a catalog of the virtues of the Blessed Virgin.

For Dante's view of the empirical church and its need for reform, the debates of the thirteenth and fourteenth centuries over poverty and property carried great importance. The discourse of Thomas Aquinas about Francis of Assisi in Canto XI of the *Paradiso* described the spiritual marriage between Francis and Lady Poverty, who had been "deprived of her first husband," Christ, and who had thereafter remained without a suitor for "eleven hundred years and more," until the coming of Francis.[40] But one of the questions being debated in the Franciscan controversies over poverty during Dante's time was whether, like Christ, Mary, too, had taken a vow of absolute poverty and, if she had, what she had done, for example, with all that gold, frankincense, and myrrh that the Wise Men from the East had brought to her and to her Child.[41] Dante's answer to the question of the poverty of Mary seemed unequivocal: "Sweet Mary!" Dante heard a voice say in Purgatory,

> In that hostel where
> you had set down your holy burden, there
> one can discover just how poor you were.[42]

The chastity of the Virgin Mary, who was, as Bernard said in the two opening words of his song, unique among women in being simultaneously Virgin and Mother,[43] was contrasted in the *Purgatorio* not only with "the force of Venus' poison," the extramarital unchastity of others, but even with the marital chastity of virtuous wedlock: "Virum non cognosco, I know not a man," as Mary had said, in Latin, to the angel of the annunciation.[44] And when Dante confronted in Purgatory those souls who had been guilty of the sins of gluttony and drunkenness in this life, he was reminded once more of the contrast with the virtue of Mary, manifested at the wedding feast in Cana of Galilee, and of her role as Mediatrix both at Cana and now in Purgatory. As a voice explained,

> Mary's care was for the marriage-
> feast's being seemly and complete, not for
> her mouth (which now would intercede for you),[45]

continuing in heaven the intercession that she had articulated while on earth.

It was likewise in the *Purgatorio* that Dante the poet first described the relation Mary bore to the angels. The two guardian angels dressed in green whom Dante the pilgrim saw, with their flaming swords shortened but their faces blinding for sheer brilliance, "both come from Mary's bosom," Sordello told him, "to serve as the custodians of the valley / against the serpent that will soon appear."[46] The other reference in the *Purgatorio* to Mary's relation with the angels appeared two cantos later. The pilgrim was contemplating an amazingly beautiful wall of white marble, adorned with carvings that put to shame not only the greatest of human sculptors but nature itself.[47] Carved on the marble wall was the figure of the angel Gabriel:

> The angel who reached earth with the decree
> of that peace which, for many years, had been
> invoked with tears, the peace that opened heaven
> after long interdict, appeared before us,
> his gracious action carved with such precision—
> he did not seem to be a silent image.
> One would have sworn that he was saying, "Ave";
> for in that scene there was the effigy
> of one who turned the key that had unlocked
> the highest love; and in her stance there were
> impressed these words, "*Ecce ancilla Dei*,"
> precisely like a figure stamped in wax.[48]

Already in Purgatory, therefore, the divinely decreed mission of the Virgin Mary to "turn the key" and become the human means for the incarnation and thereby for salvation was being announced to the souls that awaited release into Paradise; and already in Purgatory the angels were making it evident that they stood ready to serve her, and through her both her divine Son and the humanity he came to save.

Yet it was in Paradise that the special relation between Mary and the angels was disclosed in all its glory. Once again, the angel Gabriel,

> the angelic love who had descended
> earlier, now spread his wings before her,
> singing "*Ave Maria, gratia plena*."[49]

But this time it was not, as it had been in Purgatory, in a mere physical representation on cold marble, which was beautiful but was not living, but in the spiritual reality of heaven itself that Gabriel continued forever the salutation with which the history of salvation had begun[50]—not any longer in the "modest voice" of his original greeting but in full-throated praise.[51] It was from this event of the annunciation, rather than from the nativity of Christ itself, that Dante, who followed the Florentine custom, dated the beginning of the new era through the incarnation, so that the new year began on 25 March.[52] Gabriel was joined in his salutation and praise by all the angelic hosts of heaven. Dante the pilgrim saw and heard the heavenly "brightnesses" as they expressed "the deep affection each possessed for Mary" and as they sang the *Regina Coeli* so sweetly, Dante the poet added, "that my delight in that has never left me" even now as he wrote.[53] It was a song in praise of Mary in which the angels were joined by the church triumphant of the saved who had already come to Paradise.[54] As "the greatest flame,"[55] Mary, Lady of Heaven, was the object of this angelic paean:

> I am angelic love who wheel around
> that high gladness inspired by the womb
> that was the dwelling place of our Desire;
> so shall I circle, Lady of Heaven, until
> you, following your Son, have made that sphere
> supreme, still more divine by entering it.[56]

This "ineffable vision,"[57] which attributed to Mary the ability to make the glories of the supreme sphere of heaven "still more divine" through her presence, prepared Dante for the sublimely ineffable vision of Mary and the angels that wold come to him as the occasion for Bernard's discourse about the Blessed Virgin.

It was that vision that was described in the concluding tercets of Canto XXXI of the *Paradiso*. As his awe had deepened, the pilgrim had been reluctant to contemplate the full power and glory before him. Therefore, "son of grace" that he was, he had nevertheless to be admonished:

> You will not come to know this joyous state
> if your eyes only look down at the base;
> but look upon the circles, look at those
> that sit in a position more remote,

until you see upon her seat the Queen
to whom this realm is subject and devoted.[58]

The souls of the saints who had already come to heaven, including in particular "the Hebrew women,"[59] were part of the celestial realm, and Mary was their archetype. But the angels, those dread and powerful spirits who did God's bidding day and night, had been its citizens all along, and there they had remained even after their rebellious fellow angels had been cast into the Inferno, where, as the pilgrim learned, the demons had now become as foul as they once had been fair.[60] And since Mary was indeed the Queen of Heaven, she was Queen of Angels, too.

Lifting his eyes in response to the admonition, the "son of grace," in language reminiscent of the apocalyptic visions of Ezekiel, Daniel, and Saint John the Divine,

. . . as, at morning,
the eastern side of the horizon shows
more splendor than the side where the sun sets,
so, as if climbing with my eyes from valley
to summit, I saw one part of the farthest
rank of the Rose more bright than all the rest.[61]

Before the transcendent light of the glorified Queen of Heaven, the angels gathered—not an indiscriminate mob, but as distinct individuals, since, as Thomas Aquinas taught, "it is impossible for two angels to be of one species," but each had to be a species unto itself.[62] The poet described what he saw:

I saw, around that midpoint, festive angels—
more than a thousand—with their wings outspread;
each was distinct in splendor and in skill.[63]

The "midpoint" and the object of their sportive celebration was the ineffable beauty of Mary, who ruled over a realm in which both saints and angels had their place. That special place of Mary among the saints in heaven became the theme for the altarpiece that Giovanni Bellini was to create for the church of San Giobbe in Venice, *Madonna Enthroned with the Saints*, sometime in the 1480s.[64] Bellini, like Dante, was a devotee of Francis of Assisi, who was represented on the altarpiece.[65] In his portrayal of the Virgin, Bellini put into living color the very qualities of Mary that Dante described:

> And there I saw a loveliness that when
> it smiled at the angelic songs and games
> made glad the eyes of all the other saints.

Here it became the task of poetic language about transcendent reality not to describe the object but to describe its own incapacity to describe the object:

> And even if my speech were rich as my
> imagination is, I should not try
> to tell the very least of her delights.[66]

That sentence needs to be parsed with some care. As his treatises on literature and language attested, Dante was honest enough to know that he had a skill with words, and it would have been the most hypocritical kind of false modesty for him to pretend otherwise. Moreover, here he recognized in himself a "wealth of imaginative power," and he found that it in turn far exceeded all of this verbal power. Yet even if it had not, he was saying, if word could truly have been matched to imagination in some simple one-to-one correlation, that would have been inadequate for describing Mary—indeed, inadequate for describing not her regal and transcendent position in the cosmos but "the very least of her delights."

It would be easy to read all of this extravagant language about the Virgin Mary as what Protestant polemics against Medieval Catholicism came to call "Mariolatry."[67] It would be easy, but it would be superficial and mistaken. For, as Henry Osborn Taylor put it, "One may say that the *Commedia* begins and ends with the Virgin. It was she who sent Beatrice into the gates of Hell to move Virgil—meaning human reason—to go to Dante's aid. The prayer which obtains her benediction, and the vision following, close the *Paradiso*." But, he warned, "no more with Dante than with other mediaeval men is she the end of worship and devotion. Her eyes are turned to God. So are those of Beatrice, of Rachel, and of all the saints in Paradise."[68] Mary could not have been the archetype of the saved unless she herself had been saved. She had been saved in a special manner, as by now almost all the theologians of the church affirmed, although it did not become official and binding until 1854—that is, by being preserved from original sin rather than, as everyone else was, rescued from it—but saved by the same divine grace and through the same divine Redeemer as the rest of humanity.[69] Dante's attitude toward this explanation of Mary's holiness was not altogether clear, but in Canto XIII he had Thomas Aquinas declare,

> I do approve of the opinion
> you hold, that human nature never was
> nor shall be what it was in those two persons,

namely, in Adam and in Christ.[70] This does seem to justify the conclusion drawn by Alexandre Masseron: "Dante affirms that Christ and Adam are the only ones who were created perfect," the explicit position of Bernard of Clairvaux, who rejected the doctrine of the immaculate conception.[71] Such was as well the teaching of Saint Thomas Aquinas.[72] That in turn makes it necessary to consider the question of the relation of Mary to Christ in Dante's theology.[73]

Whatever may have been Dante's doctrine about the special privilege of the immaculate conception at the beginning of the life of the Blessed Virgin, he clearly did teach, as did Bernard, that at the end of her life Mary was granted the privilege of the assumption, through the grace of Christ.[74] Therefore Saint John explained very carefully concerning himself that (*pace* some legends about him) he had not received this privilege of being assumed into heaven:

> On earth my body now is earth and shall
> be there together with the rest until
> our number equals the eternal purpose.

But then John added the significant stipulation, speaking of Mary and of Christ: "Only those two lights that ascended wear / their double garment in this blessed cloister,"[75] the "double garment" being the body and the soul, not only the soul. The two were Christ, through the ascension narrated in the New Testament and confessed in the creed, and then Mary through the assumption celebrated throughout the liturgy of the Medieval church but not officially promulgated as a dogma of the church until 1950. When Dante, bidden by Beatrice, lifted his eyes to behold Mary in heaven as "the Rose in which the Word of God became / flesh,"[76] he celebrated the ascension of Christ as an event intended "to grant scope to the eyes there that had not strength for Thee," and immediately went on to recognize that through her bodily assumption into heaven Mary shared in that exaltation, becoming not only "the fair flower which I always invoke morning and evening" on earth but "the greatest of the fires" in the Empyrean.[77] Therefore it was to Mary assumed into heaven that Bernard addressed his petition on Dante's behalf, to "curb his mortal passions" and to "disperse all the clouds of his mortality," so that Dante might receive the vision of the "Eternal Light" and so "that the Highest Joy might be his to see."[78]

Seeing that "Eternal Light" was the content of the vision of God. And in the final hundred lines of the final canto of the *Paradiso*, Dante celebrated the vision of the Trinity of three divine Persons in one divine Substance:

> In the deep and bright
> essence of that exalted Light, three circles
> appeared to me; they had three different colors,
> but all of them were of the same dimension;
> one circle seemed reflected by the second,
> as rainbow is by rainbow, and the third
> seemed fire breathed equally by those two circles.[79]

Therefore it must not be forgotten that a canto opening with the celebration of the Virgin Mary by Bernard of Clairvaux went on—through her and not around her, but nevertheless beyond her—to the celebration of the Eternal Light and Eternal "Love that moves the sun and the other stars,"[80] including Mary as the sun from which "the morning star draws beauty"[81] and Mary as *Stella Maris*, the Star of the Sea and the Queen of Heaven.[82] Hence there was not, in those final hundred lines, a single explicit reference to her; or perhaps it was all a reference to her, as the fellow creature (as Bernard explicitly described her)[83] who had pioneered in this vision. And that would have been in keeping with her role throughout the poem, as the heavenly Muse whose intervention, as it had been described by Beatrice already in Canto II of the *Inferno*,[84] had made it all possible. Thus "Maria" was for Dante "the name of that fair flower which I always/invoke, at morning and at evening";[85] singing the *Salve Regina* to her already while traveling through Purgatory,[86] but becoming her most eloquent troubadour in the *Paradiso* and above all in its final cantos.

Lucas van Leyden, *The Virgin with Two Angels*, 1523. Yale University Art Gallery, Stephan Carlton Clark, B.A. 1903, Fund.

11 The Model of Faith
in the Word of God

And Mary said,
Be it unto me according to thy word.
—Luke 1:38

When a great faith disappears, Gilbert Chesterton once observed, its sublime aspects go first: the Puritans rejected the worship of the Virgin Mary but went on burning witches.[1] Like so many of Chesterton's aphorisms, this one managed to be both true and false, as a closer examination of the attitude (or, rather, the several attitudes) of the sixteenth-century Reformation toward Mary would reveal. For the Protestant Reformers contended that just as their critique of what they regarded as Medieval sacramental magic had raised and restored the Lord's Supper to its divinely instituted place, so taking from Mary the false honors with which she had been burdened in the Middle Ages was in fact a liberation of her to be a supreme model of faith in the word of God.[2] And Mary as model of faith has also been an integral element of the Mariology of Western Catholicism; for "faith as lived by Mary is total, trusting self-surrender of mind and body to God."[3] The most obvious characteristic of the picture of Mary in the Protestant Reformation was its critique and rejection of what it took to be the excesses of Medieval devotion and teaching. Taking up the familiar Latin translation of Genesis 3:15, "She

[*Ipsa*] will crush his head,"[4] in his *Lectures on Genesis,* which occupied him during the final ten years of his life, Luther found it "amazing" and "damnable" that "Satan has managed to apply this passage, which in fullest measure abounds in the comfort of the Son of God, to the Virgin Mary. For in all the Latin Bibles the pronoun appears in the feminine gender: 'And *she* will crush.' "[5] At its most radical, particularly in Switzerland, this rejection of Medieval Mariology took the form of a new iconoclasm, what Lee Palmer Wandel has called "a conception of the 'Reformed' Church in which there were no images."[6] In Charles Garside's chilling description of "the war against the idols,"

> The committee as a body went into every church in Zurich.
> Once inside, they locked the doors behind them, and then,
> free from all disturbance from the curious crowds without,
> began to dismantle the church. . . . Every standing statue was
> removed from its niche or its base and, together with the
> base, taken out of the church. It was then either broken up by
> the masons, if made of stone or plaster, or burned, if made of
> wood. Every painting was taken down from the altars and
> burned outside. All murals were chipped away or scraped off
> the walls. The altars were stripped of all images and vessels, all
> votive lamps were let down and melted outside, and all cruci-
> fixes were removed.[7]

And many of the most prominent victims of this zeal were representations of the Virgin. But even such Reformers as Martin Luther, who in 1525 protested vigorously against this iconoclasm,[8] protested no less vigorously against what Luther called the "abominable idolatry [*grewliche Abgötterey*]" of Medieval Mariology, an idolatry that was, he said, "not praising Mary, but slandering her in the extreme and making an idol of her."[9]

The context of that Reformation critique was a fundamental reconsideration of the practice of invoking the saints. Articles XIX and XX of Ulrich Zwingli's *Sixty-Seven Articles* of 1523 declared that because "Christ is the only Mediator between God and us," it followed "that we do not need any mediator beyond this life but him."[10] For, in the words of the *Heidelberg Catechism*, "He is our Mediator."[11] Also quoting the words of the New Testament, "There is one mediator between God and men, the man Christ Jesus,"[12] Article XXI of the *Augsburg Confession* of 1530, written by Luther's colleague Philip Melanchthon, entitled "The Cult of the Saints," reinforced this polemic by defining Christ as "the only highpriest, advocate, and intercessor before God. He alone has promised to hear our prayers."[13] Although Melanchthon's *Apology of the Augsburg Confession* did "grant that the saints in heaven pray for the church in general, as they prayed for the church universal while they were on earth,"[14] that did not justify the practice of invoking them for particular needs. Not even the highest of the saints, the Virgin Mary, therefore, could infringe on the sole mediatorship of Christ. For with varying degrees of severity, the Protestant Reformers were using their slogan of *solus Christus* to attack what John Henry Newman was to call the system of "created mediation,"[15] the principle that, under the sovereignty of the unique uncreated mediation of Christ, there was an entire chain of mediating powers—the sacraments, the church, the saints, and Mary—which, though created, conveyed the power of the uncreated mediation of Christ to believers.

In part this critique of the Medieval cult of Mary was the application to her cult of the far-reaching Reformation insistence on their slogan of *sola Scriptura*, the sole authority of Scripture over tradition—not simply the *supreme* authority, which almost everyone would accept, but the *sole* authority of the Bible. Thus the *Thirty-Nine Articles* of the Church of England of 1571 listed the "inuocation of Saintes" as the last in a list of "Romishe Doctrines" that were "a fonde [foolish] thing, vainly inuented, and grounded vpon no warrantie of Scripture, but rather repugnant to the worde of God."[16] Or, at greater length, Calvin in his dissertation on the idea asked: "Then who, whether angel or demon, ever revealed to any man even a syllable of the kind of saints' intervention they invent? For there is nothing about it in Scripture. What reason, then, did they have to invent it? Surely, when human wit is always seeking after assistance for which we have no support in God's Word, it clearly reveals its own faithlessness."[17] The application of the exclusionary principle of *sola*

Scriptura was directed not only against the doctrine of the intercession of
Mary and the saints but against the Medieval proliferation of stories about
Mary and the saints for which there was no biblical basis. Contrasting the
stark simplicity and credibility of the biblical account of Sarah with such
stories, Luther asserted, "The legends or accounts of the saints which we
had under the papacy were not written according to the pattern of Holy
Scripture."[18] And elsewhere he expressed the wish: "Would to God that I
had the time to cleanse the legends and examples, or that somebody else
with a higher spirit would venture to do it; they are full, full of lies and
deception."[19] Particularly deceptive, of course, were legends about biblical saints, and above all about Mary, for they crowded out the testimony
of Scripture about the very qualities that had made them saints in the first
place.

At the same time, the doctrine of Mary during the Reformation
underwent a revival of various early theologies that had been denounced
as heresy, including some of the heretical theories about Mary examined
in earlier chapters of this book. As the leading historian of the Radical
Reformation, George Huntston Williams, has pointed out, the Mariology
of Caspar Schwenckfeld issued in

> the glorification of the human nature of Christ and his scrip-
> tural discernment of Mary as indeed unique among women in
> the very words of Elizabeth after she was filled with the Holy
> Spirit: "Blessed art thou, Mary, among women and blessed is
> the fruit of thy womb," for she in Schwenckfeld's own words
> "received from the Holy Spirit natural flesh," whereby she,
> unique among women[,] fulfilled the prophecy of Jer. 3:22:
> "a new thing, a woman will encompass a man," that is, says
> Schwenckfeld, it was foreseen that Mary, "impregnated
> through the Holy Spirit, would carry and give birth to God's
> and her son, a son of such glory that his flesh could see no
> decomposition."[20]

But some Radical Reformers went even further, as when Orbe Philips,
rejecting the idea that "the body of Christ had been made by Mary (as the

world thinks and says with such want of understanding regarding it),"
asserted instead that "God, the Heavenly Father, prepared for Jesus Christ,
his only begotten Son, a body [Heb. 10:5], but not of corrupt human
seed [Luke 1:35], rather of his incorruptible seed." For, he continued, "it
is impossible for the flesh of Christ to be formed of the seed of Mary; for
neither the seed of Mary, nor that of any earthly creature can by any
means be the true living bread that came down from heaven [John 6:31–
35], or be so called."[21]

In response to such speculations among the Radical Reformers, the
Anglican, Lutheran, and Reformed confessions of faith reaffirmed the
traditional doctrine of Eastern and Western orthodoxy, which had originally been formulated in opposition to Gnosticism, that the entire human
nature of Christ, body and soul, was a creature, was derived from the
created and human body of the Virgin Mary, and was not in any sense
pre-existent. Therefore the Lutheran *Formula of Concord* of 1577, which
devoted a major part of its discussion to differentiating the Lutheran
Reformation from the Calvinist Reformation on such issues of doctrine as
the relation of the two natures in the person of Christ, the real presence in
the Eucharist, and double predestination, was in this case speaking also
for its Calvinist adversaries when it rejected the teaching "that Christ did
not assume his flesh and blood from the Virgin Mary but brought it along
from heaven."[22] In this way Mary once more became, also for the mainline Reformers, what she had always been: guarantee of the reality of the
incarnation and of the human nature of Christ.[23]

But it would be a mistake, and one into which many interpretations
of the Reformation both friendly and hostile have all too easily fallen, to
emphasize these negative and polemical aspects of its Mariology at the
expense of the positive place the Protestant Reformers assigned to her in
their theology.[24] They repeated—and in many cases used their superior
grasp of the original languages of the Bible to reinforce—the central
content of the orthodox confession of the first five centuries of Christian
history.[25] For despite the constantly repeated accusations that the doctrinal principles of the Reformation, consistently carried out, would and
did lead to a repudiation of historic Christian and Catholic orthodoxy,

especially of the dogmas of the Trinity as confessed by the Council of Nicaea in 325 and the person of Christ as confessed by the Council of Chalcedon in 451, Luther and Calvin and their colleagues indignantly insisted that, in the opening words of the *Augsburg Confession,* "we unanimously hold and teach, in accordance with the decree of the Council of Nicaea."[26] The same words could have been applied to the decree of the Council of Chalcedon, and to Reformed, Calvinist teaching, as Thomas F. Torrance has argued in pointing out that "care was taken to repudiate and avoid all the classical errors in Christology on both sides of the Chalcedonian fence."[27] The texts on which Torrance was commenting with that observation, namely, the authorized catechisms of the Reformed church in Scotland, were evidence, moreover, that this adherence to the orthodox teaching of the church was not a mere formality or political ploy by the Reformers but what was being believed, taught, and confessed in the concrete life of the churches. Thus the *Larger Catechism* of 1648 taught: "Christ the Son of God became man, by taking to Himself a true body, and a reasonable soul, being conceived by the power of the Holy Spirit in the womb of the Virgin Mary, of her substance, and born of her, yet without sin."[28]

It was thus possible for Walter Tappolet in 1962 to compile a remarkable collection of texts from Luther, Calvin, Zwingli, and Bullinger under the title "The Reformers in Praise of Mary."[29] Drawing on sermons and devotional material as well as on theological treatises, he documented, first of all, this continuing orthodoxy of the Mariology of the Reformers. Zwingli, for example, called Mary "the highest of creatures next to her Son" and "Mother of God," and Balthasar Hubmaier asserted her perpetual virginity.[30] Luther did the same—and not only in his private writings and sermons, as when he described Mary as "in childbirth and after childbirth, as she was a Virgin before childbirth, so she remained."[31] Even in the only confessional statement of faith by him that was officially adopted by the Lutheran church and incorporated into the official collection of the *Book of Concord* of 1580—as distinct from his *Small Catechism* and *Large Catechism,* which were also included but were not, strictly speaking, confessions—the *Smalcald Articles* of 1537, the Latin text contained the words (which did not, however, appear in the German version): "from Mary, pure, holy, and Ever-Virgin [ex Maria pura, sancta, Semper Virgine]."[32] But beyond the orthodoxy of their language and teaching about Mary, the Protestant Reformers one after another spoke of her with warmth and dedication, as when Luther in 1521, the year of his excommunication by Pope Leo X, could close his Commentary on the Magnificat with the words: "May Christ grant us this through the intercession and for the sake of His dear Mother Mary! Amen."[33] Such sentiments, which could easily be duplicated, belied the impression, which the Protestant Reformers themselves sometimes gave and which their opponents often magnified, that they were sweeping aside the entire accumulation of Christian devotion to Mary in the name of restoring the primitive Christianity of the apostolic church.

More than either of these principles, sola gratia, "by grace alone," or sola Scriptura, "by Scripture alone," however, the Reformation slogan that epitomized Mary's positive position in the Reformation was sola fide, "by faith alone." For in the theology of the Reformers she was the model of faith, as the Reformation redefined it.

A favorite passage of the Reformers was Paul's statement, "Faith cometh by hearing, and hearing by the word of God,"[34] which provided the title for an important twentieth-century study of Reformation theology by Ernst Bizer.[35] That connection between faith and the hearing of the word of God had, of course, been a component of the definition of faith all along. As one of the triad of faith, hope, and love set forth by the apostle Paul,[36] faith, and consequently the function of the word of God as the means by which faith was aroused and sustained, had always received its share of attention: "Since, therefore, faith comes by hearing, and hearing by the word of God [Cum ergo fides sit ex auditu, auditus autem per verbum Christi]," Thomas Aquinas could argue in his Commentary on the Sentences.[37] But the Reformers, beginning with Luther, taught that authentic Christian love was dependent on faith and therefore, despite the identification of love as "the greatest of these,"[38] assigned to faith the central position in that triad and therefore assigned to the word of God what must be called a sacramental function: as the sacraments were, in a formula that the Reformation took over from Augustine, a "visible word,"[39] so the preaching and teaching of the word of God could have been called an audible sacrament. Thus Calvin, in a carefully crafted discussion, defined "faith to be a knowledge of God's will toward us, perceived from his Word."[40]

Mary became the obvious case study of this for Luther, as the opening words of Mary's Magnificat showed him that "holiness of spirit . . . consists in nothing else than in faith pure and simple." In a characteristic summary of the Reformation doctrine of justification by faith and not by works, he insisted on the basis of Mary's faith "that works breed nothing but discrimination, sin, and discord, while faith alone makes men pious, united, and peaceable." Therefore "faith and the Gospel . . . are the highest goods . . . which no one should let go."[41] For when Mary said to the angel Gabriel (in Luther's German), "Let it happen to me as you have said [Mir geschehe, wie du gesagt hast],"[42] this was above all an expression of her faith. And "through such faith alone she was saved and freed from sin."[43]

In a bold definition of faith—which was in some ways an anticipation of Blaise Pascal's famous argument du pari, "One has to wager . . . and calculate the gain and loss of wagering whether or not God exists"— Luther asserted in 1522: "Faith does not require information, knowledge, or certainty, but a free surrender and a joyful bet on his unfelt, untried, and unknown goodness."[44] In his Commentary on Galatians, by contrast, Luther spoke more positively about the quest for certainty: "This is the reason why our theology is certain: it snatches us away from ourselves and places us outside ourselves, so that we do not depend on our own strength, conscience, experience, person, or works, but depend on that which is outside ourselves, that is, on the promise and truth of God, which cannot deceive."[45] For both of these definitions, Luther, like the apostle Paul, took Abraham as the biblical figure who especially exemplified this characteristic of faith; and in his lengthy portrait of Abraham as part of the Lectures on Genesis of 1535–45 he dwelt above all on Abraham's faith, which "was counted to him for righteousness."[46] But the faith of Abraham, which caused him to forsake Ur of the Chaldees and venture forth into the unknown in obedience to the word and promise of God and then to be willing to offer up his only son, was matched by the faith of the Virgin Mary, who also offered up her only Son. Even in the context of an attack on those who "exalt the Virgin Mary too highly and praise her for having known everything," therefore, Luther could speak of her as "blessed and endowed with every kind of grace [*gebenedeyet und hoch begnadet mit allerley gnaden*]" and describe how "God led her in such a way that he concealed many things from her," which he took as a reminder that "in Christendom nothing should be preached but the pure word of God."[47]

A particularly fascinating aspect of the relation between the Protestant Reformation and the cult of the Mary as Virgin and Queen was the cult of Elizabeth I as Virgin and Queen, as Gloriana. As Roy Strong has suggested, "The cult of Gloriana was skillfully created to buttress public order, and even more, deliberately to replace the pre-reformation externals of religion, the cult of the Virgin and saints with their attendant images, processions, ceremonies and secular rejoicing."[48] Although it has been brought into question by some scholars, who have seen it as a later theory,[49] there are at least some indications that Elizabeth consciously invoked the parallel. For example, the "Virgin Queen of Walsingham" was the name of the most widely venerated image of Mary in pre-Reformation England. Although it had been destroyed before the reign of Elizabeth, it was widely venerated into the sixteenth century;[50] and Elizabeth's title of "Virgin Queen" would seem to have been borrowed from it. Edmund Spenser did seem to be invoking the parallel, consciously and frequently, as in *The Shepheardes Calender*:

Of fayre *Elisa* be your silver song,
that blessed wight:
The flowre of Virgins, may shee florish long,
In princely plight.
For she is *Syrinx* daughter without spotte,
Which *Pan* the shepheards God of her begot:
So sprong her grace

> Of heavenly race,
> No mortall blemishe may her blotte,[51]

those final three lines sounding unmistakably like an echo of Medieval Mariology. And near the beginning of *The Faerie Queene* he addressed Queen Elizabeth in similar language:

> And with them eke, ô Goddesse heauenly bright,
> Mirrour of grace and Maiestie diuine,
> Great Lady of the greatest Isle, whose light
> Like *Phœbus* lampe throughout the world doth shine,
> Shed thy faire beames into my feeble eyne,
> And raise my thoughts too humble and too vile,
> To thinke of that true glorious type of thine,
> The argument of mine afflicted stile:
> The which to heare, vouchsafe, ô dearest dred a-while.[52]

Just as in his *Paradise Lost*, John Milton could not avoid attention to Eve, but also to Mary as the Second Eve,[53] so likewise in his *Paradise Regained* Mary had to have a place, as when he had Christ explain:

> These growing thoughts my Mother soon perceiving
> By words at times cast forth, inly rejoiced,
> And said to me apart: High are thy thoughts
> O Son, but nourish them and let them soar
> To what height sacred virtue and true worth
> Can raise them, though above example high.[54]

Thus a special case of "Protestant Mariology" was the place of Mary in sacred poetry, hymnody, worship, and devotion, which perpetuated some of these patterns of the Reformation into modern times, as I noted in an earlier chapter on the basis of John A. L. Riley's hymn of 1906, "Ye Watchers and Ye Holy Ones."[55] Again, in the hymn "Crown Him with Many Crowns," originally by Matthew Bridges but with additions and supplements by others,[56] Christ was saluted as "Fruit of the mystic Rose, / As of that Rose the stem," making Mary in Protestantism the

Mystic Rose that she had been in the piety of the Middle Ages and the Counter-Reformation.

In art as well as in poetry, Mary continued to claim a place in the affections of those who on doctrinal grounds did not share the traditional reverence for her. So it was that, as Owen Chadwick has suggested, "The *Annunciation* by Fra Angelico, for a cell of the Dominican priory of San Marco in Florence, [was] one of the two or three pictures which most helped Protestants, as well as Catholics, to remember St. Mary with affection."[57] The relation of the art of Albrecht Dürer to the Reformation continues to be the object of serious investigation.[58] Most pertinent to our theme here was his cycle of woodcuts, *The Life of Mary*.[59] A colleague and in some ways a pupil of Dürer, and even an artistic subject of his, was Lucas van Leyden.[60] Whatever his own complex relation to the Reformation may have been, his woodcut of *The Virgin with Two Angels*, dated 1523, epitomized the Reformation tension being discussed here: between a retention of the Dantean, and universally Medieval, depiction of the Virgin Mary as Queen of Angels (and therefore, at least by implication, Queen of Heaven), and a reinterpretation of her in the light of the Reformation principles of *sola Scriptura*, *sola gratia*, and above all *sola fide* as the totally human Maid of Nazareth, a peasant girl snatched by the initiative of God from her ordinary life to take her great and historic part in the drama of salvation.

Paolo and Giovanni Veneziano, *The Coronation of the Virgin*, 1358. Copyright The Frick
Collection, New York.

12 The Mater Gloriosa
and the Eternal Feminine

Mary hath chosen the better part,
which shall not be taken away from her.
—Luke 10:38–42

When truly archetypal motifs and figures of tradition cease to be the objects of the devotion to which they have been attached for many centuries, the afterglow can sometimes seem even brighter than the glow. So it has been true in a preeminent sense of the figure of Jesus that, by a phenomenon that could be labeled Christocentric agnosticism, "as respect for the organized church has declined, reverence for Jesus has grown."[1] And so it has been with his Mother. In the Romantic poetry of many countries during the nineteenth century, therefore, Mary came to glow with a halo that was in some respects no less resplendent than the one with which the unsophisticated piety of the people, the speculations of the theologians, and the liturgy of the church had adorned her. For if, with René Wellek, Romanticism is defined as "that attempt, apparently doomed to failure and abandoned by our own time, to identify subject and object, to reconcile man and nature, consciousness and unconsciousness by poetry which is 'the first and last of all knowledge,'"[2] then William Wordsworth, the poet from whose preface to the 1800 edition of *Lyrical Ballads* the closing words of that definition were taken, well illustrated the situation. Wordsworth's early "radical Protestantism," as Geoffrey Hartman has called it,[3] continued to manifest itself even in his later and more conservative *Ecclesiastical Sonnets*. As a Protestant, he seems to have been quite sure, as he said there, that "From false assumption rose, and fondly hailed / By superstition, spread the Papal power."[4] Nevertheless, he was able to address the Virgin Mary this way:

> Mother! whose virgin bosom was uncrost
> With the least shade of thought to sin allied;
> Woman! above all women glorified,
> *Our tainted nature's solitary boast;*
> Purer than foam on central ocean tost;
> Brighter than eastern skies at daybreak strewn
> With fancied roses, than the unblemished moon
> Before her wane begins on heaven's blue coast;
> Thy Image falls to earth. Yet some, I ween,
> Not unforgiven the suppliant knee might bend,
> As to a visible Power, in which did blend
> All that was mixed and reconciled in Thee
> Of mother's love with maiden purity,
> Of high with low, celestial with terrene![5]

For if Mary truly was "celestial" as well as "terrene," that seemed to come close to calling her Queen of Heaven. Here Wordsworth echoed the portrayal of "the coronation of the Virgin," which became a standard part of the iconography of Mary during the twelfth century, regularly depicted her as sitting at Christ's right hand, and it was a continuation of this understanding when later painters showed Christ or God the Father or the entire Trinity investing her with the crown.[6]

Similarly, Mary Ann Evans, as the anonymous translator into English of the radical *Life of Jesus* by David Friedrich Strauss, knew very well that it had relegated the Virgin Mary and the virgin birth to the realm of myth, for she had translated the section about this, which was entitled (in her translation) "History of the Conception of Jesus Viewed as a Mythus."[7] But later in her life, writing as George Eliot, in perhaps her greatest novel, she had Tertius Lydgate, the discredited physician, exclaim about the protagonist of the novel, Dorothea Brooke Casaubon: "This young creature has a heart large enough for the Virgin Mary. She evidently thinks nothing of her own future, and would pledge away half her income at once, as if she wanted nothing for herself but a chair to sit in from which she can look down with those clear eyes at the mortals who pray to her. She seems to have what I never saw in any woman before—a fountain of friendship towards men"; and a little later Dorothea was described as having "the pale cheeks and pink eyelids of a *mater dolorosa*" (which, for late twentieth-century American readers, the editor of *Middlemarch* felt obliged to explain in a footnote as "a title of the Virgin Mary").[8]

Similar passages could easily be added from Romantic poets of the several national literatures, because, as a German poet said,

I see thee, Mary, beautifully depicted
in a thousand pictures;
Yet none of them can portray thee
As my soul perceives thee.

I only know that ever since then
The tumult of the world has vanished like a dream,
And a heaven, ineffably sweet,
Abides eternally in my heart.

[Ich sehe dich in tausend Bildern
Maria lieblich ausgedrückt;
Doch keins von allen kann dich schildern,
Wie meine Seele dich erblickt.

Ich weiß nur, daß der Welt Getümmel
Seitdam mir wie ein Traum verweht,
Und ein unnennbar süßer Himmel
Mir ewig im Gemüte steht];[9]

and those thousand pictures came into view throughout the poetry, music, and painting of the Romantic century. It will not, however, be on that German poet, but on his more celebrated countryman, Johann Wolfgang von Goethe, that this chapter will concentrate, and specifically on Goethe's *Faust* as the supreme example of the Virgin Mary as an enduring archetype.[10] Goethe's relation to historic Christianity, too, was a complex one. In the *Conversations with Goethe in the Last Years of His Life* recorded by Johann Peter Eckermann, Goethe was reported as having said on 11 March 1832, just eleven days before his death: "Beyond the grandeur and the moral elevation of Christianity, as it sparkles and shines in the Gospels, the human mind will not advance." But the context of that declaration made it clear that he was doing anything but affirming the orthodox and catholic faith of the church.[11] Nevertheless, like Wordsworth, Goethe was profoundly fascinated by the mystical figure of the Virgin Mary, and especially by her exalted status as Mater Gloriosa and the Eternal Feminine [*das Ewig-Weibliche*]. For like Dante's *Divine Comedy*, and apparently in a conscious echoing of it, Goethe's *Faust* began in the setting of Holy Week and ended in Paradise with the vision of Mary and the Eternal Feminine. But before Mary manifested herself as the Mater Gloriosa in the closing scene of *Faust*, she had first been seen as the Mater Dolorosa.[12] In her despair, Gretchen prayed to her, in a fervent petition to the Virgin Mary inspired by the *Stabat Mater Dolorosa*.[13] As the drama turned out, then, "the young woman who is at first the object of Faust's purely sensual passion, inspired by Mephisto—Gretchen—becomes in fact Mephisto's victorious rival in the battle for Faust's soul."[14] For she was told that it was her elevation to "higher spheres" of glory that would become the means for Faust to attain to those spheres of glory, too.[15]

Those words were addressed to the Woman Penitent, Formerly Called Gretchen by the Mater Gloriosa, seen as the special refuge for those who, like Gretchen, had been "easy to seduce" and were "hard to save" but who were now "penitent women, in need of grace."[16] The Chorus of Penitents addressed the Mater Gloriosa with the praise, "Thou dost soar to the heights of the everlasting kingdoms," and with the petition, "Receive our pleading, thou incomparable one, who art full of grace!"[17] She was "full of grace," as she had been addressed by the angel of the annunciation, "Ave, gratia plena, Dominus tecum."[18] The penitents were "in need of grace," and through her grace and purity their impurity was healed. But the Mater Gloriosa did not represent the healing only of their individual lusts, nor only of Faust's conflicts; as has been said about such theological terms in this scene, "it is, of course, contrary to the sense to interpret them according to the strict sense of the terminology of the church, but it would be forcing things to exclude echoes of this completely."[19] Not only was it the case that "the several persons of Margarete-Galatea-Helen are now subsumed in the one person of Mary Mother of God";[20] but through these "echoes" of themes that had been sounding throughout the rest of the work, the several titles with which she was identified here in the closing scene may be said to have achieved a new synthesis of disparate elements, not by negating them but by exalting them to the level of the sublime, in what one scholar called "that loving fusion of pagan and Christian convictions in which Goethe . . . found his own final religious peace."[21]

Those titles were brought together by Doctor Marianus, whose importance for the outcome of the drama has been well summarized in this sensitive observation by Cyrus Hamlin: "As a sublime counter-figure to Doctor Faustus in his study at the outset of the drama, this mystical devotee of the Virgin represents the highest level of spiritual perfection attainable within the human sphere. Thematically he may be compared with Nereus in his devotion to Galatea in the final scene of the 'Classical Walpurgis Night.' Through Doctor Marianus the theme of the Eternal Feminine is re-introduced to *Faust* in its highest traditional form."[22] Doctor Marianus brought the titles together in the final two lines of the worshipful ode with which he introduced the transcendent closing hymn. The ode was spoken first to the penitents: "Look upwards to this saving look, all who have been made tender through repentance, in order to transform yourselves thankfully into your blessed destiny." Then Doctor Marianus turned to the Mater Gloriosa herself: "Let every higher sense be placed at thy service. *Virgin, Mother, Queen, Goddess*: continue to grant grace!"[23] Such a heaping up of titles was a familiar device from earlier passages in the drama.[24] These four titles had been anticipated in the other ode of Doctor Marianus, shortly preceding this one: "The Glorious One in the center, in her wreath of stars, the Queen of Heaven. I can tell from her splendor. She is the Supreme Ruler in the world!"[25] And again: "Virgin, pure in the most beautiful sense, Mother worthy of honor, our chosen Queen, equal in birth to the gods."[26] He implored her to "grant approval to that which earnestly and tenderly moves this man's breast and which with a holy passion of love he bears to thee."[27] He prayed, "Let every higher sense be placed at thy service."[28] By such petitions, the various yearnings and intuitions in "this man's breast," every "passion of love," including even Faust's original "coarse passion of love,"[29] and "every higher sense," as these had manifested themselves in Faust's development throughout the work, were being raised to the exalted plane of the Virgin Mary, and thus of Christ her Son, and thus of God the Father in heaven (where this entire "postlude in heaven parallel to the 'Prologue in Heaven'"[30] was being played, with no action in heaven between these two scenes).

"In the soteriology, as in the ethics, of Goethe's play," one commentator has suggested, "love, not egoism, is both the principal instrument of Grace and the highest value."[31] The saving power of that love through each of the three occupants of that exalted plane—Mary, her Son Jesus Christ, and God the Father—had already been explicitly adumbrated by the Woman Penitent Formerly Called Gretchen while she was still alive on earth, in her penitential sighs for grace before the "devotional image of the Mater Dolorosa," as she prayed a paraphrase of the Medieval *Stabat Mater Dolorosa*: "Incline thy countenance graciously to my need, thou who art abounding in pain. With the sword in thy heart [Luke 2:35] and with a thousand pains thou dost look up at the death of thy Son. Thou dost look to the Father and send sighs upward for [thy Son's] trial and for thine own."[32] Now at the end, having become a participant in the grace and glory of heaven, she prayed to Mary once more. Her prayer "is transposed into a radiant major key,"[33] and it was no longer addressed to the Mater Dolorosa but to the Mater Gloriosa: "Incline, oh incline, thy countenance graciously to my happiness, thou incomparable one, thou radiant one! The one whom I first loved, now no longer troubled, is coming back."[34] The sharp contrast, and yet the special bond, between Gretchen as the fallen woman, whom her own brother had called "a whore," and Mary as the "Virgin, pure in the most beautiful sense,"[35] became the subject of prayers to the Virgin on Gretchen's behalf by the three Women Penitents of this closing scene, with a devotional version of the logical argument *a maiori ad minus*, from the greater to the lesser: "Thou who dost not deny thy presence to women who have sinned greatly and dost elevate a repentant recovery to the level of eternity [which was how all three of them had been treated, despite the magnitude of their sins], grant also to this good soul, who forgot herself only once and who did not know that she was doing wrong, thy fitting forgiveness!"[36] If even they had not been denied the grace of forgiveness, so the prayers argued, she certainly ought to receive it.

It was significant for this special bond that the prayer of each of the three Penitents to Mary on behalf of Gretchen, and much earlier Faust's lamentation over Gretchen, should have contained the most detailed references anywhere in the drama to the redemptive work of Christ, who nevertheless, "significantly, does not appear and is not invoked" directly as such even here.[37] When Mephistopheles sneered about Gretchen, "She is not the first," this was apparently a verbatim quotation from the accounts of an actual case that occurred in Frankfurt in 1771, as reported by Goethe.[38] But Faust's reaction to the sneer was to explode, with its reference to "rendering satisfaction for guilt" apparently intended as an allusion to the atoning death of Christ: "Not the first! How utterly miserable! No human soul can comprehend that more than one creature has descended to the depths of this misery, that the death-agony of the first was not enough to render satisfaction for the guilt of all the others in the eyes of the One who pardons eternally!"[39] Mephistopheles always had the typical devil's horror of the cross.[40] In their original hostile encounter, Faust confronted Mephistopheles-as-poodle with the crucifix and with the death of Christ, whom he described as "the never-begotten One, the ineffable One, who was poured out through all the heavens and was blasphemously pierced" on the cross.[41] And now, before Mary as Mater Gloriosa, each of the three penitents in her turn intoned the litany, by referring to the person of Christ and citing the authority of some aspect of his life and death.[42]

The first was the Mulier Peccatrix.[43] In the exegetical tradition, though not in the text of the Gospel itself, she had been identified with Mary Magdalene[44] and was the Mary of whom the Dies Irae, sung at the Requiem Mass for Gretchen's mother, prayed: "Thou who didst absolve Mary, and listen to the petition of the thief, thou hast also granted hope to me." But it was striking that this petition, with its confident reference to divine forgiveness, was omitted from the Dies Irae in that scene in Part One, though it was echoed here in Part Two. Paraphrasing the Gospel, the Magdalene based her petition on Christ's statement that "Her sins, which are many, are forgiven; for she loved much,"[45] and addressed it to the Virgin Mary: "By the love that made tears flow as balsam on the feet of thy divinely transfigured Son, despite the scorn of the Pharisees; by the jar that so richly poured out its incense; by the locks of hair that so gently dried the sacred limbs."[46] The second was the Mulier Samaritana, who encountered Christ at the well.[47] She now made "the well to which Abraham once brought his flocks to be watered" and at which "the cup was permitted to touch and cool the Savior's lips" into an allegory of the "superabundant, eternally clear fountain" of grace "that flows from there through all the worlds."[48] And the third was Maria Aegyptica, whose life was recorded not in the New Testament but in the Acta Sanctorum, including her conversion while on a pilgrimage to the Holy Sepulcher in Jerusalem, "the consecrated place where the Lord was laid to rest," and then her forty-seven years of penance as a hermit in the desert east of Jordan.[49] Although it does seem "that according to the earliest conception of the closing scenes it was to be Christ who would free Faust's soul from hell after his victory over Lucifer,"[50] Christ himself did not appear directly and was not prayed to directly in these petitions. Rather, all of these references to the history of Christ were invoked in a prayer to Mary in support of the petition for Gretchen—a reminiscence of the closing cantos of Dante's *Paradiso*, with the description of the Virgin Mary by Bernard of Clairvaux as "the one whose face most resembles that of Christ."[51]

But she was called "Virgin"—and then "Mother." This can be taken as an echo of the "pantheistic" symbol of the Mothers in Part Two, for the theme of Nature as the All did resound here in the closing scene of *Faust*. Thus the content of redemption was defined as "being saved in the company of the All."[52] That "company of the All" was one of the very things which "earnestly and tenderly moves this man's breast and which with a holy passion of love he bears" to the Virgin Mother.[53] In keeping with this "holy passion of love," the mighty forces of Nature, according to the Pater Profundus, "are messengers of love, they proclaim that which surrounds us in eternal creativity."[54] It does not seem to be an exaggeration to conclude that "this transfigured Nature becomes a metaphor of love. It is the only theme at the conclusion of Part Two of *Faust*."[55] And just as those forces of a transfigured Nature surged everywhere and yet provided continuity and stability, "so it is almighty love that shapes and cares for the All,"[56] apparently yet another echo of Dante's *Paradiso*, this time of the closing line of its Marian vision about "the love that moves the sun and all the other stars,"[57] as well as of the words of God to the angels in the Prologue in Heaven about being "embraced by that which is becoming, which works and lives eternally, with the chaste bonds of love," and of Faust's reminiscence of his youthful sense of "the love of heaven."[58] Immediately preceding the prayer of the Pater Profundus, however, came that of the Pater Ecstaticus, which opened by calling God "the eternal torch of joy, the glowing bond of love,"[59] and closed with another reference to the theme of the All, but to a way of transcending it in eternal love, "until everything worthless is put to flight and what continues to shine is the star, the core of everlasting love."[60] That transcending even of the All in the Eternal was the fulfillment of the aspirations of Faust's science and his pantheism, for which "everything transitory is only a parable" of what abides;[61] and it was this in Mary, not only as Virgin but as Mother and as the Eternal Feminine.[62]

Yet, in the words immediately preceding these, the Eternal Feminine who was Virgin and Mother was called Queen and Goddess as well[63] and was thus the fulfillment also of the aspirations of Faust's poetic polytheism, and specifically of the typology represented in the figures of Leda, Galatea, and above all Helen of Troy. Leda had appeared in a vision as Queen.[64] Helen was repeatedly hailed simply with the title Queen,[65] even when she was being identified as the sacrificial victim.[66] Elsewhere she was labeled as "the high Queen."[67] Faust expanded on the title, speaking to her as the Queen whose arrow had found its mark in him[68] and as "the Ruler who, the moment she appeared, assumed the throne."[69] She also used the title Queen in referring to herself. The title Goddess, applied at the end of the drama to Mary, was also used earlier for various deities: the Sun, the Moon, Nike, Galatea, and the Mothers.[70] Yet to Faust, Helen was the preeminent holder of that title, too. His incredulous exclamation at the initial vision of her, calling her "the sum total of the content of all the heavens" and asking, "Is it possible that something like this can be found on earth?"[71] already put her into that realm.

But when she appeared to him in person, coming back to life out of the mists of Classical Antiquity, he told her: "To you I owe the springs of every action and the quintessence of passion. I devote myself to you in affection, love, worship, yes in madness."[72] The Poet, speaking for Faust and for all those present, proceeded to express that "worship" as, watching her kiss Faust for the first time, he described her as the Goddess. When she embraced Faust for the last time and disappeared, leaving her garment behind, the Phorcyad told him to keep the garment, because although "it is not the Goddess any more" and he had lost her, the garment was still "divine."[73] The vision of "godlike" feminine figures that Faust then experienced—followed immediately by a vision of "my most youthful summum bonum, of which I have been deprived for very long," which seems to have been an obvious reference to Gretchen—may be seen as a precognition of the closing scene: "Yes, my eyes do not deceive me! I see it, on a sunlit couch, gloriously stretched out, but truly gigantic—the godlike form of a woman! It resembles Juno, Leda, Helen. With what majestic loveliness it shimmers before my eyes!"[74] For to Faust, Helen was "the sole object of my yearning," but she was more: "The eternal being, equal in birth to the gods, as great as she is tender, as majestic as she is lovable!"[75] And "equal in birth to the gods" was the epithet used again here in the closing scene by Doctor Marianus for Mary the Virgin.[76] Under the titles Queen and Goddess, then, the Virgin was the sublime fulfillment of Faust's vision of a "the godlike form of a woman that resembles Juno, Leda, Helen" at the beginning of Act IV of Part Two, just as she was, under the title Mother, the fulfillment of his vision of Nature as Mother at the beginning of Part One and elsewhere throughout the drama, and at his visit to the Mothers. The title addressed to her by Doctor Marianus, when "in mystical rapture" he called her Supreme Sovereign of the World, likewise seemed to bring these two motifs together.[77] In a sublimely ironic way, therefore, this fulfilled eschatologically the prediction of Mephistopheles after the potion in the Witch's Kitchen that Faust would now "see Helen in every woman," except that what he now saw was not Helen, but Mary, as he traveled "from Gretchen and Helen through Sophia, which brings with it the best of our inner life, higher to Mary, who alone, as the supreme center of humanity, lifts the upward look into the miracle of the mystery."[78]

Thus the final salvation of Faust was assured as, like the Boy Souls, he was invited to "rise upward to a higher circle and go on growing imperceptibly."[79] These words, "rise upward," pointed in the same upward direction as the final words of the drama, which celebrated the Ultimate Reality in its relation to that which floated in shifting appearances, as the transcendent vision of Mary made the quest sublime. For "all that is transitory is only a parable. Here the inadequate becomes an event. Here the indescribable is accomplished. The Eternal Feminine leads us upward."[80]

The Apparition to Juan Diego, engraving from the 1685 edition of Luis Becerra Tanco, *Felicidad de Mexico en el Principio, y Milagroso Origen, que Tubo el Santuario de la Virgen Maria N. Señora de Guadalupe*. (Courtesy of the Special Collections, University of Arizona Library, Tucson)

13 The Woman Clothed with the Sun

And it shall come to pass in the last days, saith God,
I will pour out my Spirit on all flesh:
and your sons and your daughters shall prophesy,
and your young men shall see visions,
and your old men shall dream dreams.
—Acts 2:17, Joel 2:28

Although African-American spirituals, with their profound and powerful identification between the slave experience in North America and the history of Israel, contained relatively few references to Mary, probably because the churches of most of the slaves were Evangelical and Protestant rather than Roman Catholic, it is striking to find, in one of these spirituals, Mary designated as "that woman clothe' with the sun, moon under her feet."[1] For the application to the Virgin Mary of that title from the words of the Book of Revelation, "And there appeared a great wonder in heaven: a woman clothed with the sun [*mulier amicta sole*], and the moon under her feet, and upon her head a crown of twelve stars," was characteristic of the Roman Catholic rather than the Protestant tradition of New Testament interpretation.[2] More specifically, it has been used in that tradition to justify and validate the apparition, not only to the seer of the Apocalypse but to later visionaries, of that same "wonder in heaven" and of Mary as the Woman Clothed with the Sun. Literally thousands of such apparitions of the Virgin have been reported through the centuries, beginning with this one in the Book of Revelation. One of the earliest came in the fourth century, as reported by the philosophical theologian and mystic Gregory of Nyssa, in a sermon in his biography of Gregory the Wonder-Worker.[3]

In spite of the eminence of the saint and theologian who reported it, that early apparition never received official approval by responsible church authorities. In fact, although the impression has been widespread among critics that the church fosters such apparitions, along with other superstitions, in order to hawk its wares to the gullible,[4] the history of their reception clearly shows that, to the contrary, "the Church is very prudent with regard to apparitions, and accords them a low status because they are signs which reach us through our senses and are subject to the illusions of subjectivity."[5] So observed René Laurentin, the leading authority on the history of Marian apparitions, whose critical edition of the documents surrounding and following the appearances at Lourdes in 1858 is an indispensable repository of historical source material for the entire history of Marian apparitions.[6] A catalog published in 1962 of the Marian apparitions that had been ecclesiastically acknowledged to be worthy of pious belief, out of the innumerable accounts reported by individuals and groups, produces the following list of ten, in chronological order of their happening (which did not always correspond to the chronological order of their official acknowledgment):[7]

>   9–12 *December* 1531: at Guadalupe, Mexico, to Juan Diego;[8]
>
>   17 *November* 1830: at Paris, to Sister Catherine Labouré;[9]
>
>   19 *September* 1846: at La Salette in the French Alps near Grenoble, to Maximin Giraud and Mélanie Calvat;[10]
>
>   11 *February*–16 *July* 1858: at Lourdes, France, to Bernadette Soubiroux;[11]
>
>   12–13 *January* 1866: at Filippsdorf (Philippsdorf), now in the Czech Republic, to Magdalena Kade;
>
>   17 *January* 1871: at Pontmain in Brittany;
>
>   8 *July* 1876: at Pompeii, Italy;
>
>   13 *May*–13 *October* 1917: at Fátima, Portugal, to three children, Lucia, Francisco, and Jacinta;[12]

29 November 1932–3 January 1933: at Beauraing, Belgium;[13] and

15 January–2 February 1933: at Banneux, Belgium, to Mariette
   Beco.[14]

Of these ten, the three most celebrated, and the ones we shall chiefly discuss here, were Guadalupe, Lourdes, and Fátima. Of those that failed to achieve ecclesiastical recognition, the most celebrated was probably the series of apparitions that began on 3 July 1876, at Marpingen, Germany, to five young girls: Katharina Hubertus and her sister, Lischen Hubertus, Susanna Leist, Margaretha Kunz, and Anna Meisberger.[15]

For our purposes, several features were common to most of these modern apparitions. In the course of his study of Marpingen, historian David Blackbourn identified "all the elements of the classic modern apparition" as they had "fused" at Lourdes: "The simplicity of the humble visionary, the delivery of a message, the initial scepticism of the parish priest, the hostile reaction of the civil authorities, claims of miraculous cures, and finally the purposive creation of an official cult by the church"[16]—the last of these having, of course, been absent in the case of the Marpingen visions of 1876.

It would appear that the vast majority of those to whom the Virgin appeared during what deserves to be called the great century of Marian apparitions—the hundred years from the 1830s to the 1930s[17]—were not members of the elites but laypeople and peasants.[18] This has been seen as fulfilling her proclamation and prophecy in the Magnificat, "He hath scattered the proud in the imagination of their hearts. He hath put down the mighty from their seats, and exalted them of low degree. He hath filled the hungry with good things and the rich he hath sent empty away."[19] That contrasted with many of the earlier instances in the Middle Ages, when she manifested herself to religious professionals, and professional religious (as was also true, in the present list, of the apparition to Sister Catherine Labouré in 1830); among these, some, such as for example Saint Birgitta of Sweden, came from the upper classes. But when, on 13 May 1946, more than 700,000 pilgrims, almost a tenth of the population of Portugal, gathered at Fátima in honor of Mary as Queen of Peace to give thanks to her for the end of the Second World War, it was, as it had been for the thirty years preceding in the devotion to this particular Marian apparition, "scrubwomen, waiters, young and old, rich and poor, all sorts of people (but most of them humble, most of them barefoot, most of them workers and their families)," who paid tribute to the Virgin.[20] Whether the explanation for this privileging of the poor and humble was, as critics such as Emile Zola charged,[21] the manipulative power of the church over the invincible ignorance of the unenlightened masses, which would be dissipated when science and schooling prevailed, or whether it was, as defenders maintained, the predilection of the Virgin for those who were like herself,[22] both the initial reaction to the visions and the subsequent controversy over them sometimes reflected an almost textbook case of the "class struggle," in the interpretation of which its most influential advocate, though anything but a proletarian himself, took the side of the proletariat even as he scorned such manifestations of lower-class spirituality as "the opium of the masses."

The events associated with the appearance of the Virgin at Guadalupe in 1531 attached themselves to tensions that were evidence not only of class struggle but of racial struggle, as well as of struggle over religious syncretism.[23] For Juan Diego was an Indian, and those who initially refused to accept the reliability of his account were Caucasian.[24] In the difference of opinion over *Nuestra Señora de Guadalupe*, therefore, as one account inspired by twentieth-century liberation theology has put it, "it is the Indian's work or mission that the white man must acknowledge. It is the Indian's word that is at stake, and it is his mission to struggle to be recognized by the whites. In this struggle the Indian is certain that he has absolute backing from the Virgin."[25] Examination of the rise of the cult of the Virgin of Guadalupe by anthropologists has suggested many close connections with the condition of the native Indian population under Spanish colonial domination.[26] She has likewise been seen as a vindication not only of Indians' self-conscious resistance to the transformation of their homeland into "New Spain" but of "the female self-image" in resistance to the patriarchal dominance represented by the Spanish conquistadores—and by the Spanish missionaries.[27] Evidently at work in the struggle was also the identification of the site of the apparition with a native female deity, whom the Spanish Christian missionaries had sought to expel but who now seemed to them to have returned to their Indian converts in the borrowed guise of the Mother of God.[28] Yet even that situation was not without its special ironies. The very name "Guadalupe," now so closely identified with the Indian cause in Mexico that she has been called, in words quoted earlier, "the unofficial, the private flag of Mexicans,"[29] was not an Indian word but was of Spanish origin, having been the name of the Marian shrine in the province of Cáceres in Spain long before Juan Diego ever saw *Nuestra Señora de Guadalupe*; the continuing prominence of the Virgin in Spain during this period is documented by her many apparitions there in the Medieval and Early Modern periods and is well illustrated by Baroque statues of her.[30] But by her identification with the native population and with the downtrodden there and everywhere, Mary the Virgin of Guadalupe became, as the poet Octavio Paz has said, "the mother of Mexico,"[31] and, as more than one writer has called her, a "Mexican national symbol."[32] Thus the dual title of an exhibit devoted to her, "Mother of God, Mother of the Americas,"[33] summarized well the dual role she has come to occupy. And in the poetry devoted to her all these themes have been sounded.[34]

Sometimes, when the Virgin appeared, she remained silent, even enigmatically so. But more usually she communicated a message, first to the visionaries in their private devotion but then also to the church and the world. Occasionally, as in the celebrated "third message" of the Lady of Fátima,[35] that message was conveyed in secret, to be disclosed at some future time when it would be needed most; this has generally been followed by tantalizing speculations about what the secret message might contain and when it might become public. The political messages delivered by the Virgin have drawn by far the most attention, both in the popular press and in the scholarly literature. Our Lady of Guadalupe, by the sheer fact of her having singled out an Indian native rather than a Spanish conqueror as the object of her attentions, became a Mexican national symbol and has become decisive in "the formation of Mexican national consciousness."[36] But our other prime case studies, Lourdes and

Fátima, as well as Marpingen, also represented the Virgin's explicit intervention into the political affairs of the time with a message. At Lourdes, therefore, "Mary, refuge of the sick and sinners, could also be Mary the refuge of Catholic France. In her Immaculate Conception, she vanquished not only Satan but also his Republican legions and materialist ideas. Queen of heaven, she was also Queen of France, or at least the symbol of the 'true France.' Yet in her youth and simple clothes she could also be identified with the young, poor, and the humble. Mary was truly a unifying symbol that could help French people overcome their class, regional, and local differences."[37]

Similarly, when, on the twenty-fifth anniversary of the Virgin's appearance at Fátima, Pope Pius XII addressed the Portuguese people in 1942, which in the event turned out to be the midpoint of World War II, he made a direct connection between her appearance in 1917, the nadir of World War I, and the crisis of their own time during another world war: "The greater the mercies for which today you thank Our Lady of Fatima, the more assured the confidence you place in Her for the future, the nearer you feel Her to be, protecting you under Her mantle of light, the more tragic appears, by contrast, the fate of so many nations torn to pieces by the greatest calamity in history. . . . Now more than ever, only confidence in God can be of avail; voiced before the Divine Throne, by a Mediatrix such as She."[38] But for many who had passed through the fiery trial of both world wars, including the church that had passed through many wars during its history, the outcome of World War II was a fiery trial no less threatening. The domination of Eastern Europe, including not only such Eastern Orthodox lands as Russia, Serbia, and Bulgaria but also such Roman Catholic lands as Poland, Croatia, and Lithuania, by a military power and political ideology even more hostile to Christianity and all religion than the French Revolution had been was very much on the mind of Roman Catholic leaders. And it was seen as having been on the mind of the Lady of Fátima when she put in her appearance in the very year of the Russian Revolution. When Pope Paul VI came to pay his devotion to her at Fátima for the fiftieth anniversary of the apparition in 1967, therefore, he declared: "The whole world is in danger. For this reason we have come to the feet of the Queen of Peace to ask her for the gift of God which supposes his intervention, divine, good, merciful and mysterious."[39]

Concentration on the political messages of the Virgin has, however, sometimes led secular-minded journalists and historians to a reductionism that ignores the role she has assumed also in the doctrinal development of the church's message. Above all, she has been seen as intervening in support of that doctrinal development when the doctrine at issue has dealt specifically with her own person. In the next two chapters I shall turn to two of the three most important "new" doctrines to have been defined by the Roman Catholic church in the entire modern era: the dogma of the immaculate conception of the Virgin Mary in 1854 and the dogma of the bodily assumption of the Virgin Mary in 1950. (The third was the dogma of the infallibility of the pope, promulgated by the First Vatican Council in 1870, at least partly to vindicate the action of Pius IX in 1854.) It was especially to reinforce the first of these that the Virgin appeared only a few years later at Lourdes; for the mysterious Lady said to Bernadette Soubiroux (in her own native dialect): "I am the Immaculate Conception."

In the light of the conservatism of both the political and the religious messages that the Virgin has conveyed when she appeared, it may seem surprising that the official reaction at all levels has not been instantly enthusiastic. In fact, the church has at all levels proceeded with great caution in dealing with such phenomena, developing over the years a set of doctrinal and pastoral criteria for distinguishing the genuine from the illusory.[40] What Blackbourn identifies as "the initial scepticism of the parish priest [and] the hostile reaction of the civil authorities"[41] has been a commonplace of the apparition narratives.[42] Particularly impressive in one account of Marian apparitions after another, including both that of Juan Diego and that of Bernadette, has been the persistently negative reaction attributed to the local parish priest and to local magistrates.

Such reactions from the clergy and local authorities betoken the profound ambiguity of the very phenomenon of the Marian apparition as a two-edged sword. For it did serve as a weapon in the sometimes rearguard battle of the church against its modern enemies. The France of Voltaire and Diderot may have been seen by all sides at the end of the eighteenth century as the seedbed of rationalism and the stronghold of atheism; but it was to rationalistic, atheistic France that the Virgin repeatedly granted her presence during the following century, to Sister Catherine Labouré on 17 November 1830 in Paris, to Maximin Giraud and Mélanie Mathieu on 19 September 1846 in La Salette, and above all to Bernadette Soubiroux on 11 February–16 July 1858 in Lourdes. There is good reason to believe that neither the intellectual defense of Christian revelation by the apologetic enterprise in nineteenth-century Roman Catholic theology, including the revival of Thomistic philosophical apologetics, nor the political defense of the institutional church and its prerogatives against the anticlericalism of that time was as effective a campaign, particularly among the common people, as the one that the Virgin Mary waged. For it has been well said that "Rome is the head of the Church but Lourdes is its heart."[43] But therein also lay much of the ambiguity of the Marian apparitions. The authority of the parish priest in the confessional and even the solemnity of his celebration of the Mass before the local altar seemed to pale into insignificance when compared with the dramatic appeal of a personal appearance by none less than the Mother of God and her continued activity in the grotto at Lourdes. As in the period of the Reformation the peddling of papal indulgences by itinerant preachers threatened to undercut the administration of the sacrament of penance at the parish level, so a struggling parish pastor in nineteenth-century France could well resent the interference in his ministry by the "delusions" of these children that they had sighted the Blessed Virgin.

For many of the Marian shrines called into being by the apparitions, the most prominent dimension has been the miraculous, together with the mass movement of pilgrims who have been attracted primarily by the miraculous element. In the first instance, that miraculous quality applied to the visions themselves, which were attributable only to a capacity that exceeded normal sight, whether the root cause was to be ascribed to supernatural forces or to neurosis. An apparition of Mary or of Christ was in its own right a transcendent event, whose credibility would usually seem to depend on the prior credibility of miracles of any kind. Conversely, once accepted or "verified" (whatever that process of verification may have entailed), its miraculous power extended itself to the person of the visionaries or to the site of the vision or to some physical feature of the site even when, as in the case of the wonder-working water of Lourdes, it has been carried far away from the original venue of the apparition. Always, however, at least in theory, the miracles and the credit for them still belonged to the person of the Virgin, not to some magic thought to be intrinsic to the places or inherent in the things that she had touched and transformed by her presence. The frequently noted reversal over time in the role of miracles—from the ancient view of both pagans and Christians that miracles were actions that proved the authority of the miracle worker to the modern view of the Enlightenment that purported miracles depended for any credibility they might have on the already accepted authority of the holy person—does not completely apply here; for the miracles of Lourdes or Fátima have functioned both ways.

The statistics of miraculous cures, particularly in the case of Lourdes, have been variously perceived.[44] It has sometimes been estimated, whether accurately or not, that Lourdes has, in something less than a century and a half, attracted twice as many pilgrims as has Mecca in more than thirteen centuries.[45] Undoubtedly some of those who have come were sightseers or curiosity-seekers, and many others came only to pray. But tens of thousands, and perhaps millions, have made the pilgrimage to Lourdes to seek a miraculous cure for ills of body and spirit. The miraculous powers of the Virgin of Lourdes and the Virgin of Fátima have received certification at the highest level of authority. The entire civilized world, Roman Catholic or not, was shocked when Pope John Paul II was shot and gravely wounded in Saint Peter's Square on 13 May 1981 and gratified when he survived. The pope himself left no doubt regarding his view of how and why he was spared: "And again I have become indebted to the Blessed Virgin. . . . Could I forget that the event in Saint Peter's Square took place on the day and at the hour when the first appearance of the Mother of Christ to the poor little peasants has been remembered for over sixty years at Fátima in Portugal? That day . . . I felt that extraordinary motherly protection, which turned out to be stronger than the deadly bullet."[46] Pius XII on the twenty-fifth anniversary, Paul VI by his visit to the shrine on the fiftieth anniversary, and John Paul II after the attempted assassination—all three called special attention to Our Lady of Fátima, as they and other twentieth-century popes also lent their authority to the cult of Our Lady of Lourdes.

For the counterpart to the "initial scepticism" of which Blackbourn speaks as a characteristic of the history of Marian apparitions has been what he goes on to call "the purposive creation of an official cult by the church," of which Lourdes is for him the outstanding instance (and Marpingen an outstanding exception).[47] Because, as Barbara Pope has said, "Rome . . . had an interest in shoring up traditional faith within the country that it considered to be the seedbed of modern revolutions . . . . the combined motives of faith and political sensitivity moved the papacy to confirm the French Catholics' belief that they had been chosen by Mary."[48] As that description implies, the belief of French Catholics in the apparition and in their having been "chosen by Mary" took hold first on the local, regional, and national levels, from which it went on to gain papal approbation. Similarly, it was the action of the "ordinary," the responsible bishop of Leiria, in 1930, "(1) to declare worthy of credence the visions of the shepherds at the Cova da Iria, in the parish of Fátima of this diocese, on the 13th day of the months from May to October 1917 and (2) to give official permission for the cult of Our Lady of Fátima."[49] Far from being imposed on a reluctant laity by an authoritarian regime, as hostile interpreters assumed, belief in Marian apparitions has, as often as not, been imposed from below on the ecclesiastical authorities by what is in some sense a democratic process. As John Henry Newman once described the process, speaking not about the doctrine of Mary in the nineteenth century but about the doctrine of the Trinity in the fourth, it was "the orthodoxy of the faithful" that prevailed over the speculations of the theologians.[50] More realistically (or more cynically), the granting of ecclesiastical approbation and the systematic encouragement of an official cult may be seen as the effort to restrain in the legions of the

Marian faithful the excesses to which Marian devotion has been especially subject. Indeed, as one scholar judges, "Lourdes, because of its
careful guardianship by the Church since its inception, is perhaps the
most tightly controlled and orchestrated, at the levels of both meaning
and practice of all the pilgrimage cults,"[51] although it needs to be added
that in at least some respects both Guadalupe and Fátima do not seem to
have lagged far behind. It does seem safe to say that for many millions of
people no form of Marian devotion or doctrine has carried more momentous significance than her miraculous apparitions.

Diego Velázquez, *The Virgin of the Immaculate Conception*, c. 1618. National Gallery, London.

14 The Great Exception, Immaculately Conceived

Behold, I was shapen in iniquity,
and in sin did my mother conceive me.
—Psalms 51:5

A̲s we have seen in the early chapters of this book, much of the venue for the development of both devotion and doctrine connected to the Virgin Mary was the Christian East—Syriac, Coptic, Armenian, and Greek—rather than the Latin West, to which the results came from the East. To be sure, that was also true of other doctrines, such as the doctrine of the person of Christ, though it was not by any means true of all of them. To the doctrine of the Trinity, for example, Latin writers such as Tertullian in North Africa made substantial contributions, including the word *trinitas;* and at the Council of Nicaea in 325, a Western bishop, Ossius of Cordova, not only presided over the council but was a principal theological adviser to the emperor Constantine and, it seems, the source of the formula adopted by the council, that the Son of God was "one in being [*homoousios*] with the Father." But even that formula, with its origins in earlier heresies, was in Greek, and so were such formulas for Mary as Theotokos.

One issue in the historical development of the doctrine of Mary, however, was in great measure confined to the Latin West: the dogma of the immaculate conception.[1] The reason was the form that the doctrine of original sin had taken in the West, which was itself closely tied to the interpretation of Mary.[2] The assertion of the virgin birth of Jesus Christ— or, more precisely, of his virginal conception—originated in the New Testament, being found in the Gospels of Matthew and Luke but nowhere else.[3] In the first of these, as Krister Stendahl has put it, "the Virgin Birth story is theologically mute, no christological argument or insight is deduced from this great divine intervention."[4] The narrative in Luke was somewhat more specific in identifying the significance of the intervention, for the angel said to Mary: "The Holy Ghost shall come upon thee, and the power of the Highest shall overshadow thee: therefore also that holy thing which shall be born of thee shall be called the Son of God."[5] The word "therefore [dioti]" indicated that "the inference is self-evident"[6] and thus that the holiness and the divine sonship of the child had some connection, perhaps even a causal one, with the special circumstances of his conception; but it fell far short of specifying just what that connection might be.

As noted earlier, Ambrose of Milan, who in turn became the mentor of Augustine on these matters, was probably responsible for the definitive establishment of a firm "causal connection between the virginal conception and the sinlessness of Christ . . . , the combination of the ideas of the propagation of original sin through sexual union and of the sinlessness of Christ as a consequence of his virginal conception."[7] To be free from sin, Christ had to be free from the normal mode of conception; this was the conclusion Ambrose seemed to draw from the words of the prophet: "Who will tell the story of [enarrabit] his having been begotten [generationem]?"[8] As he continued the argument, his chief proof text was likewise from the Old Testament: "Behold, I was shapen in iniquity; and in sin did my mother conceive me."[9] According to the superscription of the psalm, these words were spoken by "David, when Nathan the prophet came unto him, after he had gone in to Bathsheba." As Ambrose put it, David "was regarded as righteous beyond others." If Christ was to be called truly righteous, it had to be "for no other reason than that, as one who was born of a virgin, he was not bound in any way by the ordinances against a guilty mode of having been begotten."[10] Therefore Ambrose summarized the relation between original sin and the virgin birth of Christ this way: "Even though he assumed the natural substance of this very flesh, he was not conceived in iniquity nor born in sin—he who was not born of blood nor of the will of the flesh nor of the will of a man, but of the Holy Spirit from a virgin."[11] (It bears noting in those words that Ambrose was quoting the Latin variant noted earlier, by which the words of John 1:13 were taken in the singular and applied to the birth of Christ.)[12] This doctrine of original sin was established in Western teaching through the thought of Augustine of Hippo, which in turn made necessary a special treatment of the place of Mary in the schema of sin and salvation.[13]

For where did that leave the Virgin? She had conceived without sin, but how had she in turn *been* conceived? In a famous and controversial passage of *On Nature and Grace*, one of the most important treatises that he devoted to the defense of the doctrine of original sin, Augustine had listed the great saints of the Old and New Testaments, who had nevertheless been sinners. Then he continued: "We must make an exception of the holy Virgin Mary, concerning whom I wish to raise no question when it touches the subject of sins, out of honor to the Lord. For from him we know what abundance of grace for overcoming sin in every particular [*ad vincendum omni ex parte peccatum*] was conferred upon her who had the merit to conceive and bear him who undoubtedly had no sin."[14] When he made such a statement, Augustine was being more faithful to the Greek tradition in his doctrine of Mary than he was in his doctrine of human nature. As suggested in chapter 6, the East and the West took significantly divergent directions in their handling of the distinction between nature and grace—perhaps more divergent from each other than were, for example, Thomas Aquinas and Martin Luther. In spite of these differences between Augustine's theory of original sin and the definitions of "ancestral sin [*propatrikon hamartēma*]" in the Greek fathers, however, they were agreed about the Theotokos, as this quotation from *On Nature and Grace* indicated. But Augustine did not explain this great exception, leaving it to the doctrinal development of the West over the next fourteen centuries to clarify it.

One of the earliest and most important thinkers in the Latin West to move that development along was a ninth-century Benedictine monk at Corbie, Paschasius Radbertus.[15] He is best remembered for having raised the doctrine of the real presence of the body and blood of Christ in the Eucharist to a new level of discussion and for having in significant ways anticipated the form that the doctrine was eventually to take with the adoption of the concept of transubstantiation at the Fourth Lateran Council in 1215. But Radbertus was at the same time a pioneer in Marian doctrine, with a treatise on how Mary gave birth. Radbertus is also, by almost universal consent, regarded as the author of a treatise entitled *Cogitis me* ("You compel me"), which was, however, written under the name of Jerome, who had lived more than four centuries earlier. *Cogitis me* was devoted to the question of whether it was appropriate to celebrate a festival commemorating the nativity of the Virgin Mary, not the day of her death, or "dormition,"[16] which could be celebrated as the victorious climax of her life, but the day of her physical birth. Inevitably, a consideration of that question raised the question not only of her birth but of her conception, specifically whether, like the rest of humanity, she had been conceived and born in original sin or whether she deserved to be regarded as another "great exception" to that universal rule, her Son, Jesus Christ, having been the primary exception. The treatise of Radbertus raised the question but left it unsettled.

During the High Middle Ages no one spoke more articulately or eloquently about Mary than one of the great preachers of Christian history, Bernard of Clairvaux.[17] As mentioned earlier, Dante put his praise of the Virgin at the conclusion of the *Divine Comedy* into the mouth of Bernard and in so doing quoted extensively from his writings.[18] But when it came to this question of what is being called here "the great exception," Bernard was adamant. In his famous *Epistle* 174, addressed to the canons of the cathedral of Lyons, he insisted: "If it is appropriate to say what the church believes and if what she believes is true, then I say that the glorious [Virgin] conceived by the Holy Spirit, but was not also herself conceived this way. I say that she gave birth as a virgin, but not that she was born of a virgin. For otherwise what would be the prerogative of the Mother of God?"[19] It was widely believed that the "special novelty of grace" by which Mary had given birth to Christ did not affect in any way the manner by which she herself had been born, which did not differ from the usual method of conception and birth. Yet, the virgin birth of Christ from one who had herself been conceived and born in sin did not seem to resolve the question of how he could be sinless in his birth if his mother was not. Sometimes, in the eyes of its critics and even of its supporters, such argumentation seemed to lead to the notion of an infinite regress of sinless ancestors, going back presumably to Adam and Eve, all of whom had been preserved free from sin in order to guarantee the sinlessness of Christ and of Mary. A certain kind of "superfluous curiosity" could then begin to inquire into Mary's parentage as a means of explaining how she had given birth through how she herself had been born. For if, as was by now universally assumed, Augustine's doctrine was correct in declaring those who were conceived and born in the usual way were infected by original sin, then Mary must have been unique in some way. It remained to be determined "how it was that the Virgin was purified before the conception" of Christ; this could not have been "otherwise than by him" to whom she gave birth, because he was pure and she was not. There was unanimity that Mary had been saved by Christ, so that, although she lamented his death because he was her Son, she welcomed it because he was her Savior.[20] A feast devoted to the commemoration of her conception or nativity, which was adopted from time to time in one place or another, therefore, was not appropriate, because it was not how she had been conceived but how she herself had conceived that set her apart. But Bernard also added the important stipulation that he was prepared to defer to the judgment of Rome on the entire question, both of the doctrine of the immaculate conception itself and of the commemoration of a feast of the nativity of Mary.

The iconographic tradition, like the theological one, had had a two-fold development, with the two parts not clearly harmonized. One was the pattern of emphasizing the humanity of the Virgin, therefore also her relation to her parents, Anna and Joachim. Various paintings and panels devoted to "the childhood of the Virgin" represented the legends about her life, and especially about her early life, that had been growing, such as her early vow of chastity.[21] The almost naturalistic depiction of her childhood was evident in Peter Paul Rubens's *Anna Teaching Mary*, which could be taken to be the picture of a normal bourgeois family, with the mother teaching and the daughter learning. But as it has done with the doctrine of Mary throughout history, Christian art often anticipated the development of dogma, which eventually caught up with the iconography. In a variety of artistic forms, the immaculate conception was shown both directly and indirectly, and an elaborate schema of symbols was created for it.[22] Several of those symbols, notably the moon as a symbol for the immaculate conception of the Virgin, have been woven into the early painting of Diego Velázquez, *The Virgin of the Immaculate Conception*. Although various commentators on this painting have commented on the absence of idealization in it, they have also noted its dramatic use of light as an expression of the mystery in this "great exception."

As the controversy over the immaculate conception developed already in the thirteenth and fourteenth centuries,[23] it became customary to put into juxtaposition these two passages from teachers of massive authority in the Latin West: Augustine's identification of Mary as in some way or other an "exception," and Bernard's *Epistle* 174 to the canons of Lyons, opposing the immaculate conception. When they were lined up that way, depending on the viewpoint, the author would proceed to explain one of them on the basis of the other. Gregory of Rimini, citing other passages from Augustine that made Christ the only exception to the universality of original sin, explained that in the passage under discussion he must have been referring only to actual sin, from which everyone, including Bernard, agreed that Mary was free. But this explanation could not satisfy those who interpreted Augustine's phrase "overcoming sin in every particular [*ad vincendum omni ex parte peccatum*]" as comprehending both actual and original sin, so that she alone among all the saints did not have to pray the words of the Lord's Prayer: "Forgive us our debts."

The controversial letter of Bernard was all the more troublesome because of his standing as "bearer of the flame" for the Virgin. For example, all but one of the *Sermons on the Festivals of the Glorious Virgin Mary* of Gabriel Biel, a vigorous Franciscan supporter of the immaculate conception, included at least one quotation from Bernard, just as his exposition of the doxology to Mary in the Mass quoted Bernard in every paragraph; and it was to Bernard that he turned for the doctrine of her position as Mediatrix. In the face of such eminent authority, a head-on refutation of Bernard's letter, point by point, was a difficult tactic, but some ventured to undertake it. Others found an extenuation in the large number of Patristic and Medieval doctors who had shared Bernard's ideas—they were certainly in the majority over those who had taught something like the theory of the immaculate conception—or they argued that both of the conditions stipulated by Bernard for accepting the doctrine (a feast of Mary's conception as an official day of the church year, and a pronouncement by the see of Rome on the doctrine) had now been fulfilled. There arose a legend not long after his death that Bernard had a black mark placed on his breast by God as punishment for "writing what ought not to be written about the conception of Our Lady" and that he was undergoing the cleansing punishments of purgatory for this. The legend was even used to discredit his doctrine of Mary generally, although that did seem to be going too far.

The most formidable argument that Bernard of Clairvaux and then Thomas Aquinas, as well as their later followers, had directed against the immaculate conception of Mary was the charge that if she had been conceived without original sin, she did not need redemption—which would detract from "the dignity of Christ as the Universal Savior of all." If Christ died for those who were dead, then his having died for the Virgin necessarily implied that she, too, had been dead in original sin. On the basis especially of the verse quoted earlier, "Behold, I was shapen in iniquity; and in sin did my mother conceive me,"[24] Augustine had declared the universal need of humanity for the redemption wrought by Christ. If Mary was to be included as part of humanity, albeit a very special part, did that universal statement apply to her, and if not, why not? To this specific objection it was possible to reply that she was exempt from other universal statements of Scripture, such as "All men are liars."[25]

But the fundamental reply to this entire line of reasoning was, as Heiko Oberman has put it, "the great invention of Scotus, [who] was to use this precise argument to defend the doctrine under discussion."[26] This was a speculative tour de force with few if any equals for sheer brilliance in the history of Christian thought.[27] Duns Scotus considered the question of Mary on the basis of a theological method that has been called "maximalism." It was, he said, possible for God (1) to preserve her from original sin or (2) to rescue her from it within an instant of her conception (as Thomas Aquinas taught), so that, though conceived in sin, she was born pure of sin, or (3) to purify her of it at the end of a period of time. "Which of these three . . . it was that was done," he continued, "God knows," because neither Scripture nor tradition had spoken unequivocally about it. "But," he went on, "if it does not contradict the authority of Scripture or the authority of the church, it seems preferable to attribute greater rather than lesser excellence to Mary." Or, as a later thinker put it, "I would rather err on the side of superabundance by attributing some prerogative to her than on the side of inadequacy by taking away from her some excellence that she had": better to believe and teach too much than too little. Another component of this method was the oft-repeated formula: "Whatever was both possible and eminently fitting for God to do, that he did [potuit, decuit, fecit]." The defenders of the formula conceded that it seemed to be indispensable to the doctrine of the immaculate conception, and its critics objected that the issue was "not whether it was possible for her to be conceived without [original] sin, but whether in fact she was conceived without it." On the basis precisely of "the excellence of her Son as Redeemer," Scotus insisted that the most perfect of Redeemers must have had "the most perfect possible degree of mediation with respect to one creature" and that the most fitting candidate for this honor was, obviously enough, his mother. The most perfect method of redemption, moreover, was to preserve her from original sin rather than to rescue her from it. As in the case of others "the rescuing grace of redemption does away with original sin," so in the case of Mary "preserving grace does not do away with original sin, but prevents [it]."[28] In this sense it was even possible for Scotus to assert that "Mary needed Christ as Redeemer more than anyone did," for she needed the suffering of Christ, "not on account of the sin that was present in her, but on account of the sin that would have been present if that very Son of hers had not preserved her through faith." She was immaculately conceived because what nature had not given to her, the special grace of God had accomplished in her. In spite of the counterargument that then the most perfect method of all would have been to preserve everyone from original sin, it was in her case alone that this method of redemption-by-preservation was adjudged "the most fitting," and therefore her "restoration was not an act of supplying what had been lost, but an act of increasing what [she] already had."

Contributing to the eventual resolution of the issue and of the controversy was the belief that a basic reason for the difference between Mary and all of humanity was that there was never any actual sin in her—an exemption from the universal rule that everyone had to grant, regardless of views about whether she had been conceived in original sin. The paradox of that exemption evoked from Pierre D'Ailly such an affirmation as this, addressed to Mary: "It was not by thy righteousness, but by divine grace that thou didst merit to be the only one without the woe of venial and mortal guilt, and, as is devoutly believed, without the woe of original guilt as well." His disciple Jean Gerson took the affirmation the rest of the way, paraphrasing the Apostles' Creed in Middle French: "I believe that in the sacrament of baptism God grants, to every creature who is worthy of receiving it, pardon from original sin, in which every person born of a mother has been conceived, with the sole exceptions of our Savior Jesus Christ and his glorious Virgin Mother." This was not, he explained in response to the standard objection, tantamount to putting her on the same level as Christ. In the case of Christ sinlessness was "by right," in the case of Mary it was "by privilege." Another paradox, and one that Bernard had already noted, appeared in the Gospel account of the annunciation, in which the angel had saluted Mary as "full of grace [gratia plena, in the Latin]" and thus presumably not in need of further grace, but then had gone on to explain to her,

"The Holy Spirit shall come upon thee," the Holy Ghost being the divine agent of sanctifying grace.[29] It could well be asked whether the Virgin required sanctification or, more precisely, when she had received it. Sometimes the doctrine of the immaculate conception could, and did, lead to such "superfluous" extremes as the theory that from the beginning of creation God had set aside a special portion of "prime matter" that was predestined to be eventually present in Mary at the time of the conception of the flesh of Christ, or the theory that Mary, being free of original sin, was also free of all its possible consequences, including physical weariness. Even some who favored the doctrine warned that there were certain gifts and privileges, as for example a total knowledge of the future, that Christ could have given his mother but did not. Nevertheless, the method prevailed, and by the sixteenth century even the heirs of Thomas Aquinas were using it to substantiate the immaculate conception.

The thirty-sixth session of the Council of Basel, on 18 December 1439, decreed that the immaculate conception was "a pious doctrine, in conformity with the worship of the church, the Catholic faith, right reason, and Holy Scripture." It prescribed that the doctrine "be approved, held, and professed by all Catholics," and it forbade any preaching or teaching contrary to it. That might have seemed to settle the matter, and was probably intended to do just that—except that by the time of this session Basel was itself under a cloud because of its statements and actions on the relation of the authority of the pope to that of a general council, which were subsequently condemned and which therefore made these later sessions of the Council of Basel invalid and not entitled to the designation of "ecumenical council." Therefore the decree on the immaculate conception was not canonically binding. Nevertheless, defenders of the immaculate conception in the fifteenth century used this decree to assert that although there may have been an earlier time when it was permissible to question the immaculate conception, the church had now spoken out definitively on the question, and it was "foolish and impudent" to continue to oppose it. By the end of the fifteenth century, with or without the authority of the Council of

Basel, the doctrine had become generally accepted in Western Christendom, believed by the faithful and taught by the doctors of the church.

At the Council of Trent, which was held from 1545 to 1563 at least partly in response to the attacks of the Protestant Reformation on Catholic doctrine, including the doctrine of the immaculate conception as well as other supposedly postbiblical doctrines about Mary, the extensive debates over original sin led to a consideration of the immaculate conception as an unavoidable implication.[30] When one of the draft decrees for the seventh session of the Council of Trent spoke of original sin as transmitted "to the entire human race in accordance with its universal law," the implications of this statement for the doctrine of Mary led to its deletion and, eventually at the fourteenth session, to a new paragraph at the end of the decree, specifying that it was not the council's intention to include Mary in its assertion of the universality of original sin and citing the constitutions on the Virgin promulgated by Pope Sixtus IV in 1477 and 1483 but still stopping short of defining the immaculate conception as a dogma binding, as an article of faith, on the entire church. That would not come until 8 December 1854, with the bull Ineffabilis Deus of Pope Pius IX, which declared: "The doctrine which holds that the Most Blessed Virgin Mary was preserved from all stain of original sin in the first instant of her conception, by a singular grace and privilege of Almighty God, in consideration of the merits of Jesus Christ, Savior of the human race, has been revealed by God and must, therefore, firmly and constantly be believed by all the faithful."[32] And less than four years later, on 25 March 1858, at the French village of Lourdes in the Pyrenees, a "lovely lady" appeared to the peasant girl, Bernadette Soubiroux, and announced, in the vernacular dialect: "I am the Immaculate Conception."[32]

The specific content of the promulgation of the dogma of the immaculate conception by Pius IX evoked controversy and polemics from both Eastern Orthodoxy and Western Protestantism; for as Marina Warner has said, "Although the Greeks led the way to the doctrine of the Immaculate Virgin by their cult of her miraculous birth, they opposed veneration of her as anything but the mother of the Redeemer, and were followed in this belief by the Reformed Churches."[33] But the doctrine of Mary was in some ways overshadowed by the procedural and juridical question of the authority of the pope on his own to define a dogma for the entire church, the doctrine of papal infallibility, which so dominated the agenda of the First Vatican Council in 1869–70 that further elaboration of the doctrine of Mary was largely deferred. It was a fascinating irony in the history of Western thought, therefore, that much of the weight of authority for the Augustinian doctrine of original sin had come from the teaching about the "privilege" of Mary by which Jesus Christ had been born of a Virgin and therefore was free of original sin, but that this very teaching about her "privilege" went on in later centuries to make it necessary for Augustine's Western heirs to develop an elaborate explanation of her "privilege" of being holy in a special sense. And once again, the doctrine of Mary proved to be one of the most important places to observe and test the processes by which great ideas have developed.

15 The Queen of Heaven, Her Dormition and Her Assumption

Death is swallowed up in victory.
—Isaiah 25:8, 1 Corinthians 15:54

Throughout this book, in discussing the themes and doctrines dealing with the Virgin Mary I have deliberately eschewed the many debates about her, cultural as well as theological, that have broken out during the twentieth century.[1] Rather, I merely mentioned them briefly in the Introduction, as a foil for the review that followed, which dealt only with the earlier centuries; or in some cases I have mentioned them only in order to take the account of an earlier development into its subsequent stages.[2] Nevertheless, one event in the history of Mary at the precise middle of the twentieth century, together with its aftermath, demands inclusion as the final—or, at any rate, the most recent—stage in that history: the issuance, on 1 November 1950, of the papal bull *Munificentissimus Deus*.[3] In this solemn proclamation, which presumably carried the stamp of the papal infallibility decreed by the First Vatican Council, the belief in the bodily assumption of the Virgin Mary, long held to be true both among the faithful and by theologians, was promulgated as a dogma of the Roman Catholic church by Pope Pius XII: "that the immaculate Mother of God, Mary *Semper Virgo*, when the course of her earthly

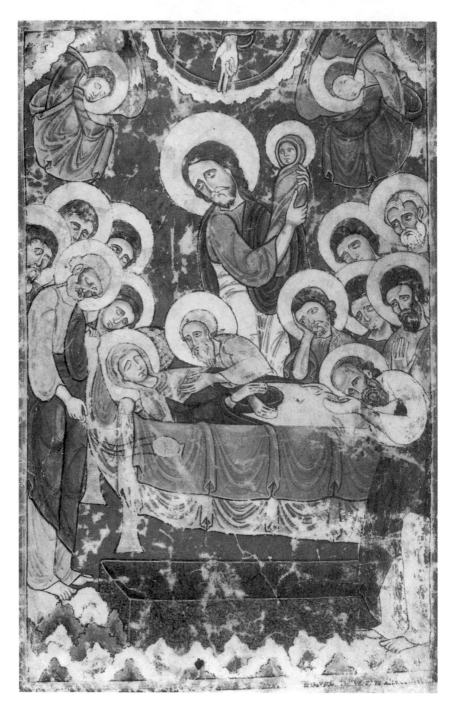

The Winchester Psalter, *The Death of the Virgin* and *The Virgin as Queen of Heaven*, MS. Cotton Nero V.IV, folios 29 and 30, c. 1145–55. London, The British Library.

life was run, was assumed *in body and soul* to heavenly glory."[4] Thus it became obligatory in 1950 for Roman Catholics to believe and teach that, as the Spanish Marian mystic Sister María de Jesús de Agreda had said in her *Life of the Virgin Mary* already in 1670, Mary "was elevated to the right hand of her Son and the true God, and situated at the same royal throne of the Most Blessed Trinity, whither neither men nor angels nor seraphs have before attained, nor will ever attain for all eternity. This is the highest and the most excellent privilege of our Queen and Lady: to be at the same throne as the divine Persons and to have a place in it, as Empress, when all the rest of humanity are only servants or ministers of the supreme King."[5]

Not at all surprisingly, the issuance of *Munificentissimus Deus* caused an uproar among Protestant theologians and clergy, both over its doctrinal content and over its dogmatic authority.[6] It was seen as sharply and confrontationally divisive, and all the more tragic because it came just when the painfully slow deepening of ecumenical awareness had begun to show signs of healing the ancient conflicts between the Eastern and the Western churches and even between Protestantism and Roman Catholicism. On the authority of Scripture and the doctrine of justification by faith, the two central doctrinal issues of the Reformation—central enough to have been identified during the nineteenth century as, respectively, the "formal principle" and the "material principle" of Reformation Protestantism—the Roman Catholic and the Protestant positions had been converging over a period of time. Roman Catholic theologians were increasingly emphasizing, significantly more than many of their sixteenth-century predecessors had in the polemical atmosphere of the Reformation and the Counter-Reformation, that the authority of Scripture, and in the original languages, established the legitimacy of a Christian doctrine (*sola Scriptura*, at least in some sense), even as Protestant theologians were paying more respect than they once did to the claims of tradition and to the role that tradition had played in the formation of Scripture. Similarly, the primacy of the initiative taken by the divine gift of grace (*sola gratia*) and the centrality of justifying faith (*sola fide*, once more only in some sense) had become a standard concern of Roman Catholic theology, just as the inseparability of good works from justifying faith was occupying a more central position in Protestant teaching. Almost as if to find new reasons to perpetuate the schism now that some of these earlier points of disagreement had at least begun to yield on both sides of the conflict, the Marian doctrines of the immaculate conception in 1854 and the assumption in 1950 came along to counter this trend. Even a well-disposed Protestant response felt constrained to warn in 1950: "While today the majority of churches with tears of penitence confess before God that they share in the guilt of a divided Body of Christ, and in common prayer and serious scholarly effort seek to diminish the area of disagreement and increase the area of agreement . . . the Roman Church would increase the area of disagreement by a dogma of the Assumption. Creation of a dogma of the Assumption would be interpreted today in the midst of the efforts at closer relationships between the churches as a fundamental veto on the part of the Roman Church."[7] For the New Testament and the early centuries of the church had been silent about "when [and how] the course of her earthly life was run," so this argument ran, although many traditions and various pious opinions about it had sprung up in subsequent centuries.[8] But to take these traditions and opinions and now to elevate them to the status of an official doctrine, binding on the entire church de fide and laying claim to the same authority as the doctrine of the Trinity, seemed to be completely presumptuous and utterly without biblical warrant.

By contrast with that reaction, the influential twentieth-century psychologist Carl Gustav Jung addressed the significance of Mary in a striking and controversial book originally published in German in 1952, entitled Answer to Job [Antwort auf Hiob].[9] The year of its original publication is relevant, for the book contained Jung's response to the bull of Pius XII. Carl Jung was the descendant of a long line of Swiss Protestant ministers and an associate and eventually an opponent of Sigmund Freud. But in his Answer to Job he basically defended the papal doctrine. The Book of Job, with its climax in the voice of God out of the whirlwind, "Who is this that darkeneth counsel by words without knowledge?"[10] had pushed the concept of divine transcendence just about as far as it could go in the direction of what Martin Luther would later call the Deus absconditus, the hidden God. But by its doctrine of the incarnation, and then even more effectively by its picture of the Virgin Mary, Catholic Christianity had mollified the austerity of this transcendence, rendering the Deity gentler and more accessible, "even as a hen gathereth her chickens under her wings."[11]

Already at the time of the promulgation of the dogma of the immaculate conception in 1854, there was widespread support in many quarters of the Roman Catholic church for a corresponding definition of the doctrine of the assumption, with 195 of the council fathers in attendance at the First Vatican Council of 1869–70 urging it. The political and ecclesiastical turmoil surrounding that council precluded the possibility of such a definition; but the doctrine of the assumption of the Virgin, though it would not become a dogma until 1950, and then only in Catholicism, did have far better support and more ancient attestation in the tradition than, for example, the doctrine of the immaculate conception had had before its definition.[12] There was a specific feast in the church year, fixed during the Middle Ages at 15 August.[13] That feast commemorated "the day when she was assumed from the world and entered into heaven," as it was called by Bernard of Clairvaux in the very epistle in which he challenged the observance of a feast of the immaculate conception.[14] By her presence, he said elsewhere, in a set of brilliant sermons on the assumption, not only the entire world but even "the heavenly fatherland shines more brightly because it is illumined by the glow of her virginal lamp."[15] Her assumption had elevated her above all the angels and archangels, and even all the merits of the saints were surpassed by those of this one woman. The assumption of the Virgin meant that human nature had been raised to a position superior to that of all the immortal spirits.

Eastern Christendom did not participate in the dogmatic definition of the assumption.[16] But that did not mean that the issue had been left without consideration in the development of doctrine in Byzantium.[17] There was a tradition repeated by the Council of Ephesus in 431, that when, in obedience to the word of Christ from the cross, "Woman, behold thy son!" and "Behold thy mother!" the disciple John "took her unto his own home,"[18] they lived in Ephesus, and that she died there; a later and quite unreliable tradition even went on to identify the House of the Virgin at Ephesus. The hour of her death or, as it was usually termed, her falling asleep or "dormition [koimēsis],"[19] was the subject of many icons. Those icons reflected the Christian art of very early times.[20] Because of its prominence in the iconographic tradition,[21] the defenders of the icons also had occasion to speak about the dormition. Theodore the Studite, for example, described it as an "ineffable" mystery, at which the twelve apostles, together with the Old Testament figures of Enoch and Elijah (both of whom had been assumed bodily into heaven),[22] attended the Theotokos at the end of her earthly life.[23] There was a homily on the subject of the dormition attributed to the seventh-century patriarch of Jerusalem, Modestos.[24] On the basis of internal evidence, however, the date of the homily has been moved forward to a century or so after Modestos, but many of the Mariological themes celebrated in it were, of course, much older.[25] For, as a later Byzantine historian reported, around the end of the sixth century the festival celebrating the dormition had, by imperial decree, been appointed for 15 August (which, as we have noted, also became the date in the Western Church for the Feast of the Assumption of the Blessed Virgin Mary).[26] Thus it eventually became one of the twelve feasts observed in the Eastern Church. It is likewise to that period that the earliest iconographic treatments of it by Byzantine artists are traced. Although an ivory plaque of the dormition came from a later period in the history of Byzantine art (perhaps as late as the twelfth century), it was an especially comprehensive treatment of the theme: the Theotokos was surrounded by the figures of the twelve apostles, in addition to two others with their faces covered (perhaps Enoch and Elijah, for the reasons indicated earlier); angels hovered overhead, hands extended to receive her into heaven.[27] At the center of the plaque—in a striking reversal of the roles they took in the conventional icons of Mother and Child—was Christ in Majesty with the infant Mary in his arms. And the adult Mary reposed in tranquility, as she was about to be received into heaven— apparently in body as well as in soul, as the East and eventually the West came to affirm—where the process by which her humanity was made divine would be completed.

In the art of the West, the dormition of the Virgin often at least implied her assumption, for example, in Caravaggio's *Death of the Virgin*.[28] A particularly dramatic depiction of the connection and the contrast between the dormition and the assumption appeared in two portrayals from the Winchester Psalter, dated "before 1161," *Death of the Virgin* and *Queen of Heaven*.[29] Angels were in attendance for both events, and once again Christ was holding the infant Mary in the moment of her dormition. But the point of the juxtaposition between the two was that the figure who was in repose at the dormition, according to the superscription of the second portrait, *Ici est faite Reine del Ciel*, "has now become Queen of Heaven." Now the angels on either side of her held banners of victory, to show that she, having vanquished the enemy and having crushed the head of the serpent as, according to the Vulgate, God had promised already in the Garden of Eden that "she [*ipsa*]" would do,[30] now participated in the victory that was accomplished not only by the passion and death of Christ but also by the resurrection of Christ. As Pope Pius XII declared in *Munificentissimus Deus*, employing in his Latin the Greek word for the resurrection, *anastasis*, "just as the glorious resurrection of Christ [*gloriosa Christi anastasis*] was an essential part and the ultimate trophy of this victory, so the struggle that the Blessed Virgin had shared in common with her Son was to be concluded with the 'glorification' of her virginal body. As the apostle says [1 Cor. 15:54, Isa.25:8], 'When . . . this mortal shall have put on immortality, then shall be brought to pass the saying that is written, Death is swallowed up in victory.' "[31]

As was evident from the pope's reference to 1 Corinthians and through it to Isaiah, "Death is swallowed up in victory," one question raised by the doctrine of the assumption had been whether Mary had ever died or whether she had, like Enoch and Elijah, been taken up alive into heaven.[32] The prophecy of Simeon to her, considered earlier as a theme of Mary the Mater Dolorosa, "Yes, a sword shall pierce through thy own soul also,"[33] seemed to imply that she would die, just as her divine and sinless Son would. As it stood, the prophecy spoke only of "sorrow, not the martyrdom of death." But this was not an adequate ground to "arouse doubt concerning her death," because she was by nature mortal. The prophecy did, moreover, appear to disprove the pious feeling of some that she who had given birth without pain should also have died without pain; for "by what authority can one suppose that she did not suffer pain in her body? . . . But whether at her death she did not feel pain, which God could grant, or whether she did feel it, which God could permit," the conclusion seemed to be that "the Blessed Virgin did undergo the vexation of the flesh by dying." Mitigating this conclusion was the widely held belief of "Christian piety" that her death had been followed immediately by a resurrection, which in turn was followed by her assumption; for she was "the firstfruits of [human] incorruptibility." Yet it was also recognized that "we do not dare to affirm that the resurrection of her body has already taken place, since we know that this has not been declared by the holy fathers." Although it was "wicked to believe that the chosen vessel" of Mary's body had been subject to corruption, still "we do not dare to say that she was raised, for no other reason than that we cannot assert it on the basis of evident proof."

The defenders and exponents of the dogma of the assumption have emphasized its consistency both with the larger body of Christian teaching and with the Mariological development that had preceded it.[34] In her function as the representative of the human race, as noted earlier, she had uniquely documented the subtle relation between divine grace and human freedom when, by her voluntary assent to God's plan of redemption through her Son, "Be it unto me according to thy word,"[35] she had set in motion the series of events that would lead to the redemption of humanity and its victory over sin and death through the death and resurrection of Christ. Her victory over all sin, original and actual, had been achieved through the unique gift, conferred on her as a consequence of the merits of Jesus Christ, of being spared the burden of original sin through her immaculate conception. It was only logical, so it could be argued, that when, as Isaiah had prophesied and Paul had proclaimed, "Death is swallowed up in victory,"[36] her death, too, should participate in that victory by Christ as an anticipation of the full participation of all the saved through the general resurrection at the end of human history. There had, after all, been such an anticipation when, at the time of the crucifixion of Christ, "the graves were opened; and many bodies of the saints which slept arose, and came out of the graves after his resurrection, and went into the holy city, and appeared unto many."[37] She was eminently more worthy of such an honor than any of these saints.

Considerations like these have made the dogma of the assumption of the Virgin perhaps the most provocative illustration of the position of Mariology in its entirety as the most controversial case study of the problems represented by "development of doctrine" as a historical phenomenon and as an ecumenical issue.[38] To those who harbored fundamental misgivings about the very idea of development of doctrine, or about the notion that the Virgin Mary should be the subject of a "doctrine" in her own right rather than be discussed as part of the doctrine of Christ or the doctrine of the church (or about both of these questions), the evolution of the assumption over a period spanning so many centuries, from a pious practice and a liturgical observance to a speculative theological theory to a dogma that was finally made official only at the middle of the twentieth century, simply proved that development of doctrine was pernicious both in theory and in fact. And even those Protestant theologians who were prepared to come to terms with the idea of development as, in the words of the Dominican scholar Yves Congar, "an inner dimension to that of tradition,"[39] balked at the assumption. One reason in the case of some of them was, undoubtedly, a basic aversion to the phenomenon of lay piety, out of which, as we have seen throughout this book, so much of the history of the development of Mariology, including the assumption, had emerged. On such aversion, the observations of a leading Protestant commentator on Roman Catholicism who was highly critical of its doctrine and its structure deserve to be quoted in full:

The worship of God "in spirit and in truth" [John 4:24] is an ideal that is only seldom attained in its entirety. Only certain individuals, as for example the great mystics, have been capable of it. Basically, all popular piety is a compromise. Only a few people grasp the idea that we can approach God only through pictures and symbols. But it would be cruel to deprive the great mass of simple souls of such pictures and symbols, for this would cut them off from any access to the being of God itself. Why should God not hear even a prayer addressed to Mary if it rises from a simple, pious heart? To use a figure, God must smile at our more spiritual forms of devotion and our high theological skill, just as we adults kindly recognize the serious purpose manifest in the games of children. . . . Many a Protestant fanatic, who flies into a rage when he sees a votive tablet with the motto "Mary has helped me," does not realize at all how petty his own basic idea of God is. Perhaps this same fanatic regards it as his sacred duty to tie God's salvation to some particular dogmatic formula. . . . No, naïve and unconscious paganism is not the real evil in Marian piety.[40]

It bears remarking that those words were written only a few years after the dogma of the assumption has been promulgated but a few years before the Second Vatican Council had been convoked.

On the eve of the Second Vatican Council it appeared reasonable to suggest that ecumenical understanding would come if Roman Catholics could recognize what made the Reformation necessary and Protestants what made it possible. On no issue of doctrine was that paradox more strikingly appropriate than on the doctrine of Mary.[41] There were observers, both hostile and friendly, who expected—or feared—that the "new" dogma of 1950 would lead a decade later to further Mariological development and to the definition of additional "new" doctrines.[42] To them, the Second Vatican Council came as a disappointment,[43] just as the issuance of the papal bull *Ineffabilis Deus* by Pope Pius IX on 8 December 1854 had been obliged to yield center stage to the First Council of the Vatican fifteen years later. For although, as Avery Dulles has said, "a separate document on the Blessed Virgin was contemplated, and was presented in draft form by the Theological Commission at the first session in 1962," the council went on to incorporate the doctrine of Mary into its first decree, the Dogmatic Constitution on the Church, *Lumen Gentium*.[44] "The Fathers," Dulles continues, "saw a danger in treating Mariology too much in isolation; they preferred to link her role more closely with the main theme of the Council, the Church."[45] They also wanted it to be seen, as they themselves put it, that they "carefully and equally avoid the falsity of exaggeration on the one hand, and the excess of narrow-mindedness on the other,"[46] partly on ecumenical grounds and partly to come to terms with the new biblical and historical scholarship within Roman Catholic circles that had inspired so many of the council's actions. What emerged from this process was no new doctrine at all but a balanced and evenhanded summary, dated 21 November 1964, of the principal themes of the entire historical development of the doctrine of Mary.

The five major headings, which the council itself supplied for its text, read:

I. *The Role of the Blessed Virgin Mary, Mother of God, in the Mystery of Christ and the Church*, according to which "because of this gift of sublime grace she far surpasses all other creatures, both in heaven and on earth"; and yet "at the same time, however, because she belongs to the offspring of Adam she is one with all human beings in their need for salvation." Nevertheless, "the Synod does not, however, have it in mind to give a complete doctrine on Mary [*completam de Maria proponere doctrinam*], nor does it wish to decide those questions which have not yet been fully illuminated by the work of theologians."

II. *The Role of the Blessed Virgin in the Economy of Salvation*, including

the way "the books of the Old Testament . . . , as they
are read in the Church and are understood in the light of
a further and full revelation, bring the figure of the
woman, Mother of the Redeemer, into a gradually
sharper focus" [Gen. 3:15, Isa. 7:14]. Through the entire
history of the Bible, "the Blessed Virgin advanced in her
pilgrimage of faith, and loyally persevered in her union
with her Son unto the cross."

III. *The Blessed Virgin and the Church*, in which "the Blessed Virgin
was eternally predestined, in conjunction with the incarnation of the divine Word, to be the Mother of God," so
that "Mary figured profoundly in the history of salvation
and in a certain way unites and mirrors within herself the
central truths of the faith [*in historiam salutis intime ingressa,
maxima fidei placita in se quodammodo unit et reverberat*]."

IV. *Devotion to the Blessed Virgin in the Church*, with the directive
"that practices and exercises of devotion toward her [*praxes
et exercitias pietatis erga Eam*] be treasured as recommended
by the teaching authority of the Church in the course of
centuries," but with the warning "that true devotion consists neither in fruitless and passing emotion, nor in a
certain vain credulity [*neque in sterili et transitorio affectu, neque
in vana quadam credulitate*]."

V. *Mary, a Sign of Sure Hope and of Solace for God's People in Pilgrimage*,
because "in the bodily and spiritual glory which she pos-
sesses in heaven, the Mother of Jesus continues in this
present world as the image and first flowering of the
Church [*imago et initium Ecclesiae*]."[47]

Many of these guiding principles were almost (if not quite) formulated
in the terms that have been employed here, in the preceding chapters of
this book, and that are summarized in the chapter to follow.

Master of the Saint Lucy Legend, *Mary, Queen of Heaven*, c. 1485. © 1996 Board of Trustees, National Gallery of Art, Washington. Samuel H. Kress Collection.

16 The Woman for All Seasons—
And All Reasons

For, behold, from henceforth all generations shall call me blessed.
—Luke 1:48

D uring nearly twenty centuries, these words of the Magnificat have come true over and over, and only the most churlish have dared to be an exception to them. Retrospective consideration of the many topics and themes of this book suggests various areas of history for which the centrality of the person of the Virgin Mary is an indispensable interpretive key. Her importance as such a key does not depend on the belief or unbelief of the observer; for even those who do not, or cannot, have faith need to grasp the faith of other ages in order to understand them.

It is impossible to understand the history of Western spirituality and devotion without paying attention to the place of the Virgin Mary. The "social history" of various ages and various places has been engaging the attention of many of the most important and productive historians during the past generation or two. Ours is, therefore, a time of great interest in the history of everyday life and therefore also in "popular religion." Scholars have zealously sought a methodology that would get beyond the dominance of "high culture" to discover the beliefs and practices of simple and illiterate people. Such a methodology has, on closer scrutiny, proven to be a far subtler problem than it might have appeared at first. How does one read the surviving evidence, much of it literary in form, in order to probe the hidden (or even concealed) material it contains about the lower classes and the other members of the silent majority? How, for example, should the social historian read the legislation of other eras? Does the repetition of prohibitions directed against certain practices necessarily imply that those practices held on among the common people, or could the repetition be evidence of the inherent tendency of laws to be left standing on the books long after the need for them has passed and the reason for them has been forgotten? Because, in the case of the church, a major component in the history of its legislation has taken the form of liturgy, creed, and dogma, should the historian in a later age automatically assume, as orthodox theologians and historians have sometimes tended to do, that what the councils of the church legislated as dogma and liturgy was what the common people actually believed? Or conversely, is the frequent and no less automatic assumption among modern secularizing historians any more plausible, that what the common people actually believed was undoubtedly quite different from dogma and creed and that the "real meaning" of popular religion is to be sought in the categories of race or class or gender or anywhere else except in creed and liturgy? It would also seem to be an essential assignment specifically for such social history to ask, and if possible to answer at least in part, questions about the movement of ideas and practices in the opposite direction, from the faith of the common people into liturgy, creed, and dogma, rather than the other way around.

At least within the history of Christianity, it is difficult to think of a more fitting theme to explore for its bearing on these issues than the Virgin Mary. Why has she maintained her hold on most of the Western world even in a secular age and even in the face of anti-religious propaganda and downright persecution during the Communist era in Eastern and Central Europe? It was not primarily because she has been the subject of solemn pronouncements of doctrine and creed since the councils of the early Christian centuries and was in fact the subject of the most recent official promulgation of a dogma by a pope, on 1 November 1950. A far more important explanation is that she has been, to paraphrase the famous words of "Light-Horse Harry" Lee about George Washington in 1799, "first in the hearts of her countrymen." Historians and comparativists, not to mention such propagandists and persecutors, have frequently remarked on the continuity and tenacity of religious devotion from one period to another, including the persistence of external devotional observance long after the death of the devotion itself. Nor would it be sound to ignore the subtle but profound changes that can take place in the meaning of words and actions across such continuities, for which, as we have seen, devotion to Mary provides many striking examples.

A special form of devotion to the Virgin Mary has been Marian mysticism. We may leave aside for the moment the highly mooted question of whether the mystical form of devotion and language has a legitimate place in the Christian faith. But if it does, it has found some of its most profound expressions in the prayers and poetry addressed to the Virgin. As it is the ambition of the mystic to rise through the visible to the Invisible and through the things of earth to the things of heaven, so these prayers to Mary take their start from her simple historical person and her humble earthly life to rise toward her special place in the kingdom of God and her unique role in the universe. This mystical vision of the Virgin, moreover, is not intended merely for passive enjoyment but has been said to carry a transforming power, as those who have had the privilege of beholding the Queen of Heaven have dedicated their lives to her service. Thus in his powerful poem, "The Blessed Virgin Compared to the Air We Breathe," Gerard Manley Hopkins spoke about

New Nazareths in us,
Where she shall yet conceive
Him, morning, noon, and eve,
New Bethlems, and he born
There, evening, noon, and morn—
Bethlem or Nazareth,
Men here may draw like breath
More Christ and baffle death;

> Who, born so, comes to be
> New self and nobler me
> In each one and each one
> More makes, when all is done,
> Both God's and Mary's Son.[1]

Here the union with Christ of which the apostle Paul spoke when he said, "I am crucified with Christ: nevertheless I live; yet not I, but Christ liveth in me,"[2] was expanded into a union also with his Mother, yet in a highly Christocentric form. Because of the reliance on trendy "psychobabble" that seems to have gained such currency also among academics, it does perhaps need to be added that this Marian mysticism has by no means been confined to celibate men such as Gerard Manley Hopkins, but has been widely cultivated among both men and women, married as well as celibate.

That observation may be the appropriate context in which to consider the psychological significance of Mary. And in the first instance that pertains above all to her significance for women. As clergy of all denominations have noted, the women were the first to render service to Christ on Easter Sunday morning—and that, they have often been tempted to add, is the way it has been on most Sunday mornings ever since. Many of the mighty women of the history of the Middle Ages, for example, are known to us chiefly or even solely through the medium of what men wrote down from them or about them. It has been pointed out earlier that the visions of Birgitta of Sweden were transmitted chiefly in Latin, and in a version intended to demonstrate her credentials as a candidate for sainthood. Or, to mention two examples from the fourth century who deserve to be compared in Plutarchian "parallel lives": Saint Macrina, sister of two of the most important theologians of the Greek East, Saint Basil of Caesarea and Saint Gregory of Nyssa, who was celebrated by the latter of these as *adelphē kai didaskalos*, "our sister and our teacher" in philosophy and theology; and Saint Monica, mother of Saint Augustine, who taught him and bore with him through the trials of his stormy youth, until Saint Ambrose of Milan, who eventually was to baptize

Augustine, told her that the child of such tears could not be lost. If we could enable the silent millions among Medieval women to recover their voices, the evidence that we do have from those relatively few who did leave a written record strongly suggests that it was with the figure of Mary that many of them identified themselves—with her humility, yes, but also with her defiance and with her victory: "*Deposuit potentes de sedibus suis, et exaltavit humiles; esurientes implevit bonis, et divites dimisit inanes*—He hath put down the mighty from their seats and exalted them of low degree; he hath filled the hungry with good things, and the rich he hath sent empty away." And he could do it again.

Because of that role that she has been playing for the history of the past twenty centuries, the Virgin Mary has been the subject of more thought and discussion about what it means to be a woman than any other woman in Western history. To an extent that many have chosen to ignore, explanations about Mary or portraits of her in words or in pictures can tell us much about how "the feminine" has been perceived. Together with Eve, with whom she has often been contrasted as the Second Eve, she has provided the subject matter for some of the best and some of the worst in that checkered history. A highly one-sided and prejudiced account of this history has been permitted to engage in a drastic kind of oversimplification that would be attacked, and rightly, if it were arguing on the opposite side. Because Mary is the Woman par excellence for most of Western history, the subtleties and complexities in the interpretation of her person and work are at the same time central to the study of the place of women in history, which has begun to claim its proper share both of scholarly and of popular attention. But some extremely valuable resources for that history are being neglected.

Another important part of this psychological significance of Mary has been her function as the symbol of those qualities, in a God who is beyond all gender, that have traditionally found expression through the feminine. Although it is fashionable today to speak about Judaism and Christianity as "patriarchal" not only in their ethics and way of life but in their picture of God, the most serious reflection of Jewish and Christian thought has transcended any such easy identification. For "the divine power," as Gregory of Nyssa wrote, "though it is exalted far above our nature and inaccessible to all approach, like a tender mother who joins in the inarticulate utterances of her babe, gives to our human nature what it is capable of receiving; and thus in the various manifestations of God to humanity, God both adapts to humanity and speaks in human language."[3] And an important bearer of this dimension in the relation of God to humanity has been the person of Mary. That has made her prominent also in the relation between Christianity and other religions. As Christianity confronted religions in which not only gods but goddesses were central, it had in Mary a way of simultaneously affirming and yet correcting what those goddesses symbolized. The most striking symbol of how she did this is probably to be found in the city of Ephesus, as noted earlier.[4] According to the Book of Acts, the preaching of the apostle Paul there posed a threat to the silversmiths of the city, who made their livelihood by fashioning silver shrines to the goddess Artemis. To combat the threat of this new deity without a face, they stirred up a riot among the people with the cry "Great is Diana of the Ephesians!"[5] And it was in that same city of Ephesus, slightly less than four centuries later, that the Third Ecumenical Council of the church in 431 solemnly decreed that Mary was to be called Mother of God, Theotokos.

Yet another dimension of her psychological significance has been pedagogical. Throughout most of the history of Christian education, at least until the Reformation, the lives of the saints served as patterns of character, and among these the life of Mary occupied a unique position, corresponding to the unique position she had occupied in the plan of God. Each of the special Christian virtues—or, as they were often designated, "theological virtues"—defined in the New Testament, "faith, hope, and charity, these three,"[6] but also each of the four classical virtues—or, as they were often designated, "cardinal virtues"—defined by Plato and then incorporated into the deuterocanonical Wisdom of Solomon, "temperance and prudence, justice and fortitude,"[7] found a special embodiment in her. Taken together, these seven virtues were fundamental to moral teaching. But in the saints, and to a special degree in the person of the Virgin Mary, these virtues were there not only to be admired and cherished but to be imitated. Individual incidents from the Gospels in which she was sometimes little more than a bit player nevertheless lent themselves to elaboration as guides to God-pleasing behavior. Above all, she served as a model of the fundamental Christian—and particularly monastic—virtue of humility. "Quia respexit humilitatem ancillae suae" was how the Latin Vulgate translated, or really mistranslated, her words in the Magnificat,[8] which are more accurately rendered, for example, in the New Revised Standard Version with "For he has looked with favor on the lowliness of his servant." Mistranslation or not, however, this humilitatem in the Vulgate became the occasion for some of the most profound explorations of the concept of humility—not in the sense in which Uriah Heep of Charles Dickens's David Copperfield could say, "I am well aware that I am the 'umblest person going. . . . My mother is likewise a very numble person. We live in a numble abode," but in the sense in which Augustine could say, "All strength is in humility, because all pride is fragile. The humble are like a rock: the rock seems to lie downwards, but nevertheless it is firm."[9]

Nor has it been only for morality and life that Mary has been important. By one of the most dramatic reversals in the history of ideas, this humble peasant girl from Nazareth has been made the subject of some of the most sublime and even extravagant theological speculation ever thought up, considerable portions of which have been occupying these pages. It is a fascinating question to ask just why and how a particular subject "becomes a doctrine." It cannot be simply because it is spoken of in the Bible: there are hundreds of references to "mountains" in the Bible, and many hundreds to the flora and fauna of the Near East; yet no one has ever seriously suggested that there be a "doctrine" of birds or trees or hills. One decisive criterion has probably been the connection of a particular topic with the central themes of the biblical message. Thus angels qualified as a doctrine not simply because angels were mentioned in the Bible or because they were identified as creatures of God but because, from the angel who was posted at the gate of the Garden of Eden after the fall to the angel who came to strengthen Christ in the Garden of Gethsemane on the night before his death,[10] angels were not only messengers but actors, dramatis personae, on the biblical stage; the two gardens, of Eden and of Gethsemane, in contrast, were only part of the scenery in the drama.

The explicit references in the New Testament to Mary the mother of Jesus were few in number, and most were quite brief. Even when, by typology or allegory, various statements were applied to her that were taken from earlier biblical books, relatively little amplification was supplied. From this sparse evidence, however, Christian thought almost from the beginning was moved to reflect on its hidden and deeper meanings and on its potential implications. The methods of such reflection were many and various, but at their core they constituted an effort to find and to formulate her place within the themes of the biblical message. Concerning no other merely human being, none of the prophets or apostles or saints, has there been even a small fraction of the profound theological reflection that has been called forth by the person of the Blessed Virgin Mary. It has been a continuing question as we have looked at "Mary through the centuries" just why this should have been so, and just how the bits of information about her provided by the Bible of both Testaments could have been expanded into a full-blown Mariology. Conversely, it also bears asking what has happened in those theological systems, such as those of Protestantism since the Reformation, in which, without any denial of the uniqueness of the Virgin Birth of Christ, the person of his Mother as such has not been accorded special significance. For in a curious way these systems, too, are part of the unbreakable hold that she has continued to have on the imagination of the West.

That imagination has expressed itself above all, of course, through the place of the Virgin in the history of the arts, as this is symbolically depicted in the serenade of the angelic orchestra amusingly and profoundly portrayed by the fifteenth-century Flemish Master of the Saint Lucy Legend. From the many that have been cited or alluded to earlier, let just three examples suffice now in conclusion. Among the hundreds of lovely settings of the *Ave Maria*, that of Franz Schubert may be the most familiar and the most beloved. The paintings of Madonna and Child have been so frequent that it would be possible to write a history of the idea of children on the basis of them. And one of the great churches of the West is Rome's Santa Maria Maggiore, constructed in direct response to the proclamation by the Council of Ephesus in 431 that she was to be called Theotokos. Even more universally than Goethe might have meant it, then, "the Eternal Feminine leads us upward."[11]

Bibliographic Note

The bibliography about the Virgin Mary is truly enormous. The on-line catalog of the Yale University Library at the end of 1995 listed 2,424 books on the subject (a few of them duplicates), and that did not include either articles or most works from before this century. Among books about her, some should be listed here, because they could have been cited in every chapter: Juniper Carol, ed., *Mariology*, 3 vols. (Milwaukee: Bruce, 1955–61); Carol Graef, *Mary: A History of Doctrine and Devotion*, 2 vols. (New York: Sheed and Ward, 1963–65); Walter Delius, *Geschichte der Marien-verehrung* (Munich: Ernst Reinhardt Verlag, 1963); the 1,042-page encyclopedic dictionary by Wolfgang Beinert and Heinrich Petri, *Handbuch der Marienkunde* (Regensburg: F. Pustet, 1984); and the massive festschrift to René Laurentin, *Kecharitōmenē: Mélanges René Laurentin* (Paris: Desclée, 1990).

The subject of Mary has been engaging me as scholar and author for more than four decades. As Herman Kogan has described in *The Great EB*, my long and fruitful association with *Encyclopaedia Britannica* began in the 1950s, when I was called in for crisis management after several successive drafts for the article MARY by various authors had been rejected by one or another outside reviewer. That article continues to appear in the set to the present; and thirty years later, employing its basic structure, I wrote an essay that appeared, in German in 1985 and in English in 1986, on "Mary—Exemplar of the Development of Christian Doctrine" as part of Jaroslav Pelikan, David Flusser, and Justin Lang, *Mary: Images of the Mother of Jesus in Jewish and Christian Perspective*, published in the United States by Fortress Press. My *Riddle of Roman Catholicism*, written on the eve of the Second Vatican Council and honored with the Abingdon Award in 1959, contained a chapter entitled "Ave Maria." The publication of the English translation of Otto Semmelroth, *Mary, Archetype of the Church* (New York: Sheed and Ward, 1963), gave me the opportunity to prepare a brief essay as a foreword entitled "The Basic Marian Idea." In the Thomas More Lectures, published by Yale University Press in 1965, *Development of Christian Doctrine: Some Historical Prolegomena*, I had analyzed "Athanasius on Mary," especially his idea of the Theotokos. The Mason Gross Lectures at Rutgers University, which I delivered in 1989 and which were published in 1990 by Rutgers University Press as *Eternal Feminines: Three Theological Allegories in Dante's "Paradiso"*, included a chapter on Dante's vision of the Virgin Mary. The Andrew W. Mellon Lectures at the National Gallery of Art, delivered for the twelve-hundredth anniversary of the Second Council of Nicaea in 1987 and published by Princeton University Press also in 1990 as *Imago Dei*, contained a discussion of early Byzantine iconography of Mary and of its theological justification. *Faust the Theologian*, my Willson Lectures at Southwestern University published by Yale University Press in 1995, climaxed, as does Goethe's *Faust*, with the picture of Mary as the Mater Gloriosa and the Eternal Feminine. Moreover, throughout the five volumes of *The Christian Tradition*, which appeared at the University of Chicago Press between 1971 and 1989, the doctrines of Mary from various periods repeatedly came in for close attention.

All of these previous treatments of Mary have made their contribution to this book, and I am grateful for the opportunity (and, where appropriate, the permission) to recycle them here for the first time in a full-length and connected historical account; simple references to the books, as distinct from such passages, are introduced with "See." In the documentation for all these books, and above all for the last one cited, the hundreds of citations from primary sources underlying the historical narrative have also been identified in full, and it did seem supererogatory to repeat most of them here.

Abbreviations

ADB   *Anchor Dictionary of the Bible.* Edited by David Noel Freedman et al. 6 vols. New York: Doubleday, 1992.

Bauer-Gingrich   Bauer, Walter, F. Wilbur Gingrich, et al., eds. *A Greek-English Lexicon of the New Testament and Other Early Christian Literature.* 2d ed. Chicago: University of Chicago Press, 1979.

Deferrari-Barry   Deferrari, Roy J., and Inviolata M. Barry, eds. *A Lexicon of St. Thomas Aquinas Based on the "Summa Theologica" and Selected Passages of His Other Works.* Washington, D.C.: Catholic University of America Press, 1948.

Denzinger   Denzinger, Henricus, and Adolfus Schönmetzer, eds. *Enchiridion symbolorum editionum et declarationum de rebus fidei et morum.* 36th ed. Freiburg and Rome: Herder, 1976.

DTC   *Dictionnaire de théologié catholique.* 15 vols. and indexes. Paris: Letouzey et Ané, 1909–72.

Lampe   Lampe, Geoffrey W. H., ed. *A Patristic Greek Lexicon.* Oxford: Clarendon Press, 1961.

Liddell-Scott-Jones   Liddell, Henry George, Robert Scott, and Henry Stuart Jones, eds. *A Greek-English Lexicon.* 9th ed. Oxford: Clarendon Press, 1940.

OED   *The Oxford English Dictionary.* 16 vols. Oxford: Oxford University Press, 1933–86.

PG   *Patrologia Graeca.* 162 vols. Paris: J. P. Migne, 1857–66.

PL   *Patrologia Latina.* 221 vols. Paris: J. P. Migne, 1844–64.

Schaff   Schaff, Philip, ed. *Creeds of Christendom, with a History and Critical Notes.* 3 vols. 6th ed. Reprint edition. Grand Rapids, Mich.: Baker Book House, 1990.

Sophocles   Sophocles, E. A., ed. *Greek Lexicon of the Roman and Byzantine Periods.* Boston: Little, Brown and Company, 1870.

Tanner   Tanner, Norman P., ed. *Decrees of the Ecumenical Councils.* 2 vols. Washington, D.C.: Georgetown University Press, 1990.

Notes

Introduction

1. Jaroslav Pelikan, *Jesus Through the Centuries: His Place in the History of Culture* (New Haven and London: Yale University Press, 1985), 1.
2. James Arnold Hepokoski, *Otello* (Cambridge: Cambridge University Press, 1987), 71–75. I am indebted for this reference to Philip Gossett.
3. William Shakespeare, *Othello*, V.ii.25.
4. Alexandra to Aleksandr Syroboiarsky, 29 November 1917, in Mark D. Steinberg and Vladimir M. Khrustalëv, eds., *The Fall of the Romanovs* (New Haven and London: Yale University Press, 1995), 206. Her letters, as well as those of the czar, are replete with such references to the Virgin Mary.
5. CBS News, 23 January 1995 (the day after her death at the age of 104).
6. Richard Rodriguez, *Days of Obligation: An Argument with My Mexican Father* (New York: Penguin Books, 1993), 16–20.
7. William F. Maestri, *Mary Model of Justice: Reflections on the Magnificat* (New York: Alba House, 1987), xi.
8. See, e.g., Isabel Bettwy, *I Am the Guardian of the Faith: Reported Apparitions of the Mother of God in Ecuador* (Steubenville, Ohio: Franciscan University Press, 1991); see also chapter 13, below.
9. Richard Foley, *The Drama of Medjugorje* (Dublin: Veritas, 1992); Medjugorje is located within the context of the nineteenth-century apparitions by Sandra L. Zimdars-Swartz, *Encountering Mary: From La Salette to Medjugorje* (Princeton, N.J.: Princeton University Press, 1991).
10. Elizabeth Rubin, "Souvenir Miracles: Going to See the Virgin in Western Herzegovina," *Harper's*, February 1995, 63–70.

11. See the recent study of Jill Dubisch, In a Different Place: Pilgrimage, Gender, and Politics at a Greek Island Shrine (Princeton, N.J.: Princeton University Press, 1995).

12. F. Adeney Walpole, Women of the New Testament (London: James Nisbet, 1901), 835.

13. Wolfhart Schlichting, Maria: Die Mutter Jesu in Bibel, Tradition und Feminismus (Wuppertal: R. Brockhaus, 1989).

14. Alvin John Schmidt, Veiled and Silenced: How Culture Shaped Sexist Theology (Macon, Ga.: Mercer University Press, 1989), 95.

15. Simone de Beauvoir, The Second Sex, tr. H. M. Parshley (New York: Alfred A. Knopf, 1971), 171.

16. Els Maeckelberghe, Desperately Seeking Mary: A Feminist Appropriation of a Traditional Religious Symbol (Kampen, The Netherlands: Pharos, 1991).

17. Maurice Hamington, Hail Mary? The Struggle for Ultimate Womanhood in Catholicism (New York: Routledge, 1995).

18. Elizabeth Schüssler Fiorenza, "Feminist Theology as a Critical Theology of Liberation," in Churches in Struggle: Liberation Theologies and Social Change in North America, ed. William K. Tabb (New York: Monthly Review Press, 1986), 57, 59.

19. Paul Evdokimov, Woman and the Salvation of the World: A Christian Anthropology on the Charisms of Women, tr. Anthony P. Gythiel (Crestwood, N.Y.: St. Vladimir's Seminary Press, 1994).

20. J. Gresham Machen, The Virgin Birth of Christ (New York: Harper and Brothers, 1930).

21. See Pelikan, Flusser, and Lang, Mary; Hans Küng and Jürgen Moltmann, eds., Mary in the Churches (New York: Concilium, 1983).

22. Hans Urs von Balthasar, Theodrama: Theological Dramatic Theory, tr. Graham Harrison (San Francisco: Ignatius Press, 1992), 3:293.

Chapter 1   Miriam of Nazareth

1. Louis Ginzberg, Legends of the Bible (New York: Simon and Schuster, 1956), xxi.

2. The Catholic Encyclopedia, 15:464E.

3. Bauer-Gingrich, 491.

4. See chapters 11 and 15, below.

5. Raymond E. Brown, Karl P. Donfried, Joseph A. Fitzmyer, and John Reumann, eds., Mary in the New Testament: A Collaborative Assessment by Protestant and Roman Catholic Scholars (Philadelphia and New York: Fortress Press and Paulist Press, 1978), 28–29.

6. Matt. 28:18–19.

7. Denzinger, 125.

8. John Courtney Murray, The Problem of God Yesterday and Today (New Haven and London: Yale University Press, 1964), 55.

9. Matt. 26:26–28; Mark 14:22–25; Luke 22:19–20; 1 Cor. 11:23–25.

10. Tanner, 230–31, 695.

11. Matt. 16:18.

12. Denzinger, 875.

13. Jaroslav Pelikan, "Canonica Regula: The Trinitarian Hermeneutics of Augustine," in Proceedings of the PMR Conference 12/13 (1987–88): 17–30; Collectanea Augustiniana, vol. 1: Augustine: "Second Founder of the Faith," ed. Joseph C. Schnaubelt and Frederick Van Fleteren (New York: Peter Lang), 329–43.

14. Matt. 28:19; John 1:1.

15. John 1:1, 14:28.

16. Matt. 1:18; Luke 1:34–35.
17. John 1:14.
18. John 1:12–13.
19. *The New Jerusalem Bible* (Garden City, N.Y.: Doubleday, 1985), 1745.
20. See chapter 2, below.
21. Schaff, 2:53.
22. Luke 1:28 (Vg).
23. Bauer-Gingrich, 877–78; Lampe, 1514–18.
24. See chapter 15, below.
25. LTK 1:1141, with bibliography (Josef Andreas Jungmann).
26. Luke 1:28, 42.
27. Gal. 4:4.
28. Job 14:1.
29. William Shakespeare, *Macbeth*, V.viii.12–16.
30. Rom. 5:19.
31. Luke 3:15.
32. John 1:29; 27.
33. Luke 1:42–43.
34. Cf. Luke 1:36.
35. Ferdinand Hahn, *Christologische Hoheitstitel: Ihre Geschichte im frühen Christentum* (Göttingen: Vandenhoeck und Ruprecht, 1963).
36. Deut. 6:4; Mark 12:29.
37. Luke 1:26–27.
38. See Jean Pétrin, *Le sens de l'oeuvre de Saint Luc et le mystère marial* (Ottawa: Séminaire Saint-Paul, 1979).
39. See Joseph Fischer, *Die davidische Abkunft der Mutter Jesu* (Vienna: A. Opitz Nachfolger, 1910).
40. Luke 2:3.
41. Matt. 1:23; Isa. 7:14.
42. Luke 1:1–3.
43. *ADB* 4:398–402 (Eckhard Plümacher).
44. Col. 4:14; 1 Cor. 15:8.
45. Gisela Kraut, *Lukas malt die Madonna: Zeugnisse zum künstlerischen Selbstverständnis in der Malerei* (Worms: Wernersche Verlagsgesellschaft, 1986); see *Imago Dei*, pl. 22.
46. LTK 6:618–19 (Karl Hermann Schelke).
47. John 19:26–27.
48. Origen *Commentary on John* I.6.
49. Luke 2:35.
50. Heb. 11:38, 1.
51. Rom. 10:17, 1:5, 16:26.
52. Rom. 3:28; James 2:24.
53. Heb. 11:8–12; Rom. 4:1; James 2:21–23.
54. Rom. 4:11.
55. Gen. 3:20.
56. Luke 1:38.
57. Luke 1:48.
58. Matt. 26:13.

Chapter 2   The Daughter of Zion

1. The Catholic Encyclopedia, 15:464E.
2. The definitive study of this issue is Henri de Lubac, Exégèse médiévale: Les quatre sens de l'écriture, 2 vols. in 4 (Paris: Aubier, 1959–64).
3. Brown et al., Mary in the New Testament, 29.
4. Luke 2:4.
5. Matt. 1:1–17; Luke 3:23–38.
6. Luke 3:23.
7. Song of Songs 1:5 (Vg; AV).
8. Rodriguez, Days of Obligation, 16–20.
9. Gen. 3:15.
10. Irenaeus Against Heresies V.xxi.1–3.
11. Tibor Gallus, Die "Frau" in Gen 3,15 (Klagenfurt: Carinthia, 1979).
12. See, e.g., Vermeer's Allegory of [the] Faith, at chapter 6, below.
13. Prov. 31:10 (Vg).
14. L. N. Tolstoy, War and Peace, Book I, ch. 22 (tr. Ann Dunnigan).
15. Edwin Hatch and Henry A. Redpath, eds., A Concordance to the Septuagint, 3 vols. (Oxford: Clarendon Press, 1897–1906), 3:108.
16. Ex. 15:20–21.
17. Isa. 7:14; Matt. 1:22–23.
18. Luke 1:34.
19. Matt. 12:46; Matt. 13:55; Mark 3:31; John 2:12; John 7:3, 5.
20. 1 Cor. 9:5; Gal. 1:19.
21. Song of Songs 4:12 (AV; Vg).
22. Jerome Against Jovinian I.31.
23. Matt. 27:60; Luke 23:53; John 19:41.
24. Gen. 2:7 (LXX).
25. 1 Cor. 13:12.
26. Num. 6:24–26.
27. 2 Cor. 4:6.
28. Ps. 27:8.
29. Gen. 22:12.
30. Murray, Problem of God, 5.
31. Ex. 3:2, 14.
32. Isa. 6:1, 21:2.
33. Amos 1:1; Obad. 1; Nah. 1:1.
34. Ezek. 11:24, 12:27, 37:2, 47:1; Dan. 8:1.
35. Luke 3:2; John 1:14; Matt. 11:13.
36. Acts 2:17; Joel 2:28.
37. Acts 10:9–16.
38. Acts 16:9, 18:9–10, 26:19.
39. Luke 10:18.
40. Luke 22:43.
41. Matt. 1:20, 2:12, 19.
42. Rev. 1:13.
43. Rev. 12:1.

44. Brown et al., *Mary in the New Testament*, 339.

45. Rev. 14:6–7.

46. See *The Christian Tradition*, 3:223–29.

47. Ps. 51:5.

48. Luke 24:27.

49. Isa. 25:8; 1 Cor. 15:54.

50. Theodore the Studite *Orations* V.2–3 (PG 99:721–724); see chapter 15, below.

51. Gen. 5:24; 2 Kings 2:11–12.

52. *ADB* 2:508–26 (Richard S. Hess, George W. E. Nickelsburg, Francis I. Andersen).

53. *ADB* 2:465–69 (Siegfried S. Johnson, Orval S. Wintermute).

54. Matt. 17:3.

55. Luke 10:38–42.

56. Ps. 68:18; Eph. 4:8.

57. John 12:26.

Chapter 3   The Second Eve

1. See the exhaustive collection of source material for this and subsequent chapters in Sergio Alvarez Campo, ed., *Corpus Marianum Patristicum*, 5 vols. (Burgos: Aldecoa, 1970–81).

2. Plato *Laws* 709B (tr. Benjamin Jowett).

3. Constantine Despotopoulos, *Philosophy of History in Ancient Greece* (Athens: Academy of Athens, 1991), 78–80.

4. See Norma Thompson, *Herodotus and the Origins of the Political Community* (New Haven and London: Yale University Press, 1996).

5. Ex. 3.

6. John 1:1, 14.

7. James 1:17.

8. Marcus Aurelius *Meditations* XII.14 (tr. Maxwell Staniforth).

9. Lino Cignelli, *Maria nuova Eva nella patristica greca, sec. II–!V* (Assisi: Studio teologico Porziuncola, 1966).

10. Gen. 3:5.

11. Matt. 4:2–3.

12. Rom. 5:12, 15.

13. 1 Cor. 15:45, 47.

14. Irenaeus *Proof of the Apostolic Preaching* 33 (tr. Joseph P. Smith, revised).

15. In Brown et al., *Mary in the New Testament*, 257 (italics added).

16. See *The Christian Tradition*, 1:108–20.

17. Gen. 3:20.

18. See chapter 6, below.

19. Mary Christopher Pecheux, "The Concept of the Second Eve in *Paradise Lost*," *PMLA* 75 (1960): 359.

20. John Milton *Paradise Lost* V.385–87.

21. Milton *Paradise Lost* XII.379–81.

22. See *The Christian Tradition*, 1:141–46.

23. Isaiah Berlin, "The Hedgehog and the Fox," in *Russian Thinkers*, ed. Henry Hardy and Aileen Kelly (New York: Penguin Books, 1979), 22–81.

24. Tolstoy, *War and Peace*, Second Epilogue, ch. 12 (tr. Aylmer and Louise Maude).

25. Charles Norris Cochrane, *Christianity and Classical Culture* (Oxford: Clarendon Press, 1944), 483–84, summarizing the argument in Book XII of Augustine's *City of God*.

26. Irenaeus *Proof of the Apostolic Preaching* 33 (ET Joseph P. Smith, revised).

27. 1 Cor. 15:45, 47.

28. Ginzberg, *Legends of the Bible*, xxi.

29. H. R. Smid, *Protevangelium Jacobi: A Commentary* (Assen: Van Gorcum, 1975), is useful and balanced.

30. Brown et al., *Mary in the New Testament*, 248–49.

31. *Protevangel of James* 19:3–20, 17:20, 9:2.

32. Irenaeus *Against Heresies* I.vii.2, III.xi.3.

33. Gregor Martin Lechner, *Maria Gravida: Zum Schwangerschaftsmotiv in der bildenden Kunst* (Munich: Schnell und Steiner, 1981).

34. Adolf von Harnack, [*Grundrisz der*] *Dogmengeschicht*, 4th ed. (Tübingen: J. C. B. Mohr [Paul Siebeck], 1905), 192.

35. See chapter 4, below.

36. Matt. 4:3, 6.

37. Ignatius *Epistle to the Trallians* 9.

38. A useful corrective on standard interpretations of Mozart's relation to religious faith is Hans Küng, *Mozart: Traces of Transcendence*, tr. John Bowden (London: SCM Press, 1992).

39. Jaroslav Pelikan, *Christianity and Classical Culture: The Metamorphosis of Natural Theology in the Christian Encounter with Hellenism* (New Haven and London: Yale University Press, 1993), 328.

40. Luke 23:26.

41. ap.Irenaeus *Against Heresies* I.xxiv.4.

42. Virginia Corwin, *St. Ignatius and Christianity in Antioch* (New Haven: Yale University Press, 1960), 170.

43. See the table in Schaff, 1:53.

44. Schaff, 1:53.

45. ap.Irenaeus *Against Heresies* I.vii.2.

46. Tertullian *Against Marcion* III.xi.

47. Richard Crashaw, "The Shepherds' Hymn," in *The New Oxford Book of English Verse, 1250–1950*, ed. Helen Gardner (Oxford: Oxford University Press, 1972), 314.

48. *Imago Dei*, 129, 71.

49. Gregory of Nyssa *Against Eunomius* IV.3 (PG 45:637).

50. See the discussion of these views in William P. Haugaard, "Arius: Twice a Heretic? Arius and the Human Soul of Christ," *Church History* 29 (1960): 251–63.

51. Quoted by Irenaeus *Against Heresies* III.xxxi.1.

52. John of Damascus *On Heresies* 31 (PG 94:697).

53. Peter Robert Lamont Brown, *The Body and Society: Men, Women, and Sexual Renunciation in Early Christianity* (New York: Columbia University Press, 1988), 111–14.

54. Ignatius *Epistle to the Trallians* ix.1.

55. Gal. 4:4; see chapter 1, above.

56. Gen. 3:20 (LXX).

Chapter 4   The Theotokos

1. *Imago Dei*, 134–38.

2. Liddell-Scott-Jones, 792, cites no pre-Christian instance of it.

3. Athanasius Orations Against the Arians III.29 (PG 26:385).

4. Guido Müller, ed., Lexicon Athanasianum (Berlin: Walter de Gruyter, 1952), 650.

5. Julian Against the Galileans 262.

6. Theodora Jenny-Kappers, Muttergöttin und Gottesmutter in Ephesos: Von Artemis zu Maria (Zurich: Daimon, 1986).

7. Acts 19:23–41.

8. Council of Ephesus (Tanner, 59).

9. Carlo Pietrangeli, Santa Maria Maggiore a Roma (Florence: Nardini, 1988).

10. John of Damascus The Orthodox Faith III.12 (PG 94:1029–32).

11. John of Damascus Orations on the Holy Icons II.11 (PG 94:1293–96).

12. Theodore the Studite On the Images 1 (PG 99:489); see chapter 7, below.

13. Development of Christian Doctrine: Some Historical Prolegomena, 105–19.

14. Hugo Rahner, "Hippolyt von Rom als Zeuge für den Ausdruck Theotokos," Zeitschrift für katholische Theologie 59 (1935): 73–81. See the discussion and bibliography in Walter Burghardt, "Mary in Eastern Patristic Thought," in Carol, ed., Mariology, 2:117, n. 147.

15. John Henry Newman, An Essay on the Development of Christian Doctrine, 6th ed., Foreword by Ian Kerr (Notre Dame, Ind.: University of Notre Dame Press, 1989), 145.

16. Alexander of Alexandria Epistle to Alexander of Constantinople 12 (PG 18:568).

17. See, e.g., Arnold J. Toynbee, A Study of History, 12 vols. (Oxford: Oxford University Press, 1934–61), 7-B:717.

18. Burghardt, "Mary in Eastern Patristic Thought," in Carol, ed., Mariology, 2:120.

19. Athanasius Orations Against the Arians III.29 (PG 26:385).

20. The controversy is well summarized in Aloys Grillmeier, Christ in Christian Thought: From the Apostolic Age to Chalcedon (451), tr. J. S. Bowden (New York, 1965), 193–219, where most of the recent literature is discussed.

21. DTC 7-I:595–602 (Anton Michel).

22. 1 John 1:7; Acts 20:28.

23. Grillmeier, Christ in Christian Thought, 357.

24. Phil. 2:5–7.

25. Athanasius Orations Against the Arians I.42 (PG 26:100).

26. Athanasius Orations Against the Arians III.29 (PG 26:385).

27. John Henry Newman, "The Orthodoxy of the Body of the Faithful during the Supremacy of Arianism," Note V to The Arians of the Fourth Century, 3d ed. (London: E. Lumley, 1871), 454–72; the note originally appeared as a separate article in 1859.

28. Bernard Capelle, "Autorité de la liturgie chez les Pères," Recherches de théologie ancienne et médiévale 22 (1954): 5–22.

29. Cf. Georg Ludwig, Athanasii epistula ad Epictetum (Jena: Pohle, 1911), a careful textual analysis; on the role of the epistle to Epictetus at Ephesus and Chalcedon, 22–25. Ludwig's textual observations are supplemented by Hans-Georg Opitz, Untersuchungen zur Überlieferung der Schriften des Athanasius (Berlin: Walter de Gruyter, 1935), 173–74.

30. Cf. Grillmeier, Christ in Christian Thought, 204–5, 214–17, on the significance of the Epistle to Epictetus.

31. Athanasius Epistle to Epictetus 9 (PG 26:1064).

32. Athanasius Epistle to Epictetus 4 (PG 26:1056–57).

33. Athanasius Epistle to Maximus the Philosopher 3 (PG 26:1088).

34. See chapter 3, above.

35. In 2 Peter 1:15, tēn toutōn mnēmēn poieisthai is translated "to recall these things."

36. Basil *Epistles* 93 (PG 32:484).
37. See chapter 15, below.
38. Martin Jugie, "La première fête mariale en Orient et en Occident: L'Avent primitif," *Echos d'Orient* 22 (1923):129–52.
39. Martin Jugie, *La mort et l'assomption de la Sainte Vierge: Etude historico-doctrinale* (Vatican City: Studi e Testi, 1944), 172–212.
40. Graef, *Mary*, 1:133–38.
41. Athanasius *Orations Against the Arians* III.29 (PG 26:385).
42. Athanasius *Epistle to Epictetus* 12 (PG 26:1069).
43. Henry Melville Gwatkin, *Studies of Arianism* (Cambridge: Cambridge University Press, 1881), 265.
44. Quoted in Athanasius *Orations Against the Arians* I.5 (PG 26:20).
45. Gwatkin, *Studies of Arianism*, 134–35, n. 3.
46. Quoted in Athanasius *On the Councils of Ariminum and Seleucia* 16 (PG 26:709).
47. Athanasius *Defense of the Nicene Council* 9 (PG 25:432).
48. But see William P. Hauggard, "Arius: Twice a Heretic? Arius and the Human Soul of Jesus Christ," *Church History* 29 (1960): 251–63.
49. Athanasius *On the Councils of Ariminum and Seleucia* 26 (PG 26:729).
50. Quoted in Theodoret *Ecclesiastical History* I.12–13.
51. Athanasius *Orations Against the Arians* I.43 (PG 26:100).
52. Athanasius *On the Incarnation of the Word* 54 (PG 25:192); cf. Jaroslav Pelikan, *The Light of the World: A Basic Image in Early Christian Thought* (New York: Harper and Brothers, 1962), 120, nn. 18–21.
53. Newman, *Essay on the Development of Christian Doctrine*, 138–39, contains certain suggestions of this line of development.
54. Adolf von Harnack, *Lehrbuch der Dogmengeschichte*, 5th ed., 3 vols. (Tübingen: J. C. B. Mohr [Paul Siebeck], 1931), 2:477.
55. Athanasius *Letter to the Virgins*.
56. Maurice Gordillo, *Mariologia Orientalis* (Rome: Pontifical Institute of Oriental Studies, 1954), 7–8, n. 56; Gérard Gilles Meersseman, *Der Hymnos Akathistos im Abendland* (Freiburg in der Schweiz: Universitäts-Verlag, 1958), 1:14–15.

Chapter 5   The Heroine of the Qur'ān

1. LTK 8:613 (Max Bierbaum).
2. See chapter 8, below.
3. Elisabeth Ott, *Thomas Merton, Grenzgänger zwischen Christentum und Buddhismus: Über das Verhältnis von Selbsterfahrung und Gottesbegegnung* (Würzburg: Echter Verlag, 1977).
4. This sentence and the balance of the paragraph are adapted from my "Introduction" to the Qur'ān in Jaroslav Pelikan, ed., *Sacred Writings*, 6 vols., with companion volume, *On Searching the Scriptures—Your Own or Someone Else's* (New York: Book of the Month Club, 1992), 3:xiv.
5. Qur'ān 21:107–8.
6. I am, throughout this chapter, following the translation of the Qur'ān by the late Pakistani poet and scholar Ahmed Ali, which I had the privilege of incorporating into the collection *Sacred Writings*.
7. Gen. 3:20.

8. Yvonne Y. Haddad and Jane I. Smith, "The Virgin Mary in Islamic Tradition and Commentary," *Muslim World* 79 (1989): 162.

9. See chapter 1, above.

10. Ludwig Hagemann, *Maria, die Mutter Jesu, in Bibel und Koran* (Würzburg: Echter Verlag, 1992).

11. Neal Robinson, "Jesus and Mary in the Qur'an: Some Neglected Affinities," *Religion* 20 (1990): 169–71.

12. Qur'ān 66:12.

13. See also Nilo Geagea, *Mary of the Koran*, tr. Lawrence T. Farnes (New York: Philosophical Library, 1984); C. H. Becker, *Christianity and Islam*, tr. H. J. Chytor (New York: Burt Franklin Reprints, 1974), 22.

14. *ADB* 3:889 (Paul W. Hollenbach).

15. Qur'ān 19:12.

16. Gen. 21:18.

17. Qur'ān 3:42–43.

18. Luke 1:32–33.

19. Qur'ān 3:45–46.

20. Norman Cohn, *The Pursuit of the Millennium* (New York: Academy Library, 1969).

21. Luke 1:34.

22. Gen. 4:1, 25.

23. Qur'ān 3:47.

24. Luke 1:37.

25. Luke 1:35.

26. Gen. 16:6, 21:9–21.

27. See chapter 3, above.

28. Qur'ān 19:16, 41, 51.

29. R. Travers Herford, *Christianity in Talmud and Midrash* (New York: Ktav Publishing House, 1975), 358.

30. N. J. Dawood, ed. and tr., *The Koran*, 5th ed. rev. (London: Penguin Books, 1995), 215, n. 1.

31. John 1:17.

32. Matt. 17:3.

33. Qur'ān 14:39.

34. Qur'ān 5:78.

35. Bartholomew of Edessa *Refutation of the Hagarene* (PG 104:1397).

36. Norman Daniel, *Islam and the West: The Making of an Image* (Edinburgh: Edinburgh University Press, 1960), 175.

37. Qur'ān 19:35.

38. See chapter 6, below.

39. Qur'ān 19:21.

40. Qur'ān 5:75.

41. Placid J. Podipara, *Mariology of the East* (Kerala, India: Oriental Institute of Religious Studies, 1985).

42. See, e.g., Charles Belmonte, *Aba ginoong Maria: The Virgin Mary in Philippine Art* (Manila: Aba Ginoong Maria Foundation, 1990).

43. See chapter 13, below.

44. Song of Songs 1:5 (tr. Marvin Pope); see also chapter 2, above.

45. See the massive illustrated study of Stanisław Chojnacki, Major Themes in Ethiopian Painting: Indigenous Developments, the Influence of Foreign Models, and Their Adaptation from the Thirteenth to the Nineteenth Century (Wiesbaden: F. Steiner, 1983).
46. Marie Durand-Lefèbvre, Etude sur l'origine des Vierges noires (Paris: G. Durassié, 1937).
47. Marvin H. Pope, Song of Songs: A New Translation with Introduction and Commentary (New York: Doubleday, 1977), 307–18.
48. A. J. Delattre, Le culte de la Sainte Vierge en Afrique: d'après les monuments archéologiques (Paris: Société St-Augustin, 1907).
49. Maria Tarnawska, Poland the Kingdom of Mary, tr. Rosamund Batchelor (Lower Bullingham, Hereford: Zgromazdenie księży Marianow, 1982).
50. See also chapter 9, below.

Chapter 6   The Handmaid of the Lord

1. A specialized study in art history, which on closer examination turns out not to be so specialized after all, is Don Denny, The Annunciation from the Right: From Early Christian Times to the Sixteenth Century (New York: Garland, 1977).
2. Imago Dei, 131–34.
3. David Metheny Robb, "The Iconography of the Annunciation in the Fourteenth and Fifteenth Century," Art Bulletin 18 (1936): 480–526.
4. See the comments and bibliography in Alice Bank, Byzantine Art in the Collections of Soviet Museums, tr. Lenina Sorokina, 2d ed. (Leningrad: Aurora Art Publishers, 1985), 289.
5. Frank Edward Brightman, ed., Liturgies Eastern and Western, vol. 1: Eastern Liturgies (Oxford: Clarendon Press, 1896), 318–320.
6. On its place in the Gospel tradition, see Lucien Legrand, L'Annonce à Marie (Lc 1, 26–38): Une apocalypse aux origines de l'Evangile (Paris: Cerf, 1981).
7. John 1:14.
8. John 1:14 (Vg).
9. Gal. 4:4.
10. Xavier Léon-Dufour, "L'Annonce à Joseph," in Etudes d'évangile (Paris: Seuil, 1965), 65–81.
11. Luke 1:38.
12. Isa. 45:9, 64:8; Rom. 9:21.
13. E.g., Rom. 1:1.
14. LTK 9:695–96 (Remigius Bäumer).
15. Phil. 2:6–7.
16. Joel 3:2; Acts 2:18.
17. Acts 1:14.
18. Sterling Stuckey, "Through the Prism of Folklore: The Black Ethos in Slavery," in America's Black Past, ed. Eric Foner (New York: Harper and Row, 1970), 79.
19. Gregory of Nyssa Epistles 3 (PG 46:1021).
20. Richard Griffiths, ed., Claudel: A Reappraisal (London: Rapp and Whiting, 1968), 5.
21. Hans Urs von Balthasar, Theodrama: Theological Dramatic Theory, tr. Graham Harrison (San Francisco: Ignatius Press, 1992), 300.
22. 2 Kings 19:35.
23. Gregory of Nyssa On the Making of Man 23 (PG 44:212).
24. Luke 1:38.
25. See chapter 3, above.

26. Irenaeus *Against Heresies* V.xix.1. Although written in Greek, this treatise is preserved in its entirety only in a Latin translation; hence the Latin terms in this quotation.

27. Augustine *On the Proceedings of Pelagius* 20.44.

28. Acts 9:1–31, 22:1–16, 26:9–23; Gal. 1:11–24.

29. Krister Stendahl, *Paul among Jews and Gentiles* (Philadelphia: Fortress Press, 1976).

30. Augustine *Confessions* VIII.xii.29.

31. Rom. 13:13–14.

32. Augustine *Confessions* VII.xxi.27.

33. Rom. 1:17 (Vg).

34. *Luther's Works: The American Edition*, ed. Jaroslav Pelikan and Helmut Lehmann, 55 vols. (Saint Louis and Philadelphia: Concordia Publishing House and Fortress Press, 1955–), 34:337.

35. Maximus Confessor *Questions to Thalassius* 61 (PG 90:637).

36. On this concept, see chapter 7, below.

37. Lars Thunberg, *Microcosm and Mediator: The Theological Anthropology of Maximus the Confessor* (Lund: C. W. K. Gleerup, 1965), 457–458; italics his.

38. Basil *Epistles* 223.3.

39. PG 31:563–90.

40. Pelikan, *Christianity and Classical Culture*.

41. Luke 1:28.

42. Lampe, 1519.

43. 2 Cor. 6:1.

44. Luke 1:48.

45. Prov. 31:10 (Vg).

46. Gen. 3:15 (Vg).

47. E. F. Sutcliffe, "Jerome," in *The Cambridge History of the Bible: The West from the Fathers to the Reformation* (Cambridge: Cambridge University Press, 1969), 98–99.

48. *The Christian Tradition*, 3:71, 166.

49. Mary Clayton, *The Cult of the Virgin Mary in Anglo-Saxon England* (Cambridge: Cambridge University Press, 1990).

50. Bede *Commentary on Genesis* 1.

51. Ambrosius Autpertus *Commentary on the Apocalypse* 2.

52. Its evolution has been described and documented by Franz [Leander] Drewniak, *Die mariologische Deutung von Gen. 3:15 in der Väterzeit* (Breslau: R. Nischowsky, 1934); see also Nicholas Perry and Loreto Echeverría, *Under the Heel of Mary* (London: Routledge, 1988).

53. Bernard of Clairvaux *In Laud of the Virgin Mother* 2.4.

54. Arthur K. Wheelock, Jr., and Ben Broos, "The Catalogue," *Johannes Vermeer* (Washington, D.C., and New Haven: National Gallery of Art and Yale University Press, 1996), 190.

55. John Michael Montias, *Vermeer and His Milieu: A Web of Social History* (Princeton, N.J.: Princeton University Press, 1989), 129.

56. See Eugene R. Cunnar, "The Viewer's Share: Three Sectarian Readings of Vermeer's *Woman Holding a Balance*," *Exemplaria* 2 (1990): 501–36.

57. Isa. 40:15.

58. *The Documents of Vatican II*, ed. Walter M. Abbott (New York: Guild Press, 1966), 85–96.

59. See chapter 13, below.

60. *The Christian Tradition*, 3:162.

61. Num. 24:17.

62. Ernst Robert Curtius, *European Literature and the Latin Middle Ages,* tr. Willard R. Trask (Princeton, N.J.: Princeton University Press, 1953), 129.

63. F. J. E. Raby, ed., *The Oxford Book of Medieval Latin Verse* (Oxford: Clarendon Press, 1959), 94.

Chapter 7 The Adornment of Worship

1. See chapter 6, above.

2. Ps. 68:25.

3. Augustine *Expositions on the Book of Psalms* 67.26.

4. Louis Bouyer, "Le culte de Marie dans la liturgie byzantine," *Maison-Dieu* 38 (1954): 122–35.

5. Lampe, 57.

6. Alexandra Pätzold, *Der Akathistos-hymnos: Die Bilderzyklen in der byzantinischen Wandmalerei des 14. Jahrhunderts* (Stuttgart: F. Steiner, 1989).

7. Maxime Gorce, *Le Rosaire et ses antécédents historiques* (Paris: Editions à Picard, 1931).

8. OED "B" 724, with many examples.

9. LTK 9:45–49 (Günter Lanczkowski, Angelus Walz, Ekkart Sauer, and Konrad Hofmann).

10. DTC 1:1273–77 (Ursmer Berlière).

11. Luke 1:26–28.

12. *Imago Dei,* 137–45.

13. Vasiliki Limberis, *Divine Heiress: The Virgin Mary and the Creation of Christian Constantinople* (London: Routledge, 1994).

14. Nicephorus *Refutation* II.4 (PG 100:341).

15. Nicephorus *Refutation* I.9 (PG 100:216).

16. Warren Treadgold, *The Byzantine Revival* (Stanford, Calif.: Stanford University Press, 1988), 88.

17. John of Damascus *Orations on the Holy Icons* I.14, III.27–28 (PG 94:1244, 1348–49).

18. Lampe, 408 (including cognates).

19. Luke 23:46.

20. Acts 7:59.

21. Phil. 2:10–11.

22. Denzinger, 301.

23. John of Damascus *Orations on the Holy Icons* III.27–28 (PG 94:1348–49).

24. Augustine *City of God* X.1.

25. Lampe, 384, 793.

26. Augustine *Confessions* I.xiii.20–xiv.23.

27. Augustine *On the Trinity* VII.vi.11.

28. Liddell-Scott-Jones, 1518.

29. Charles Diehl, "Byzantine Civilization," in *The Cambridge Medieval History,* vol. 4 (Cambridge: Cambridge University Press, 1936), 755.

30. The ambiguity appears also in earlier English usage, for example in the Authorized Version of Luke 14:10: "Then shalt thou have *worship* in the presence of them that sit at meat with thee."

31. DTC 3:2404–27, esp. 2406–9 (Jean-Arthur Chollet).

32. Deferrari-Barry, 346, 627–28, 494.

33. See chapter 11, below.

34. Demosthenes Savramis, "Der abergläubliche Mißbrauch der Bilder in Byzanz," *Ost-kirchliche Studien* 9 (1960): 174–92.
35. Theodore the Studite *Orations* XI.iv.24 (*PG* 99:828).
36. Christopher Walter, "Two Notes on the Deesis," *Revue des études byzantines* 26 (1968): 326–36.
37. Liddell-Scott-Jones, 372.
38. Sophocles, 347.
39. Lampe, 334.
40. Lampe, 1144.
41. See Cyril Mango, *Materials for the Study of the Mosaics of St. Sophia at Istanbul* (Washington, D.C.: Dumbarton Oaks, 1962), 29.
42. Matt. 11:13.
43. Justin Martyr *Dialogue with Trypho* 51 (*PG* 6:589).
44. Therefore the Greek term was used in patristic Greek both for the annunciation to Zechariah (Luke 1:8–23) and for the annunciation to Mary (Luke 1:26–38): Lampe, 559.
45. Gregory of Nyssa *On Virginity* 6.
46. Matt. 11:11; Luke 7:28 (NEB).
47. Gregory of Nyssa *On Virginity* 2 (*PG* 46:324).
48. See chapter 8, below.
49. Anders Nygren, *Agape and Eros*, tr. Philip S. Watson (Philadelphia: Westminster Press, 1953), 412.
50. L. Bieler, *Theios anēr: Das Bild des "göttlichen Menschen" in Spätantike und Frühchristentum*, 2 vols. (Vienna: O. Höfels, 1935–36).
51. Lampe, 649–50.
52. Nygren, *Agape and Eros*, 734.
53. Boethius *The Consolation of Philosophy* III.pr.x.23–25.
54. Ps. 82:6.
55. John 10:35.
56. 2 Peter 1:4.
57. Athanasius *Orations Against the Arians* III.24 (*PG* 26:373).
58. Ioann B. Sirota, *Die Ikonographie der Gottesmutter in der Russischen Orthodoxen Kirche: Versuch einer Systematisierung* (Würzburg: Der Christliche Osten, 1992).
59. James Mearns, *The Canticles of the Christian Church Eastern and Western in Early and Medieval Times* (Cambridge: Cambridge University Press, 1914).
60. Phil. 2:6–7.
61. William Loerke, "'Real Presence' in Early Christian Art," *Monasticism and the Arts*, ed. Timothy George Verdon (Syracuse, N.Y.: Syracuse University Press, 1984), 47.
62. John of Damascus *Orations on the Holy Icons* II.15 (*PG* 94:1301).
63. Dorothy G. Shepherd, "An Icon of the Virgin: A Sixth-Century Tapestry Panel from Egypt," *Bulletin of the Cleveland Museum of Art* 56 (March 1969): 93.
64. James H. Stubblebine, "Two Byzantine Madonnas from Calahorra, Spain," *Art Bulletin* 48 (1966): 379–81.

Chapter 8   The Paragon of Chastity

1. Luke 1:42.
2. Bernhard Lohse, *Askese und Mönchtum in der Antike und in der alten Kirche* (Munich: R. Olden-bourg, 1969).

3. Lampe, 244.

4. Marcus Aurelius *Meditations* II.17 (tr. Maxwell Staniforth).

5. Above all, Eph. 6:10–17; but also 1 Tim. 6:12 and 2 Tim. 4:7, and other places.

6. 1 Cor. 9:24–27.

7. Plutarch *Parallel Lives, Numa,* 10.

8. Jaroslav Pelikan, *The Excellent Empire: The Fall of Rome and the Triumph of the Church* (New York: Harper and Row, 1987), 59.

9. Peter Robert Lamont Brown, *The Body and Society: Men, Women, and Sexual Renunciation in Early Christianity* (New York: Columbia University Press, 1988).

10. Num. 6:2.

11. Judges 13:5.

12. Philo *On the Contemplative Life* 68 (tr. C. D. Yonge).

13. Eusebius *Ecclesiastical History* II.xvii.18–19 (tr. Arthur Cushman McGiffert, Sr.).

14. Athanasius *Life of Antony* 5.

15. Augustine *Confessions* VIII.vi.14–15.

16. *Development of Christian Doctrine: Some Historical Prolegomena,* 100–104.

17. Peter Brown, *Augustine of Hippo* (London: Faber, 1969), 274.

18. Jerome *Epistles* 127.5.

19. Jerome *Epistles* 108.33.

20. Jerome *Epistles* 108.20.

21. See Pelikan, *Excellent Empire,* 43–52.

22. Jerome *Epistles* 128.3.

23. Johannes Quasten, *Patrology,* 4 vols. (Westminster, Md.: Newman Press and Christian Classics, 1951–86), 4:239; the treatise appears PL 23:211–338.

24. Jerome *Against Helvidius* 2.

25. Jerome *Against Helvidius* 12.

26. See chapter 2, above.

27. Jerome *Against Helvidius* 16.

28. ap.Jerome *Against Helvidius* 20.

29. 1 Cor. 7:1–2, 38.

30. Jerome *Against Helvidius* 22.

31. Jerome *Against Helvidius* 22.

32. Jerome *Against Helvidius* 21.

33. Joseph Huhn, *Das Geheimnis der Jungfrau-Mutter Maria nach dem Kirchenvater Ambrosius* (Würzburg: Echter Verlag, 1954), 79–80.

34. See chapter 14, below.

35. Ambrose *Epistles* 63.111.

36. Ambrose *Epistles* 63.7.

37. Quasten, *Patrology,* 4:167.

38. Ambrose *Concerning Virgins* II.ii.6.

39. Ambrose *Concerning Virgins* II.ii.15.

40. W. J. Dooley, *Marriage According to St. Ambrose* (Washington, D.C.: Catholic University of America, 1948).

41. Ambrose *De virginibus* II.ii.9.

42. Ambrose *De virginibus* II.ii.8–9.

43. Eph. 5:32.

44. See *The Christian Tradition,* 3:211–12.

45. John Ruskin, *Giotto and His Works in Padua: Being an Explanatory Notice of the Series of Woodcuts Executed for the Arundel Society After the Frescoes in the Arena Chapel* (London: Arundel Society, 1854).

46. See chapter 10, below.

47. LTK 5:1140–41 (Joseph Wenner).

48. John 2:1–11.

Chapter 9   The Mater Dolorosa

1. Ernst Robert Curtius, *European Literature and the Latin Middle Ages*, tr. Willard R. Trask (Princeton, N.J.: Princeton University Press, 1953), 598.

2. Charles Homer Haskins, *The Renaissance of the Twelfth Century* (New York: Meridian Books, 1957).

3. Otto von Simson, *The Gothic Cathedral: Origins of Gothic Architecture and the Medieval Concept of Order* (New York: Pantheon Books, 1956), 172.

4. M. Kotrbová, *České gotické madony*, photographs by V. Fyman (Prague: Charita, 1985).

5. Luke 2:35.

6. See also chapter 15, below.

7. John 19:25–26.

8. Raby, *Oxford Book of Medieval Latin Verse*, 435.

9. Avery Thomas Sharp, "A Descriptive Catalog of Selected, Published Eighteenth-through Twentieth-Century Stabat Mater Settings for Mixed Voices, with a Discussion of the History of the Text" (Ph.D. diss., University of Iowa, 1978).

10. Johann Wolfgang von Goethe, *Faust*, 3588–95.

11. See chapter 12, below.

12. See also chapter 5, above.

13. Sandro Sticca, *The "Planctus Mariae" in the Dramatic Tradition of the Middle Ages*, tr. Joseph R. Berrigan (Athens: University of Georgia Press, 1988).

14. Margaret Alexiou, *The Ritual Lament in Greek Tradition* (Cambridge: Cambridge University Press, 1974); Gregory W. Dobrov, "A Dialogue with Death: Ritual Lament and the thrēnos Theotokou of Romanos Melodos," *Greek, Roman, and Byzantine Studies* 35 (1994): 385–405.

15. Dobrov, "Dialogue with Death," 393–97.

16. Jutta Barbara Desel, *"Vom Leiden Christi oder von dem schmertzlichen Mitleyden Marie": Die vielfigurige Beweinung Christi im Kontext thüringischer Schnitzretabel der Spätgotik* (Alfter: VDG—Verlag und Datenbank für Geisteswissenschaften, 1994).

17. Gerda Panofsky-Soergel, *Michelangelos "Christus" und sein römischer Auftraggeber* (Worms: Wernersche Verlagsgesellschaft, 1991).

18. On the relation of Michelangelo's Pietà to other depictions of the scene, see the collection of photographs in Paolo Monti, *La Pietà: A Rondini di Michelangelo Buonarroti* (Milan: P. Battaglini, 1977).

19. Matt. 27:46.

20. Matt. 1:21.

21. Hans Urs von Balthasar, *The Threefold Garland: The World's Salvation in Mary's Prayer*, tr. Erasmo Leiva-Merikakis (San Francisco: Ignatius Press, 1982), 102.

22. This theme will occupy us again in chapter 13, below.

23. Aron Anderson, ed., *The Mother of God and St Birgitta: An Anthology* (Rome: Vatican Polyglot Press, 1983), 33.

24. Domenico Pezzini, "'The Meditacion of oure Lordis Passyon' and Other Bridgettine Texts in MS Lambeth 432," *Studies in Birgitta and the Brigittine Order*, ed. James Hogg (Lewiston, N.Y.: Edwin Mellen Press, 1993), 1:293.

25. Teresa of Avila, *Spiritual Relations*, in *Complete Works of Saint Teresa of Jesus*, tr. and ed. E. Alison Peers, 3 vols. (London: Sheed and Ward, 1950), 1:363–64.

26. *The Christian Tradition*, 3:160–74.

27. Anselm *On the Virginal Conception and on Original Sin*, preface, *Sancti Anselmi opera omnia*, ed. F. S. Schmitt (Edinburgh: Thomas Nelson, 1938–61), 2:139.

28. Meyer Schapiro, *The Parma Ildefonsus: A Romanesque Illuminated Manuscript from Cluny, and Related Works* (New York: College Art Association, 1964), 71.

29. Guibert of Nogent *On His Own Life* 1.16 (PL 156:871).

30. Bernard of Clairvaux *Sermons on Diverse Topics* 52, *Sancti Bernardi Opera*, ed. Jean Leclercq and Henri Rochais, 8 vols. (Rome: Editiones Cistercienses, 1957–77), 6-I:276.

31. 1 Peter 2:5; Rev. 1:6.

32. Thomas Aquinas, *The Three Greatest Prayers: Commentaries on the Our Father, the Hail Mary and the Apostles' Creed*, tr. Laurence Shapcote (Westminster, Md.: Newman Press, 1956), 32–33.

33. See chapter 11, below.

34. See chapter 14, below.

35. See chapter 13, below.

36. See chapter 15, below.

37. See chapter 8, above.

Chapter 10   The Face That Most Resembles Christ's

1. *Eternal Feminines*, 101–19.

2. H. Barré, "Saint Bernard, docteur marial," *Saint Bernard théologien* (Rome: Analecta Sacri Ordinis Cisterciensis, 1953), 92–113.

3. Steven Botterill, *Dante and the Mystical Tradition: Bernard of Clairvaux in the "Commedia"* (Cambridge: Cambridge University Press, 1994), 167.

4. Par.XXXII.85–87. Here and throughout this chapter, I have employed the translation in blank verse by Allen Mandelbaum, and I have therefore also printed it as verse, by contrast with my own prose translations of verse in chapter 12, below.

5. Par.XXIII.136–37.

6. Alexandre Masseron, *Dante et Saint Bernard* (Paris: A. Michel, 1953), 82.

7. Par.XXXIII.1–2.

8. Inf.II.95–105.

9. Par.XXI.123.

10. Par.XXXII.104.

11. Par.XXIII.128.

12. Par.XXXII.119.

13. Botterill, *Dante and the Mystical Tradition*, 169.

14. Par.XXXIII.1; see chapter 14, below.

15. Par.IV.28–33.

16. Par.II.118, 122.

17. Par.XIX.98.

18. Par.III.85, 88–90.

19. Gen. 3:20.

20. Barbara Newman, *Sister of Wisdom: St. Hildegard's Theology of the Feminine* (Berkeley: University of California Press, 1987), 89–120.

21. Par.XXXII.4–6.

22. Par.XXXII.7–9.

23. Par.XV.133.

24. Purg.V.101.

25. Par.III.121–23.

26. Par.XXXIII.21.

27. Par.XXXIII.10–12.

28. So, e.g., Par.XXXII.37–39, where she would seem to be the supreme example of the faith that is spoken of.

29. 1 Cor. 13:13.

30. Manfred Bambeck, *Studien zu Dantes "Paradiso"* (Wiesbaden: Steiner, 1979), 147–54.

31. Purg.XXXII.73.

32. Peter, James, and John were the only ones present at the raising of the daughter of Jairus (Mark 5:37), on the Mount of Transfiguration (Matt. 17:1–9), and in the Garden of Gethsemane (Matt. 26:36–37).

33. Purg.X.121, 44; Luke 1:38.

34. Purg.XIII.37–38, 50.

35. Purg.XV.106, 88–89; Luke 2:48.

36. Purg.XVIII.107, 100.

37. Purg.XX.14, 19.

38. Purg.XXIII.65, XXII.142–44.

39. Purg.XXV.121–28.

40. Par.XI.58–66.

41. Matt. 2:11.

42. Purg.XX.19–24; Luke 2:7.

43. Par.XXXIII.1.

44. Purg.XXV.128–35, quoting Luke 1:34 (Vg).

45. Purg.XXII.142–44, citing John 2:3.

46. Purg.VIII.25–39.

47. Purg.X.31–33.

48. Purg.X.34–45.

49. Par.XXXII.94–96.

50. Par.XVI.34.

51. Par.XIV.36.

52. Par.XVI.34–39.

53. Par.XXIII.124–29.

54. Par.XXIII.130–32.

55. Par.XXIII.90.

56. Par.XXIII.103–8.

57. Masseron, *Dante et Saint Bernard*, 82–83.

58. Par.XXXI.112–17.

59. Giuseppe C. Di Scipio, *The Symbolic Rose in Dante's "Paradiso"* (Ravenna: Longo, 1984), 57–85.

60. Inf.XXXIV.34.

61. Par.XXXI.118–23.

62. *Summa Theologica* I.50.4.

63. Par.XXXI.130–32.

64. Rona Goffen, *Giovanni Bellini* (New Haven and London: Yale University Press, 1989), 143–60.

65. His relation to Franciscan theology is carefully analyzed in John V. Fleming, *From Bonaventure to Bellini: An Essay in Franciscan Exegesis* (Princeton, N.J.: Princeton University Press, 1982).

66. Par.XXXI.133–38.

67. OED "M," 6-II:165; see chapter 11, below.

68. Henry Osborn Taylor, *The Mediaeval Mind*, 2 vols., 4th ed. (London: Macmillan, 1938), 2:581–82.

69. See chapter 14, below.

70. Par.XIII.85–87.

71. Masseron, *Dante et Saint Bernard*, 139–41.

72. S.T.III.27.2.

73. The entire discussion "The Mother of God" in Newman, *Sister of Wisdom*, 156–95, bears on the subject of this chapter.

74. See chapter 15, below.

75. Par.XXV.127–28.

76. Par.XXIII.73–74.

77. Par.XXIII.86–90.

78. Par.XXXIII.31–43.

79. Par.XXXIII.115–20.

80. Par.XXXIII.145.

81. Par.XXXII.107–8.

82. See chapter 6, above.

83. Par.XXXIII.21.

84. Inf.II.85–114.

85. Par.XXIII.88–89.

86. Purg.VII.82.

Chapter 11   The Model of Faith

1. G. K. Chesterton, "Introduction" to Everyman Library edition of Charles Dickens, *Oliver Twist*.

2. See the discussion of Horst Gorski, *Die Niedrigkeit seiner Magd: Darstellung und theologische Analyse der Mariologie Martin Luthers als Beitrag zum gegenwärtigen lutherisch-römisch katholischen Gespräch* (Frankfurt: Peter Lang, 1987).

3. John Paul II, *Mary: God's Yes to Man*, commentary by Hans Urs von Balthasar (San Francisco: Ignatius Press, 1988), 168.

4. See chapter 6, above.

5. Martin Luther, *Lectures on Genesis*, in *Luther's Works*, ed. Pelikan and Lehmann, 1:191.

6. Lee Palmer Wandel, *Voracious Idols and Violent Hands: Iconoclasm in Reformation Zurich, Strasbourg, and Basel* (Cambridge: Cambridge University Press, 1995), 21–22.

7. Charles Garside, *Zwingli and the Arts* (New Haven: Yale University Press, 1966), 159.

8. *Luther's Works*, ed. Pelikan and Lehmann, 40:84.

9. Martin Luther, *House Postil*, in *Luthers Werke: Kritische Gesamtausgabe*, 57 vols. (Weimar: Hans Böhlau, 1883–), 52:689.

10. Schaff, 3:200.

11. *Heidelberg Catechism*, question 36 (Schaff, 3:319).

12. 1 Tim. 2:5.

13. *Augsburg Confession* XXI.2 (tr. Theodore Tappert), *The Book of Concord* (Philadelphia: Fortress Press, 1959), 47.

14. *Apology* XXI.9 (tr. Jaroslav Pelikan), *Book of Concord*, 230.

15. Newman, *Essay on the Development of Christian Doctrine*, 138–39.

16. *Thirty-Nine Articles*, XXII (Schaff, 3:501).

17. John Calvin, *Institutes of the Christian Religion*, III.xx.21, ed. John T. McNeill (Philadelphia: Westminster Press, 1960), 879.

18. Martin Luther, *Lectures on Genesis* (16:4), in *Luther's Works*, ed. Pelikan and Lehmann, 3:51.

19. Martin Luther, *The Misuse of the Mass*, in *Luther's Works*, ed. Pelikan and Lehmann, 36:195.

20. George Huntston Williams, *The Radical Reformation*, 3d ed. (Kirksville, Mo.: Sixteenth Century Essays and Studies, 1992), 797–98.

21. Orbe Philips in George Huntston Williams, ed. *Spiritual and Anabaptist Writers* (Philadelphia: Westminster Press, 1957), 238–39n.

22. *Formula of Concord*, Solid Declaration, XII.25, *Book of Concord*, 635.

23. See chapter 3, above.

24. For contemporary efforts at a restatement of this positive place, see Heiko Augustinus Oberman, *The Virgin Mary in Evangelical Perspective* (Philadelphia: Fortress Press, 1971); and David Wright, *Chosen by God: Mary in Evangelical Perspective* (London: Marshall Pickering, 1989).

25. A splendid and learned summary, which like so many of his studies, could have become a full-length book, is the work of my late colleague and friend, Arthur Carl Piepkorn, "Mary's Place within the People of God according to Non-Roman Catholics," *Marian Studies* 18 (1967): 46–83.

26. *Augsburg Confession*, I.1, *Book of Concord*, 27.

27. Thomas F. Torrance, "Introduction" to *The School of Faith: The Catechisms of the Reformed Church* (New York: Harper and Brothers, 1959), lxxx.

28. *Larger Catechism*, question 37, in *School of Faith*, 191.

29. Walter Tappolet, ed., *Das Marienlob der Reformatoren* (Tübingen: Katzmann Verlag, 1962).

30. See *The Christian Tradition*, 4:261.

31. Luther, "Sermon on the Presentation of Christ in the Temple," in *Luthers Werke*, 52:688–99.

32. *Smalcald Articles*, I.4, in *Die Bekenntnisschriften der evangelisch-lutherischen Kirche* (Göttingen: Vandenhoeck und Ruprecht, 1952), 414.

33. Martin Luther, *Commentary on the Magnificat*, in *Luther's Works*, ed. Pelikan and Lehmann, 21:355.

34. Rom. 10:17.

35. Ernst Bizer, *Fides ex auditu: Eine Untersuchung über die Entdeckung der Gerechtigkeit Gottes durch Martin Luther* (Neukirchen Kreis Moers: Verlag der Buchhandlung des Erziehungsvereins, 1958).

36. 1 Cor. 13:13.

37. Thomas Aquinas *Commentary on the Sentences* IV.vi.2.2.1a.

38. 1 Cor. 13:13.

39. This concept is carefully examined by Joseph C. McLelland, *The Visible Words of God: An*

Exposition of the Sacramental Theology of Peter Martyr Vermigli, A.D. 1500–1562 (Grand Rapids, Mich.: Wm. B. Eerdmans, 1957).

40. Calvin *Institutes* III.ii.6. McNeill ed., 549.

41. Martin Luther, *Commentary on the Magnificat*, in *Luther's Works*, ed. Pelikan and Lehmann, 21:304, 305, 338.

42. Luke 1:38.

43. Martin Luther, *House Postil*, in *Luthers Werke*, 52:624–34.

44. Martin Luther, *Sermon for 25.vii.1522*, in *Luthers Werke*, 10-III:239.

45. Martin Luther, *Commentary on Galatians*, in *Luther's Works*, ed. Pelikan and Lehmann, 26:387.

46. Gen. 15:6; Rom. 4:3; Gal. 3:6.

47. Martin Luther, "Sermon on Luke 2:41–52," in *Luthers Werke*, 12:409–19.

48. Roy Strong, *The Cult of Elizabeth: Elizabethan Portraiture and Pageantry* (London: Thames and Hudson, 1977), 16.

49. The most thorough investigation of the supposed parallels, Helen Hackett, *Virgin Mother, Maiden Queen: Elizabeth I and the Cult of the Virgin Mary* (Houndmills: Macmillan, 1995), questions the existence of a direct connection, attributing the idea more to the twentieth century than to the seventeenth.

50. Margaret Aston, *Lollards and Reformers: Images and Literacy in Late Medieval Religion* (London: Hambledon Press, 1984), 325n.

51. *The Yale Edition of the Shorter Poems of Edmund Spenser*, ed. William A. Oram et al. (New Haven and London: Yale University Press, 1989), 72.

52. Edmund Spenser, *The Faerie Queene*, I, 4, ed. Thomas P. Roche, Jr. (New Haven and London: Yale University Press, 1981), 40.

53. Milton, *Paradise Lost*, V.385–87; see chapter 3, above.

54. Milton, *Paradise Regained*, I.227–32.

55. See chapter 7, above.

56. John Julian, *Dictionary of Hymnology*, reprint ed. (New York: Dover Publications, 1957), 270.

57. Owen Chadwick, *A History of Christianity* (New York: St. Martin's Press, 1996), 166.

58. David Price, "Albrecht Dürer's Representations of Faith: The Church, Lay Devotion and Veneration in the *Apocalypse*," *Zeitschrift für Kunstgeschichte* 57 (1994): 688–96.

59. Albrecht Dürer, *Das Marienleben* (Leipzig: Insel-Verlag, 1936).

60. LTK 6:1169 (Wolfgang Braunfels).

Chapter 12   The Mater Gloriosa

1. Pelikan, *Jesus Through the Centuries*, 232.

2. René Wellek, *Concepts of Criticism* (New Haven: Yale University Press, 1963), 221.

3. See Geoffrey H. Hartman, *Wordsworth's Poetry, 1787–1814* (New Haven and London: Yale University Press, 1971), 273.

4. William Wordsworth, *Ecclesiastical Sonnets*, Part II, Sonnet ii, *The Poems*, 2 vols. (New Haven and London: Yale University Press, 1977), 2:464.

5. Wordsworth, *Ecclesiastical Sonnets*, Sonnet xxv, 2:474; italics added.

6. Emile Mâle, *The Gothic Image: Religious Art in France of the Thirteenth Century*, tr. Dora Nussey, reprint ed. (New York: Harper, 1958), 254–58.

7. David Friedrich Strauss, *The Life of Jesus Critically Examined*, tr. George Eliot, 5th ed. (London: Swan Sonnenschein, 1906), 140–43.

8. George Eliot, *Middlemarch*, ed. Bert G. Hornback (New York: W. W. Norton, 1977), 530, 544.

9. Novalis, *Werke und Briefe [von] Novalis*, ed. Alfred Kelletat (Munich: Winkler-Verlag, [1962]), 102.

10. *Faust the Theologian*, 115–28.

11. Johann Peter Eckermann, *Gespräche mit Goethe in den letzten Jahren seines Lebens*, ed. Fritz Bergemann, 3d ed. (Baden-Baden: Insel Verlag, 1955), 716–20. Translations throughout this chapter are my own.

12. See chapter 9, above.

13. Johann Wolfgang von Goethe, *Faust*, 3588–95; although in chapter 10 I have, in quoting Mandelbaum's translation of Dante into blank verse, printed the quotations in verse forms, these translations into prose, which are my own, have been woven into the text.

14. Reinhard Buchwald, *Führer durch Goethes Faustdichtung: Erklärung des Werkes und Geschichte seiner Entstehung*, 7th ed. (Stuttgart: Alfred Kröner, 1964), 59.

15. *Faust*, 12094–95.

16. *Faust*, 12013–19.

17. *Faust*, 12032–36.

18. Luke 1:28 (Vg).

19. Günther Müller, "Die organische Seele im Faust," *Euphorion* 34 (1933): 161n.

20. Stuart Atkins, *Goethe's Faust: A Literary Analysis* (Cambridge, Mass.: Harvard University Press, 1958), 172.

21. Harold Stein Jantz, *The Form of Goethe's "Faust"* (Baltimore, Md.: Johns Hopkins University Press, 1978), 48.

22. Cyrus Hamlin, ed., Johann Wolfgang von Goethe, *Faust, A Tragedy: Backgrounds and Sources*, ed. Cyrus Hamlin, tr. Walter Arndt (New York: W. W. Norton, 1976), 304 n. 9. On the meaning of the title "Doctor Marianus," see Ann White, *Names and Nomenclature in Goethe's "Faust"* (London: University of London Institute of Germanic Studies, 1980), 37–38.

23. *Faust*, 12096–103. On the Mater Gloriosa and these titles, Gerhard Möbus, *Die Christus-Frage in Goethes Leben und Werk* (Osnabrück: A. Fromm, 1964), 291–95, urges that these lines not be read as Christian and Catholic.

24. For example, *Faust*, 1334, 9028–30, 9364.

25. *Faust*, 11993–97.

26. *Faust*, 12009–12.

27. *Faust*, 12001–4.

28. *Faust*, 12100–12101.

29. *Faust*, 1114.

30. Jantz, *Form of Goethe's "Faust,"* 101.

31. Robert E. Dye, "The Easter Cantata and the Idea of Mediation in Goethe's *Faust*," *PMLA*, 92:974.

32. *Faust*, 3588–95; see also chapter 9, above.

33. Hermann Fähnrich, "Goethes Musikanschauung in seiner Fausttragödie—die Erfüllung und Vollendung seiner Opernreform," *Goethe: Neue Folge des Jahrbuchs der Goethe-Gesellschaft* 25 (1963): 257.

34. *Faust*, 12069–75. See the comments of Max Kommerell, *Geist und Buchstabe der Dichtung*, 3d ed. (Frankfurt: Vittorio Klostermann), 125–26.

35. *Faust*, 3730, 12009.

36. *Faust*, 12061–68.

37. Wilhelm Emrich, *Die Symbolik des Faust II*, 2d ed. (Bonn: Athenäum-Verlag 1957), 418–19.

38. *Faust*, "Trüber Tag," 15.

39. *Faust*, "Trüber Tag."

40. *Faust*, 10703–9.

41. *Faust*, 1298–1309.

42. *Faust*, 12037–60.

43. Luke 7:36–50.

44. *ADB* 4:579–81 (Raymond F. Collins).

45. Luke 7:47.

46. *Faust*, 12037–44.

47. John 4:4–26.

48. *Faust*, 12045–52.

49. *Faust*, 12053–60.

50. Ernst Grumach, "Prolog und Epilog im Faustplan von 1797," *Goethe: Neue Folge des Jahrbuchs der Goethe-Gesellschaft* ¹⁴/₁₅ (¹⁹⁵²/₅₃): 63–107.

51. See chapter 10, above.

52. *Faust*, 11807–8.

53. *Faust*, 12001–4.

54. *Faust*, 11882–83.

55. Heinz Schlaffer, *Faust zweiter Teil: Die Allegorie des 19. Jahrhunderts* (Stuttgart: Metzler, 1981), 163.

56. *Faust*, 11872–73.

57. *Par.*XXXIII.145.

58. *Faust*, 346–47, 771.

59. *Faust*, 11854–55.

60. *Faust*, 11862–65.

61. *Faust*, 12104–5.

62. *Faust*, 12102, 12110.

63. *Faust*, 12102–3.

64. *Faust*, 6914.

65. *Faust*, 8592, 8640, 8904.

66. *Faust*, 8924, 8947, 8954.

67. *Faust*, 7294.

68. *Faust*, 9258–59.

69. *Faust*, 9270–73.

70. *Faust*, 1084; 7915, 8289; 5450; 8147; 6213, 6218.

71. *Faust*, 2439–40.

72. *Faust*, 6498–6500.

73. *Faust*, 6510, 9948–50.

74. *Faust*, 10055–66, 10047–51.

75. *Faust*, 7412, 7440–41.

76. *Faust*, 12012.

77. *Faust*, 11997.

78. *Faust*, 2603–4; Hans Urs von Balthasar, *Prometheus: Studien zur Geschichte des deutschen Idealismus*, 2d ed. (Heidelberg: F. H. Kerle Verlag, 1947), 514.

79. *Faust*, 11918–25.
80. *Faust*, 12104–11.

Chapter 13   The Woman Clothed with the Sun

1. "Wasn' That a Wonder," *Slave Songs of the Georgia Sea Islands*, ed. Lydia Parrish (New York: Creative Age Press, 1942), 139.
2. Rev. 12:1; see Altfrid Th. Kassing, *Die Kirche und Maria: Ihr Verhältnis im 12. Kapitel der Apokalypse* (Düsseldorf: Patmos-Verlag, 1958).
3. PG 46:909–13.
4. See Edmond Paris, *Les mystères de Lourdes, La Salette, Fatima: Les marchands du temple, mercantilisme religieux, marché d'illusions* (La Chaux-de-Fonds: Union de défense protestante suisse, 1971).
5. René Laurentin and René Lejeune, *Messages and Teachings of Mary at Medjugorje* (Milford, Ohio: Riehle Foundation, 1988), 15.
6. René Laurentin, ed., *Lourdes: Documents authentiques* (Paris: L. Lethielleux, 1966).
7. LTK 7:64–65 (Hermann Lais).
8. Rubén Vargas Ugarte, *Historia del culto de María en Ibero-américa y de sus Imágenes y Santuarios más celebrados*, 2 vols., 3d ed. (Madrid: Talleres Gráficos Jura, 1956), 1:163–207; the vast literature is cataloged in the bilingual work of Gloria Grajales and Ernest J. Burrus, eds., *Guadalupan Bibliography* (Washington, D.C.: Georgetown University Press, 1986).
9. Edmond Carpez, *La Vénérable Catherine Labouré, fille de la Charité de Saint Vincent de Paul (1806–1876)*, 6th ed. (Paris: Lecoffre, 1913).
10. Sandra L. Zimdars-Swartz, *Encountering Mary: From La Salette to Medjugorje* (Princeton, N.J.: Princeton University Press, 1991).
11. René Laurentin, *Lourdes: Histoire authentique des apparitions*, 6 vols. (Paris: Lethielleux, 1961–64); more recent is Stéphane Baumont, *Histoire de Lourdes* (Toulouse: Editions Privat, 1993).
12. Cyril C. Martindale, *The Message of Fatima* (London: Burns, Oates, and Washbourne, 1950).
13. Beinert and Petri, *Handbuch der Marienkunde*, 533 (René Laurentin); a critical psychological examination of these two visisons in Belgium is that of Gerd Schallenberg, *Visionäre Erlebnisse* (Augsburg: Pattloch Verlag, 1990), 83–95.
14. Since the publication of this list of ten apparitions, two additional ones have been "approved": Akita in Japan and Betania in Venezuela.
15. See now David Blackbourn, *Marpingen: Apparitions of the Virgin Mary in Nineteenth-Century Germany* (New York: Alfred A. Knopf, 1994).
16. Blackbourn, *Marpingen*, 5. Because this roster of elements corresponds so closely to the one I had formulated in the first draft of this chapter, before reading (and reviewing) Blackbourn's study, I am gratefully adapting it here to my rather different historical purposes.
17. On the significance of this proliferation in the modern era, see René Laurentin, *Multiplication des apparitions de la Vierge aujourd'hui: est-ce elle? Que veut-elle dire?* 3d ed. (Paris: Fayard, 1991).
18. See, in general, Werner Freitag, *Volks- und Elitenfrömmigkeit in der frühen Neuzeit: Marienwallfahrten im Fürstbistum Münster* (Paderborn: F. Schöningh, 1991).
19. Luke 1:51–53.
20. William Thomas Walsh, *Our Lady of Fatima* (New York: Macmillan, 1947), 214, 140.

21. Emile Zola, *Lourdes*, tr. Ernest Alfred Vizatelly (Dover, N.H.: A. Sutton, 1993).

22. Antonio González Dorado, *Mariología popular latinoamericana: De la María conquistadora a la María liberadora* (Asunción, Paraguay: Ediciones Loyola, 1985).

23. Anna Gradowska, *Magna Mater: El sincretismo hispanoamericano en algunas imágenes marianas* (Caracas: Museo de Bellas Artes, 1992).

24. Christopher Rengers, *Mary of the Americas: Our Lady of Guadalupe* (New York: Alba House, 1989).

25. Ivone Gebara and Maria Clara Bingemer, *Mary, Mother of God, Mother of the Poor* (Maryknoll, N.Y.: Orbis Books, 1989), 152.

26. William B. Taylor, "The Virgin of Guadalupe in New Spain: An Inquiry into the Social History of Marian Devotion," *American Ethnologist* 14 (1987): 9–25.

27. Ena Campbell, "The Virgin of Guadalupe and the Female Self-Image: A Mexican Case History," *Mother Worship*, ed. James J. Preston (Chapel Hill: University of North Carolina Press, 1982), 5–24.

28. Adela Fernandez, *Dioses prehispánicos de Mexico: Mitos y deidades de panteón Nahuatl* (Mexico, D.F.: Panorama Editorial, 1983), 108–12.

29. Rodriguez, *Days of Obligation*, 16–20.

30. William A. Christian, Jr., *Apparitions in Late Medieval and Renaissance Spain* (Princeton, N.J.: Princeton University Press, 1981); María Dolores Díaz Vaquero, *La Virgen en la escultura cordobesca del barocco* (Cordova: Monte de Piedad y Caja de Ahorros de Córdoba, 1987).

31. Octavio Paz, *The Labyrinth of Solitude*, tr. Lysander Kemp (New York: Grove Press, 1965), 85.

32. Eric R. Wolf, "The Virgin of Guadalupe: A Mexican National Symbol," *Journal of American Folklore* 71 (1958): 34–38; Stafford Poole, *Our Lady of Guadalupe: The Origins and Sources of a Mexican National Symbol, 1531–1797* (Tucson: University of Arizona Press, 1995).

33. Edwin Eduard Sylvest, ed., *Nuestra Señora de Guadalupe: Mother of God, Mother of the Americas* (Dallas, Tex.: Bridwell Library, 1992).

34. Joaquín Antonio Peñalosa, ed., *Poesía guadalupana: siglo XIX* (Mexico City: Editorial Jus, 1985).

35. Peter Laszlo, *La troisième secret de Fatima enfin connu* (Montreal: Guérin, 1987).

36. Jacques Lafaye, *Quetzalcóatl and Guadalupe: The Formation of Mexican National Consciousness, 1531–1813* (Chicago: University of Chicago Press, 1974), 211–57.

37. Barbara Pope, "Immaculate and Powerful: The Marian Revival in the Nineteenth Century," in *Immaculate and Powerful: The Female in Sacred Image and Social Reality*, ed. Clarissa W. Atkinson, Constance H. Buchanan, and Margaret R. Miles (Boston: Beacon Press, 1985), 173, 183–84, 189.

38. Finbar Ryan, *Our Lady of Fatima* (Dublin: Brown and Nolan, 1942), 228–29.

39. Paul VI, *Pilgrimage to Fatima—Addresses* (Washington, D.C.: United States Catholic Conference, 1968), 6.

40. These criteria were systematically formulated by the Sacred Congregation for the Doctrine of the Faith (the Holy Office) on 25 February 1978.

41. Blackbourn, *Marpingen*, 5.

42. See, e.g., Cornelia Göksu, *Heroldsbach: Eine verbotene Wallfahrt* (Würzburg: Echter Verlag, 1991).

43. Andrea Dahlberg, "The Body as a Principle of Holism, Three Pilgrimages to Lourdes," *Contesting the Sacred: The Anthropology of Christian Pilgrimage*, ed. John Eade and Michael J. Sallnow (New York: Routledge, 1991), 35.

44. An early attempt at an assessment was A. Marchand, *The Facts of Lourdes: And the Medical Bureau*, tr. Francis Izard (London: Burns, Oates, and Washbourne, 1924).

45. B. Pope, "Immaculate and Powerful," 173.

46. *L'Osservatore Romano*, 12 October 1981.

47. Blackbourn, *Marpingen*, 5.

48. B. Pope, "Immaculate and Powerful," 183–84.

49. Joseph A. Pelletier, *The Sun Danced at Fatima* (New York: Doubleday Image Books, 1983), 146–47.

50. John Henry Newman, "The Orthodoxy of the Body of the Faithful during the Supremacy of Arianism," Note V to *The Arians of the Fourth Century*, 3d ed. (London, E. Lumley, 1871), 454–72.

51. Dahlberg, "The Body as a Principle of Holism," 10–11.

Chapter 14   The Great Exception

1. Edward Dennis O'Connor, *The Dogma of the Immaculate Conception: History and Significance* (Notre Dame, Ind.: University of Notre Dame Press, 1958), contains important historical and iconographic materials on this dogma.

2. *The Christian Tradition*, 1:286–90.

3. Matt. 1:18; Luke 1:34. See chapter 8, above.

4. Krister Stendahl, "Quis et unde? An Analysis of Mt 1–2," in *Judentum Urchristentum Kirche: Festschrift für Joachim Jeremias*, ed. Walter Eltester (Berlin: Alfred Töpelmann, 1960), 103.

5. Luke 1:35.

6. Bauer-Gingrich, 197.

7. Huhn, *Das Geheimnis der Jungfrau-Mutter Maria nach dem Kirchenvater Ambrosius*, 79–80.

8. Isa. 53:8 (Vg).

9. Ps. 51:5.

10. ap.Augustine *Against Two Epistles of the Pelagians* IV.xi.29.

11. Ambrose *Commentary on Psalm 37* 5.

12. See chapter 1, above.

13. Brunero Gherardini, *Dignitas terrae: Note di mariologia agostiniana* (Casale Monferrato: Piemme, 1992).

14. Augustine *On Nature and Grace* xxxvi.42.

15. *The Christian Tradition*, 3:71–74.

16. See chapter 15, below.

17. *The Christian Tradition*, 3:171.

18. See chapter 10, above.

19. Bernard of Clairvaux *Epistles* 174.7.

20. *The Christian Tradition*, 3:169.

21. A splendid collection, pertinent to this chapter and to this entire book, is Jacqueline Lafontaine-Dosogne, *Iconographie de l'enfance de la Vierge dans l'Empire byzantin et en Occident* (Brussels: Académie royale, 1992).

22. Mirella Levi D'Acona, *The Iconography of the Immaculate Conception in the Middle Ages and Early Renaissance* (New York: College Art Association, 1957).

23. *The Christian Tradition*, 4:38–50.

24. Ps. 51:5.

25. Ps. 116:11.

26. Heiko A. Oberman, *The Harvest of Medieval Theology* (Cambridge, Mass.: Harvard University Press, 1963), 289.

27. Roberto Zavalloni and Eliodoro Mariani, *La dottrina mariologica di Giovanni Duns Scoto* (Rome: Antonianum, 1987).

28. Carolus Balić, *De debito peccati originalis in B. Virgine Maria: Investigationes de doctrina quam tenuit Ioannes Duns Scotus* (Rome: Officium Libri Catholici, 1941), 84.

29. Luke 1:28, 35 (Vg).

30. *The Christian Tradition*, 4:302–3.

31. Denzinger, 2803–4.

32. See chapter 13, above.

33. Marina Warner, *Alone of All Her Sex: The Myth and Cult of the Virgin Mary* (New York: Alfred A. Knopf, 1976), 251.

Chapter 15   The Queen of Heaven

1. See Jan Radkiewicz, *Auf der Suche nach einem mariologischen Grundprinzip: Eine historisch-systematische Untersuchung über die letzten hundert Jahre* (Constance: Hartung-Gorre, 1990).

2. See the brief summary of Edward Schillebeecks and Catharina Halkes, *Mary: Yesterday, Today, Tomorrow* (New York: Crossroad, 1993).

3. It will be evident how much the following presentation owes to the trenchant essay of Karl Rahner, "The Interpretation of the Dogma of the Assumption," in *Theological Investigations*, tr. Cornelius Ernst (Baltimore: Helicon Press, 1961), 215–27.

4. Denzinger, 3903.

5. María de Agreda, *Vida de la Virgen María según la Venerable Sor María de Jesús de Agreda* [Madrid, 1670] (Barcelona: Montaner y Simón, 1899), 365; translation adapted from Nanci Gracía.

6. A sympathetic but still critical account was that of Raymond Winch and Victor Bennett, *The Assumption of Our Lady and Catholic Theology* (London: Macmillan, 1950).

7. Edmund Schlink et al., "An Evangelical Opinion on the Proclamation of the Dogma of the Bodily Assumption of Mary," tr. Conrad Bergendoff, *Lutheran Quarterly* 3 (1951): 138.

8. On the silence, O. Faller, *De priorum saeculorum silentio circa Assumptionem Beatae Mariae Virginis* (Rome: Gregorian University, 1946).

9. Carl G. Jung, *Answer to Job*, tr. R. F. C. Hull (Princeton, N.J.: Princeton University Press, 1969).

10. Job 38:2.

11. Matt. 23:37.

12. *The Christian Tradition*, 3:172–73.

13. See the studies collected in Michel van Esbroeck, *Aux origines de la Dormition de la Vierge* (Aldershot: Variorum, 1995).

14. Bernard of Clairvaux *Epistle* 174.3.

15. Bernard of Clairvaux *Sermons on the Assumption* 1.1.

16. *Imago Dei*, 145–50.

17. Antoine Wenger, *L'Assomption de la trés sainte Vierge dans la tradition byzantine du VIe au Xe siècle* (Paris: Institut Français d'Etudes Byzantines, 1955).

18. John 19:26–27.

19. Lampe, 760.

20. Christa Schaffer, *Aufgenommen ist Maria in den Himmel: Vom Heimgang der Gottesmutter in Legende, Theologie und liturgischer Kunst der Frühzeit* (Regensburg: F. Pustet, 1985).

21. See chapter 7, above.
22. Gen. 5:24; 2 Kings 2:11.
23. Theodore the Studite *Orations* V.2–3 (*PG* 99:721–24).
24. Modestos *On the Dormition of the Blessed Virgin Mary* (*PG* 86:3277–312).
25. Jugie, *La mort et l'assomption de la Sainte Vierge*, 214–24.
26. Nicephorus Callistus *Ecclesiastical History* XVII.28 (*PG* 147:292).
27. See *Imago Dei*, pl. 41.
28. Pamela Askew, *Caravaggio's "Death of the Virgin"* (Princeton, N.J.: Princeton University Press, 1990).
29. C. R. Dodwell, *The Pictorial Arts of the West* (New Haven and London: Yale University Press, 1993), 360–61.
30. Gen. 3:15 (Vg); see chapter 6, above.
31. Denzinger, 3901.
32. See the helpful study of Walter J. Burghardt, "The Testimony of the Patristic Age Concerning Mary's Death," *Marian Studies* 8 (1957): 58–99, together with the articles that follow in the same issue of that journal, by J. M. Egan on the Middle Ages (100–124) and by T. W. Coyle on the present status of the question (143–66).
33. Luke 2:35; see chapter 9, above.
34. *LTK* 1:1068–72 (Michael Schmaus).
35. Luke 1:38.
36. Isa. 25:8; 1 Cor. 15:54.
37. Matt. 27:52–53.
38. See chapter 1, above.
39. Yves M.-J. Congar, *Tradition and Traditions: An Historical and a Theological Essay*, tr. Michael Naseby and Thomas Rainborough (New York: Macmillan, 1966), 211.
40. Walther von Loewenich, *Der moderne Katholizismus*, 2d ed. (Witten: Luther-Verlag, 1956), 276–77.
41. See *The Riddle of Roman Catholicism*, 128–42.
42. See the analysis of Ina Eggemann, *Die "Ekklesiologische Wende" in der Mariologie des II. Vatikanums und "Konziliare Perspektiven" als neue Horizonte für das Verständnis der Mittlerschaft Marias* (Altenberge: Oros Verlag, 1993).
43. The evolution of the Dogmatic Constitution on the Church as it dealt with the doctrine of Mary is well summarized in Gérard Philips, "Die Geschichte der dogmatischen Konstitution über die Kirche 'Lumen Gentium,'" in *Das Zweite Vatikanische Konzil*, ed. Herbert Vorgrimler, 3 vols. (Freiburg: Herder, 1966–68), 1:153–55.
44. The close theologial connection between the doctrine of Mary and the doctrine of the church has been set forth in Yves M.-J. Congar, *Christ, Our Lady, and the Church*, tr. Henry St. John (Westminster, Md.: Newman Press, 1957); and in Otto Semmelroth, *Mary, Archetype of the Church*, Foreword by Jaroslav Pelikan (New York: Sheed and Ward, 1963).
45. Avery Dulles, "Introduction" to *Lumen Gentium*, in *The Documents of Vatican II*, ed. Walter M. Abbott (New York: Guild Press, 1966), 13.
46. *Lumen Gentium* 67.
47. Abbot, *Documents*, 85–96.

Chapter 16 The Woman for All Seasons

1. W. H. Gardner, ed., *Poems of Gerard Manley Hopkins*, 3d ed. (New York: Oxford University Press, 1948), 101.

2. Gal. 2:20.

3. Gregory of Nyssa *Against Eunomium* II.419.

4. Theodora Jenny-Kappers, *Muttergöttin und Gottesmutter in Ephesos: Von Artemis zu Maria* (Zurich: Daimon, 1986).

5. Acts 19:23–41.

6. 1 Cor. 13:13.

7. Wis. 8:7; Plato *Laws* I.631C.

8. Luke 1:48 (Vg).

9. Augustine *Expositions on the Book of Psalms* XCII.3.

10. Gen. 3:24; Luke 23:43.

11. *Faust*, 12104–11.

Index of Proper Names

Index of Biblical References

About the Author

Jaroslav Pelikan, Sterling Professor Emeritus of History at Yale University, has received more than thirty-five honorary degrees from universities all over the world, as well as awards and medals from numerous scholarly societies and institutions. He was named a Senior Fellow at the Carnegie Foundation for the Advancement of Teaching in 1982–83 and again in 1990–91. The Jefferson Award, the highest honor given by the U.S. government to a scholar in the humanities, was conferred on him in 1983, and he was honored with the Haskins Medal from the Medieval Academy of America in 1985. He received the American Academy of Religion's Award for Excellence in 1989 and in 1990 was awarded the Newberry Library's "Umanità" medal. The New York Public Library honored him with its "Literary Lions" Award in 1992, and in the same year he received the Jan Amos Komenský medal of the Czech and Slovak Federal Republic. He has served on the U.S. President's Committee on the Arts and the Humanities since 1994 and is currently President of the American Academy of Arts and Sciences.

Among the many lectureships Pelikan has held are the Gauss Lectures, Princeton University; the Gifford Lectures, University of Aberdeen; the Jefferson Lectures, National Endowment for the Humanities; the Jerome Lectures, American Academy in Rome and University of Michigan; the Mellon Lectures, National Gallery of Art; and the William Clyde De Vane Lectures, Yale University.

Mary Through the Centuries is the thirty-fourth book Jaroslav Pelikan has written. His first book, From Luther to Kierkegaard, was published in 1950. His five-volume work, The Christian Tradition: A History of the Development of Doctrine, 1971–89, is widely acknowledged as the foremost history of its kind. Among the many edited volumes he has overseen is the twenty-two-volume edition of Luther's Works, 1955–71. Other books by Pelikan published by Yale University Press are Development of Christian Doctrine, 1969; The Vindication of Tradition, 1984; Jesus Through the Centuries, 1985; Imago Dei, 1990; The Idea of the University—A Reexamination, 1992; Christianity and Classical Culture, 1993; Faust the Theologian, 1995; and The Reformation of the Bible/The Bible of the Reformation, 1996.